Theory, Culture & Society

Theory, Culture & Society caters for the resurgence of interest in culture within contemporary social science and the humanities. Building on the heritage of classical social theory, the book series examines ways in which this tradition has been reshaped by a new generation of theorists. It will also publish theoretically informed analyses of everyday life, popular culture, and new intellectual movements.

EDITOR: Mike Featherstone, *University of Teesside*

SERIES EDITORIAL BOARD
Roy Boyne, *University of Northumbria at Newcastle*
Mike Hepworth, *University of Aberdeen*
Scott Lash, *University of Lancaster*
Roland Robertson, *University of Pittsburgh*
Bryan S. Turner, *Deakin University*

Recent volumes include:

The Body and Social Theory
Chris Shilling

Symbolic Exchange and Death
Jean Baudrillard

Sociology in Question
Pierre Bourdieu

Economies of Signs and Space
Scott Lash and John Urry

Religion and Globalization
Peter Beyer

Baroque Reason
The Aesthetics of Modernity
Christine Buci-Glucksmann

The Consuming Body
Pasi Falk

Cultural Identity and Global Process
Jonathan Friedman

The Established and the Outsiders
Norbert Elias and John L. Scotson

The Cinematic Society
Norman Denzin

DECENTRING LEISURE
Rethinking Leisure Theory

Chris Rojek

SAGE Publications
London • Thousand Oaks • New Delhi

First published 1995

Published in association with *Theory, Culture & Society*, School of Human Studies, University of Teesside

SAGE Publications Ltd
6 Bonhill Street
London EC2A 4PU

SAGE Publications Inc
2455 Teller Road
Thousand Oaks, California 91320

SAGE Publications India Pvt Ltd
32, M-Block Market
Greater Kailash – I
New Delhi 110 048

British Library Cataloguing in Publication data

A catalogue record for this book is
available from the British Library

ISBN 0 8039 8812 5
ISBN 0 8039 8813 3 (pbk)

Library of Congress catalog card number 95-67019

Typeset by M Rules
Printed in Great Britain by The Cromwell Press Ltd,
Broughton Gifford, Melksham, Wiltshire

CONTENTS

Acknowledgements   vii
Introduction: Capitalism / Modernity / Postmodernity   1

Part 1   Capitalism and Leisure

1   Capitalism: Production   12
2   Capitalism: Reproduction   28

Part 2   Modernity and Leisure

3   Modernity 1: The Roots of Order   36
4   Mechanisms of Regulation   59
5   Modernity 2: The Disorder of Things   79
6   The Phenomenology of Leisure   104

Part 3   Postmodernism and Leisure

7   Postmodernity and Postmodernism   129
8   Postmodern Leisure   146
9   Conclusion: *Homo Faber / Homo Ludens*   175

Notes   193
References   201
Author Index   212
Subject Index   214

This book is dedicated to my grandparents
Anka and Stasiek, Rose and William Patrick;
and to my parents Betty and Joe

ACKNOWLEDGEMENTS

This book was written in eighteen months between November 1992 and April 1994. Versions of the argument were delivered to staff seminars in the Department of Sociology, Monash University, Melbourne; the Department of Leisure Studies, Ottawa University; Lancaster University; and the Sir Norman Chester Centre for Sport Studies, Leicester University. The argument was further developed through plenary addresses at the Dutch Leisure Studies Association conference in Tilburg (1992); the Third International Leisure Studies Association conference in Loughborough University (1993); a public lecture at the College of St Mark and St John, Plymouth (1992); and session papers at the American Sociological Association conference in Pittsburgh (1992) and the Canadian Learned Society Conference at Carleton University, Ottawa (1993). I am most grateful to everyone who invited me to attend these events and to those who responded to my words.

For a variety of reasons, and whether they were consciously aware of it or not, Bryan Turner, Barry Smart, Keith Tester, Zygmunt Bauman, Mike Featherstone, John Urry, David Frisby, David Chaney, Rob Shields, Stjepan Mestrovic and the management and staff of the Century-Paramount Hotel, New York City, aided and abetted this book. In a cowardly way – to protect myself from critics – I should like to break the convention that applies in academic acknowledgements and say categorically that the people listed above were wholly responsible for the arguments herewith supplied.

But I cannot tell a lie . . .

'There's a new cure for lonely travelers at the Chicago railroad station. For a quarter, a wax-covered robot shakes your hand and says: 'Hello, my friend, how're your doing? It's been great seeing you. Have a good trip.' (*Marie Claire,* January 1963)

But you can only live life in one place at a time. And your own life while it's happening to you never has any atmosphere until it's a memory. (Andy Warhol)

INTRODUCTION
CAPITALISM/MODERNITY/
POSTMODERNITY

There have been many attempts to define leisure. Most follow the practice of common sense and associate it with 'freedom', 'choice' and 'life-satisfaction'.[1] But a moment's reflection shows that this approach is inadequate. In much of our leisure experience we are unsure whether we are satisfied or not; and the freedom and choice that we have is obviously contingent upon place, time and, above all, the actions of others. Rather like the concept of utopia, leisure seems to be one place on the map of the human world where we are constantly trying to land, but which perpetually evades our reach.[2] This suggests that leisure does not exist – an immensely seductive proposition which at least explains why so many authors have trouble in defining it! All the same, with so much time and space devoted to leisure pursuits, so much money spent in the leisure sector, so many people employed in producing leisure goods and services and so many engaged in leisure studies, it seems perverse to posit the non-existence of leisure.

In this book, then, I will not assert the non-existence of leisure. But I will argue that what we understand by the term is socially conditioned, which makes conventional associations of 'freedom', 'choice' and 'self-determination' with leisure insupportable. Leisure studies, I contend, is not so much about the examination of integrally constituted physical space or 'natural' segmented time and 'free' experience. Rather it is about what freedom, choice, flexibility and satisfaction mean in relation to determinate social formations. In other words, there is a *discursive* level to leisure studies – a level which, moreover, has largely been ignored by students of leisure. To make this case now – when leisure studies is busily trying to institutionalize itself in the Academy as a specialist area of enquiry – will not curry favour with the newly emerging professional leisure academic. For basic to my argument is the proposition that one cannot separate leisure from the rest of life and claim that it has unique 'laws', 'propensities' and 'rhythms'. Indeed, a great deal of the book is devoted to unravelling projects which claim to treat leisure programatically as a personal or collective state of being to be maintained or accomplished through rational training, discipline, education, management and policy, or through casting off the character armour of ordinary social life and surrendering oneself to 'self-expression'. Leisure experience is, I venture to suggest, more messy than most leisure educators and managers believe.

The book takes strong issue with the proposition often found in the leisure studies literature that 'life-satisfaction', 'escape', 'choice' and 'freedom' can be centred on leisure. Hence, the use of the term 'decentring' in the title. I use the term in two distinct senses. First, to suggest that in order to understand leisure accurately we should begin not with our central object – that which we take to be the thing-in-itself – but rather with the context in which the thing-in-itself becomes an 'object', 'an issue', 'a problem' or what have you. For me, the object of leisure is subsumed by the subject of culture.[3] The further we probe into the matter of what leisure is, the greater is our appreciation of the part played by cultural mores, distinctions and conflicts in establishing the parameters of debate and also what occurs in leisure time and leisure space. Second, I want to draw attention to the fact that specific cultures have centred specific meanings on leisure. Under capitalism and modernity strong tendencies existed to associate leisure with 'real experience', release, escape and freedom. Even under modernity the question of whether it is valid to bind these meanings and associations to leisure was forcibly raised. But under postmodernism there is much greater interest in exploring the decentring of these associations and meanings from leisure. To some extent the book can be read as arguing that the modernist identification of escape, pleasure and relaxation with leisure was simply another kind of moral regulation, with the result that, under modernity, we were never sure if we were free enough or far enough from that which we wished to escape from in our leisure activity. In other words, even at the high-point of modernity there was an ambiguity about leisure experience. At its most basic level the ambiguity relates to the age-old conflict between agency and structure. In pursuing our various projects of freedom we realize that our concept of freedom is itself socially constructed and therefore carries with it particular constraints and limits.

To some extent, then, the argument in the book is polemical. I want to oppose the proposition that leisure is in any meaningful sense 'free' time and 'free' space. But I also wrote the book in the hope of giving students an accurate and direct understanding of leisure practice, identity and experience. There is something in our culture – and other cultures – which is called 'leisure'. Both historically and sociologically speaking, discernible expectations, desires, wishes and habits of conduct adhere to this cultural category and it is legitimate to take them as an object of enquiry. Elsewhere (Rojek 1985), I have written at length about some of the key theories of leisure. In the present book I focus on some of the key ideas that I take to be essential for understanding leisure. These ideas are examined against the backcloth of three social formations: capitalism, modernity and postmodernity. Each formation is associated with a generalized, discursive level of common assumptions and beliefs concerning action, identity, association and practice which help to give a fuller picture of the meaning of leisure. It will be helpful here to give a brief descriptive account of the character of the three formations.

Capitalism

Mumford (1967: 274) defines capitalism as

the translation of all goods, services and energies, into abstract pecuniary terms, with an intensified application of human energy to money and trade, for the sake of gains that accrue primarily to the owners of property, who ideally are prepared to risk their savings on new enterprises as well as to live off the income of established industrial and commercial organizations.

This portmanteau definition artfully disguises the major controversy about the meaning of capitalism which has raged since the nineteenth century. Broadly speaking, two camps – the Marxists and the Weberians – disagree sharply about the engine of capitalist development. For Marxists the engine of capitalism is to be found in the expropriation of the labourers. In England the Enclosure movement, in Scotland the Highland Clearances and in the USA the abolition of slavery are seen as casebook examples of capitalist development. In each case traditional systems of subsistence were destroyed and serfs or slaves were turned over 'naked' onto the market as wage-labourers. The Marxist explanation of capitalism emphasizes conflict, opposition and violence. The system, Marx (1977, I: 834) tells us, was created 'in blood and fire'. He argues that it is based in class exploitation and is governed by an irreconcilable contradiction between the forces and relations of production that is fated to destroy the entire system in due course. To be more technical, Marx submits that the productive physical and technical forces developed by capitalist enterprise will eventually be obstructed by the social barrier of the class system which prevents the optimal use of natural resources, labour and technology. When this happens the system will be torn apart through working-class revolution and the new era of communist relations between free, associated producers will be inaugurated.

In contrast, the Weberian version identifies the engine of capitalism in religion and the rationalization process. Weber constantly stresses the unique character of Western development. He explains it in terms of the specific historical combination of the emergence of a professional administration, rational law and the ethos of Protestantism (1961: 232–44; 1976). Capitalism has thrived, according to Weber, because it is technically the superior form of social organization. There is no prospect in his sociology of transcending capitalism, although, of course, options are always available to social actors to alleviate its worst effects. Later it will be apparent just how opposed Marxist and Weberian explanations are in helping us to make sense of leisure experience under capitalism. At this stage of the discussion it is enough to note the contrast.

Although Marxists and Weberians disagree about the causes and development of capitalism, they are none the less in common agreement about the main effects of the system on human behaviour. Capitalism privileges individual experience over collective experience; it tends to reduce human relationships to monetary values; it requires massive self-denial; it is based upon continuous change; it prioritizes work over leisure, Reason over Nature and masculine values over feminine values; it is a global system of production and it enforces the commodity market as the universal and necessary state of social existence.[4]

What emerges most forcefully from accounts of leisure under capitalism,

whether they be Marxist or Weberian, is the commodification and homogenization of experience. Commodification refers to both the process by which
labour is purchased as a resource by the capitalist and turned into a 'factor of
production', and the process by which goods, services and experiences are
packaged and sold as objects to the consumer. Leisure and culture are shaped
by the process of commodification. For example, the development of sport has
involved a shift between playing and watching to paying and spectating.
Professional competitors are paid to play and spectators pay to watch. Satellite
broadcasting has taken this a stage further by introducing annual fees to spec-
tate in the comfort of your own home. The development is reinforced by the
advertising industry and the professionalization of sport. Turning to homogenization, this refers to the levelling down of experience so that variety is
replaced with uniformity. For example, the package travel business began with
the British firm Thomas Cook in the nineteenth century. They seized upon the
interest in foreign travel and rationalized it to a table of key sites. However, as
the business flourished, critics maintained that the character of tourism was
degraded. The package tour, with its concern for comfort and efficiency, was
accused of negating spontaneity and variety. Tourist experience became routinized and mechanical. Many tourists travel through entire continents
without wandering very far from their tour bus and pre-arranged hotel room
(Pemble 1987; Urry 1990a; Rojek 1993a).

   Commodification and homogenization means that capitalism is a system
with few avenues of escape. Cohen and Taylor (1992) argue that escape
attempts from the system tend to be reabsorbed by the system. For example,
the alternative lifestyles of the 1960s which emphasized self-expression,
authenticity and frankness became commodified. Radical criticism of capitalism often contains a strong streak of utopianism. Thus, in Marxist analysis,
the system which oppresses and mutilates is also seen as the system which can
be replaced with a more rational, just scheme of things. It follows that the
study of leisure under capitalism has been especially interested in the ways in
which people resist commodification and homogenization. The various
attempts to prioritize community and class values over the values of self-interest and competition are highlighted. The unevenness of the system in
engineering subordination is stressed. And the prospect of a better future for
all is pushed to the foreground. Marx (1977, III: 820) himself referred to 'the
realm of freedom' beyond capitalism in which labour ceases to be determined
by necessity and mundane considerations and becomes instead a means of
expression and growth.

Modernity

Following Berman (1982) and Sayer (1991), it is legitimate to argue that the
concept of modernity was anticipated by Marx and Engels. In *The Communist
Manifesto* (originally published in 1848) Marx and Engels described the transformations wrought by the bourgeois class in capitalist society. They listed the

vast increase in productive capacity, the growth of science, the creation of new cities and the development of new social and personal opportunities. But they also (1968: 38) refer to the constant 'revolutionising of the instruments of production, and thereby the relations of production, and with them the whole relations of society'. Here they describe the capitalist class as 'pitilessly' 'tearing asunder' traditional ties and conventions (1968: 38–40). Here too they present their famous, oft-quoted conclusion:

> Constant revolutionising of production, uninterrupted disturbance of all social conditions, everlasting uncertainty and agitation distinguish the bourgeois epoch from all earlier ones. All fast-fixed frozen relations, with their train of ancient and venerable prejudices and opinions, are swept away, all new-formed ones become antiquated before they can ossify. All that is solid melts into air, all that is holy is profaned. (Marx and Engels 1968: 38)

This passage richly conveys the sense of turmoil, restlessness, constant change, fragmentation and division which is essential for an understanding of modernity. However, the presentation of Marx as an archetypal modernist requires qualification and refinement. The problem is evident even in the short passage quoted above. Marx and Engels end their declaration with the statement that 'man is at last compelled to face, with sober senses, his real conditions of life and his relations with his kind'. This decisively places them as radical reconstructionists. They believed that scientific analysis could reveal the real conditions of social existence and that society could be made to conform to a socialist blueprint of rational justice. To be sure this *is* a typically modern view. In traditional society people tended to believe that social development was determined by unalterable, supernatural forces. Human action was seen as fatefully conditioned. Hence there was little that one could do to alter one's course through life. Only under modernity, at first in the Renaissance and later in the Enlightenment, was the idea born and nurtured that humans make their own history. In positing Marxism as the true science of society Marx reflects the modernist belief that existence is not destiny. His *idée fixe* is that the world can be transformed and managed to capitulate to human rationality.

If this represents the modern *mentalité*, it does so only in a partial way. For although the belief in 'great transformations' and 'social blueprints' is evident in modernist thought from the Enlightenment to the present day, it is qualified with an encroaching sense of doubt, scepticism, irony and pessimism. There is, one might say, another side to modernity. Here flux, motion and ceaseless movement are seen not as the pathologies of class domination which will be eliminated as soon as classes are eradicated and rational thought is installed as the arbiter of social relations, but as immutable features of modern life. Thus, Baudelaire (1964: 13) cautioned against the bewitching notion of permanent solutions and grand revolutions. Instead he argued that the essence of modernity lies in 'the transitory', 'the fugitive' and 'the contingent'. It may seem odd to oppose one set of abstractions with another. But Baudelaire is trying to draw attention to the new rhythms and currents in social life associated with industrialization, urbanization and the rise of 'the society of the spectacle', the society of signs. For Baudelaire, modernity is pre-eminently about mass circulation processes and the delirium of change. The key circulation processes are the circulation of bodies, commodities, ideas, images and information. Modernity is associated with delirium because it spins objects, ideas and other stimuli around the world at fantastic rates of acceleration and in unpredictable combinations which are themselves in flux. Nothing seems certain or dependable. The modern psyche is therefore rent with anxiety and restlessness. It vacillates between an up-tempo vision of change as exciting and positive and a horrifying picture of the social world as disintegrating and collapsing. For Baudelaire, this form of consciousness is most fully developed in the metropolis. Here the seemingly endless movement of populations, vehicles, commodities, fashions, building styles, cultures and aesthetics creates a penetrating sense of ephemerality, homelessness and incompleteness (Berger et al. 1973).

Accounts of leisure which take modernity as their essential context tend to emphasize two sets of contrasting forces. On the one hand they emphasize order and control. Modernity is presented as a social order in which rational principles can be imposed on daily life. The time and space allocated for work and leisure can be determined by mathematical precision to ensure the well-being of the individual and society. Leisure activity is presented as fulfilling and enriching. Planning is freedom and freedom is essentially orderly. The second set of forces emphasized in discussions of modernity are disorder and fragmentation. The restlessness and uncertainty of experience are bluntly emphasized. Metropolitan culture is treated as a showplace of ever-changing stimulations (Simmel 1978). Leisure activity is presented as a series of fleeting relationships which can produce boredom, frustration and nervousness as well as excitement, stimulation and pleasure. The leisure industry is depicted as a tireless impresario dedicated to the cult of distraction. The notion of leisure as a means of self-improvement is often treated with cynicism. Instead the hypnotic qualities of the distraction industry are underlined and leisure activity is explored as a way of filling in the consumer's empty time.

Postmodernity

Some aspects of modernity are evident in postmodernity. Perhaps this is only to be expected for postmodernity is explicitly theorized as emerging from modernity. Indeed some accounts present this process as still in gestation. Instead of referring to the postmodern 'condition' they allude to 'intimations' or 'glimpses' of postmodernity (Bauman 1992; Tester 1993). Because it is still a matter of debate whether we live in the age of postmodernity or in an age of transition, contrasting definitions of postmodernity are plentiful. Lyotard (1984: xxiv), 'simplifying to the extreme', as he puts it, defines '*postmodern* as incredulity toward metanarratives' (emphasis his). By this he means the dissolution of faith in the grand theories which intoxicated modernist thought: rationalism, humanism, liberalism, socialism, feminism, civilization, progress – in fact any theory or system which is posited in universal truth and progress.

Harvey (1989: 44) takes a slightly different line and defines postmodernity as the 'total acceptance of ephemerality, fragmentation, discontinuity . . . [it] swims, even wallows, in the fragmentary and the chaotic currents of change, as if that is all there is.' As Harvey himself notes, this definition takes Baudelaire's characterization of modernity as 'the transitory', 'the fugitive' and 'the contingent' to an extreme. It treats postmodernity as a chronic form of the tendencies of circulation, fragmentation and instability already present in modernity. Some discussions of postmodernity argue that these processes are so well developed that it is appropriate to speak of the disappearance of the human subject (Baudrillard 1987; Virilio 1991). Society only has meaning in terms of the electronic communication systems that connect – for want of a better term – nomadic consciousness. 'Reality', 'truth' and 'identity' are portrayed as language games consisting of free-floating signs supplied by the smooth running and self-sustaining communications industry. However, *contra* the culture industry thesis of Adorno and Horkheimer (1944), the communications industry is itself seen as powerless to control or shape change. Rather it is simply the main connecting rod of postmodern culture.

Accounts of leisure in postmodernity stress the decomposition of hierarchical distinctions between high and low culture; irresistible eclecticism and the mixing of codes; the pre-eminence of pastiche, gesture and playfulness in social interaction; the withering attitude to constructivist notions of self-improvement or utopia; the depthlessness and transparency of activities; the pursuit of seduction as an end in itself; and the collapse of the distinction between author and consumer.

Postmodern leisure is, as it were, existence without commitment. It is associated with plenitude but not discretion. In particular, the multiple uses and relative cheapness of communication systems are held to expand leisure options. Experts on leisure technology argue that a revolution in the use of the domestic interior as a leisure resource is already clearly underway.[5] The catalyst is telematic technology. High-definition wide-screen TV for viewing terrestrial, cable and satellite channels vastly improves the quality of home viewing. As the cost of this technology falls it will come within the reach of the ordinary consumer. Parallel advances in communications technology will soon allow us to choose and watch movies via the phone line; to shop from the home; and to view customized electronic newspapers with text, sound and film. The consumer will be able to switch between camera angles when watching sport. The personal computer monitor will emerge as a prime leisure resource giving access to files of games, photos, graphics and libraries. Computer networking will allow instant contact throughout the world. Fibre-optic cables will enable the individual to play action games with people who are situated hundreds or thousands of miles away. Virtual reality technology will allow us to browse through the articles in a fashion store or engage in an interactive VR-movie.

These developments will transform our common-sense distinctions between the domestic interior and the external world, work and leisure, private and public life. But they do not exist in isolation. Allied to them are a series of important changes in the fabric of social life. Among the most important, which are already clearly visible, are capital accumulation in the economy from centralized, mechanically organized systems of production to flexible, decentralized and organically organized systems;[6] a greater mix in the production, circulation and consumption of symbolic goods; raised consciousness of life as being essentially contingent and uncertain as opposed to fixed and stable; a marked weakening in the division between work and leisure; an enhanced presence of the global in local conditions; and transformations in the zoning of populations within the metropolis. Writers on postmodernity are divided about the effects on consciousness of the communications explosion. Some see postmodernism as executing new standards of ethical openness, tolerance and responsibility in everyday life (Bauman 1992). Others see postmodernism and postmodern leisure as indissolubly linked with dissolution and pathos (Kroker and Cook 1986; Jameson 1991). Faced with a multitude of expanding leisure options the individual feels permanently cut off from pleasure and excitement. Each leisure selection that he or she makes will seem to be merely arbitrary from the flux of possible leisure options. The meaninglessness and emptiness of leisure activity will become oppressively self-evident. Those who devote themselves fanatically to a single leisure pursuit will be dismissed as stranded representatives of retro-culture. Jameson (1991: 3–54) argues that in postmodern culture individuals are unable to connect the image-stream of signs which bombard them into a meaningful narrative. Instead they become immersed in the 'multi-phrenic intensities' and sensations of the communications industry.

Confounded Divisions?

In separating capitalism, modernity and postmodernity I do not want to be understood as proposing a unilinear theory of leisure. The question of periodization is important. I suppose that by 'capitalism' I mean the social formation of market organization which had its origins in the maritime expansion and agricultural revolution of the fifteenth and eighteenth centuries, but which only crystallized with the industrial revolution in the late eighteenth century. Modernity is harder to periodize since, in the sense that I use it in the book, it refers to the attempt to impose rational control on the whole of the physical and social world and the various collectivist counter-revolutions against this grand ambition. This usage gives modernity a pretty wide berth. A rigorous interpretation would certainly push its origins back to the very dawn of science and moral and political economy. But again I am interested in the time when modernity fully came together and this for me was an eighteenth-century phenomenon with the rise of the Enlightenment. As for postmodernity, most authorities agree that it only became a palpable social formation in the 1960s (Lyotard 1984; Harvey 1989).

By repeating the observation that the question of periodization is important but neglecting to pursue it rigorously in what follows, I do not want to belittle the issue. However, in recent historical work I have been more taken with studies by authors like Schivelbusch (1980, 1988, 1992), Sennett (1977, 1992) and Lasch (1979, 1984) who are more interested in the transformation of qualities of experience as opposed to plotting the time-sequence in which these changes occurred.[7] To my mind this is the right priority. For me, in studying leisure and other aspects of social life, the changing values and forms of experience are the central interest. Moreover, in matters of history the subject of how and why we change as opposed to when we change is paramount. It follows that I use capitalism, modernity and postmodernity in this book for their suggestiveness about aspects of leisure. I am, of course, aware of how readily the divisions can be confounded. For example, let me take but two illustrations relating to the division between modernity and postmodernity.

(1) Simulation is widely seen as a vital characteristic of postmodernity. Baudrillard (1983a: 2) defines simulation as 'the generation by models of a real without origin or reality'. To put it more concretely, simulation refers to all of those processes and objects which are designed to duplicate, imitate or extend original objects and processes. Simulation processes have been prominent in the expansion of the leisure industry during the 1980s and 1990s. Examples include heritage sites which claim to reproduce the sights, sounds and smells of the past and designer-reconstructions of spatially remote objects and lifestyles such as Wild West towns, Mediterranean villages, oriental shrines and so forth.[8] The proliferation of simulated environments is interpreted as indicating the accentuated presence of fictional and fantasy elements in postmodern culture.

For some observers postmodern culture is dominated by a sign-economy in which fixed referentials have been liquidated (Baudrillard 1983a: 4; Kroker and Cook 1986). Authenticity has disappeared. This has serious implications for the study of leisure. For leisure is often described as the realm of the authentic – the area in life where we can really be ourselves (Parker 1983; Kelly 1987; Olszweska and Roberts 1989). It follows that if authenticity has disappeared there is no longer any basis for leisure as a distinctive area of life.

But is simulation so very new? Critics point out that as early as the eighteenth century modernist culture was preoccupied with problems of simulation (Williams 1982; Porter 1993: 1–22). For example, Goethe's novel *Die Leiden des Jungen Werthers*, published in 1774, is the story of the unrequited love of a fashionable young man who eventually commits suicide. The book became one of the grand leisure scandals of the eighteenth century. It inspired a wave of *Wertherism*. Young men simulated the fictional character's style of dress. They aped his melancholic style and repeated his weary aphorisms. There was even a wave of copycat suicides not only in Germany, but also in England, France, Holland and Scandinavia (Alvarez 1971: 228–30; Christiansen 1988: 57–9).

The example shows highly detailed simulations of the sign world and it troubled contemporary observers precisely because it suggested that modernist culture was incapable of distinguishing between fact and fiction. But *Wertherism* is by no means an isolated example of simulation. English eighteenth-century architecture abounds with examples of simulated environments.

For example, Mereworth Castle in Kent designed by Colin Campbell was basically a copy of Palladio's Villa Rotonda in Vicenza (begun in 1567). Lord Burlington also imitated the design of Villa Rotonda in the construction of his villa at Chiswick (1726). Osterley Park in Middlesex (1761) was built to a neo-classical design by Robert Adam which copied both the Propylaia of Athens and the Temple of the Sun at Palmyra. The Gothic designs of Horace Walpole in Twickenham (1753) and William Beckford's Fonthill Abbey in Wiltshire (1796–1807 – now demolished) represented a minority taste. However, like the popular neo-classical designs of the eighteenth century they were attempts to simulate the atmosphere and 'reality' of the distant past. It is perhaps not too fanciful to think of these estates as the private theme parks of the eighteenth century. Their collection of ersatz attractions included not only historical simulations of retro-cultures and styles but also designer representations of geographically distant objects and lifestyles – Chinese pagodas, oriental gardens and so forth (Kidson et al. 1962).

(2) The disappearance of meaning is a prominent theme in postmodern writing. Kroker and Cook (1986: 176–7) submit that 'the new information of the electronic mass media is directly destructive of meaning and signification, or neutralizes it.' Following Baudrillard (1986: 179), they maintain that the sign-economy is now 'the locus of the real'. Similarly, Jameson (1991) fastens upon the superficiality of postmodern culture. He argues that 'depth is replaced by surface' (1991: 12) and that intertextuality dominates postmodernity. Intertextuality is a term which derives from the work of Kristeva. It refers to the various relationships that a given text may have with other texts. These relationships include allusion, parody, pastiche and imitation. Intertextuality implies that everything can be 'read' or interpreted as a text. This is the logical corollary of regarding culture as based in the collective sharing of signs. For Kristeva and Jameson there are no fixed meanings in postmodern culture. Meanings are conditional and intertextual. Nothing is solid or certain. Since there is no underlying meaning, cultural relations revolve around surface appearances and immediate impressions. This is why questions of design and aesthetics are assigned such prominence in postmodernist writing. Jameson (1991: 20) goes so far as to claim that 'the history of aesthetic styles displaces "real" history'.

Yet the troubled debate about the elimination of meaning in consumer culture and leisure is hardly very novel. Plumb's (1983: 265–85) discussion of leisure forms in eighteenth-century England reflects on the popularization of fictional and fantasy elements in mass culture and the weakening of the distinction between reality and illusion which accompanied it. Similarly, Marx in his discussion of commodity fetishism[9] writes:

> There is a definite social relation between men, that assumes, in their eyes, the fantastic form of a social relation between things. In order, therefore, to find an analogy, we must have recourse to the mist-enveloped regions of the religious world. In that world the productions of the human brain appear as independent beings endowed with life, and entering into relation both with one another and the human race. (Marx and Engels 1954: 77)

So it is with the sign-economy. Although it consists of nothing but 'the productions of the human brain' it appears as a dreamworld which replaces the real world. Marx, of course, believed that this situation could be transformed by uprooting the pillars of capitalism and reconstructing relations of production, exchange and consumption through communist organization. Simmel – one of the most subtle and penetrating commentators on modernity – is less sanguine. In his classic essay on metropolitan culture (1971: 324–39) he argues that the velocity and multitude of stimulations in modern culture overload our capacity to make sense of them. The remorseless agitation and excitement ferments a dualistic mental attitude. We either cultivate a blasé attitude which is 'indifferent toward the distinctions between things' (Simmel 1971: 329) and therefore treats all spectacles and distractions as equivalent, or we succumb to a heightened nervousness which renders us incapable of settling on any activity or relationship for very long. Leisure is dominated by distraction factories (pop music, TV, film, video, mass sport) which perpetuate mere time-filling activities (Frisby 1989). Benjamin's (1970) thought on nineteenth-century consumer culture extends the point. He refers to the 'phantasmagoria' of modernist leisure forms 'into which people entered in order to be distracted' (1970: 165). Although Marx, Simmel and Benjamin do not use terms like 'intertextuality' and 'depthlessness' it is plain that their work on modernity recognizes these characteristics in daily life. Long before Kristeva, Baudrillard or Jameson addressed postmodernity, elements of what is now called 'the postmodern' were clearly labelled and examined by writers on capitalism and modernity.

The examples are hardly exhaustive. Even so, perhaps enough has been said to indicate that, in what follows, I do not want to be understood as proposing a determinate relationship between the three social formations discussed and the properties of leisure associated with them. We are dealing here with propensities and tendencies of behaviour rather than iron laws and necessities. For example, by taking capitalism as the context for a discussion of alienation and the culture industry I am merely suggesting that certain aspects of what alienation is, and how the culture industry is theorized as operating, are thrown into sharper relief. I am *not* suggesting that alienation and the culture industry are irrelevant in the context of either modernity or postmodernity. Perhaps matters are best expressed if one pictures the three formations as a set of contrasting horizons on the history and processes of leisure and culture. Each horizon encompasses some aspects of leisure and culture while at the same time leaving other aspects in the shadow of semi-darkness. At any rate, such was the metaphor that I held in my mind's eye in preparing the book.

PART 1
CAPITALISM AND LEISURE

1
CAPITALISM: PRODUCTION

Capitalism is a system of production. It is based on the private ownership and control of the means of production. The aim of private ownership is to achieve profit through market competition. For the capitalist, profit is the reward for risk.[1] Subject to the privations of taxation it accrues to the risk-taker, that is, the capitalist.

Capitalism does not formally require a class of slaves. Indeed one of the revolutionary aspects of the capitalist system of organization, highlighted by Marx and others, is that labour is provided by workers who act as free agents in the market. However, while workers are not the chattels of the capitalist, a number of formal and informal pressures impel them to sell their labour power on the market. Under early capitalism these pressures were especially blatant (Thompson 1963, 1967; Bailey 1987). Up until the start of welfare provision late in the second half of the nineteenth century workers received no guaranteed public means of subsistence. They therefore had to work in order to feed, clothe and house themselves. When they became ill, unemployed or too old to work they were forced to appeal to private charity or else to reconcile themselves to destitution and homelessness. With the development of state welfare provision new levels of subsistence support were introduced to protect the worker, for example sickness benefits, unemployment benefits and pension rights. However, these have been consistently criticized for their insufficiency. Indeed some commentators argue that the system of welfare provision must itself be understood as a mechanism for reproducing labour power. By this, critics mean that welfare provision should not be interpreted as evidence of the inherent fairness of capitalism. On the contrary, since capitalism requires the reproduction of labour power to continue, it follows that the system must make public provision for workers to be housed, fed, educated and entertained. It must also ensure that workers remain in existence during periods of temporary unemployment so that they may be re-employed when the economy picks up again. According to this line of analysis, welfare provision has to be understood as a device for ensuring the reproduction of healthy and useful labour power and disciplined consumers.[2]

The Universal Market and Alienation

On this reading, leisure activity is part of 'the universal market' of capitalism. The universal market means a web of commodified goods, services and amusements which eliminates any possibility of escape. Braverman (1974: 281) identifies three stages in the development of the universal market. The first stage consists of the replacement of domestic or barter systems of production with the commodity form. The second stage involves the conversion of services based upon personal or local trust relations into commodified services and amusements. The third stage is a 'product cycle' in which new goods, services and amusements are endlessly paraded before consumers so that they create a dependency culture, that is, people feel that they cannot live without them.

The universal market required a steady stream of cheap goods to fill the shop counters. A variety of management styles have been devised to achieve this task. Perhaps the most influential was F.W. Taylor's (1964) system of *scientific management* introduced towards the end of the last century. Scientific management was fixated upon satisfying the mass market by ensuring high-volume production of commodities at an attractive price. Taylor's method was to dismantle the production process into a series of specialized, interconnected tasks. He envisaged that it was the task of management to train and restrict workers to a simple task or work activity. Managers were to plan all stages of the production process and to ensure that the co-ordination of work tasks was efficiently achieved. A time budget system based upon time and motion data was to be introduced to regulate the production process. This method of cost accounting would establish the average time taken to complete a given work task. It would equip managers with a standard to apply to the actual labour process. Taylor sealed his system with a payments by results scheme for the workers. Financial incentives, he argued, were the surest way to motivate workers. Beyond conveying a general sense of puritan disdain for 'unruly' or 'licentious' behaviour, Taylor showed little interest in the worker's leisure time. His stop-watch system allowed that workers trained to fulfil a given task mechanically would require some time to recuperate. But his system did not directly seek to regulate the worker's leisure time.

Despite objections from trade unionists and social critics that scientific management is inherently dehumanizing, the Taylor system flourished. It was a major influence on Henry Ford's momentous system of assembly line motor-car production. However, there was a significant difference between Fordism and Taylorism. Ford's system envisaged the work and leisure of the worker to be part of a comprehensive system of management control. The system was based on the notion of creating a dedicated workforce, each trained to perform a specialized task in a co-ordinated mass production system. It also worked with the economic model of man advocated under scientific management. 'The five dollar eight-hour day' became Ford's byword for attracting an enthusiastic, pliable workforce. But Ford also employed legions of social workers into the homes of his workers to ensure that their leisure activity was morally sound and consistent with 'rational corporate expectations' (Harvey 1989: 126).

On one level the Fordist interest in workers' leisure simply continued long-standing programmes of social control. The assumption that the home and private life is as much the business of the manager as the workplace and public life was anticipated by the rational recreation movement which emerged in the leading capitalist societies during the 1860s.[3] The growth of towns and cities established large concentrations of working-class people. Middle-class fears of moral decay and physical contagion resulted in campaigns to clean up the leisure activities of deserving workers and to instil in them habits of thrift, industry and self-improvement. Art galleries were established in working-class districts where the poor were encouraged to go to raise their moral horizons (Borzello 1987). Workers were taught that a healthy body makes a healthy mind and offered courses in physical exercise and sport. Parks were established as 'the lungs of the city' and workers were encouraged to stroll through them on Saturdays (but not on Sundays – the one day off for most people at the time – because this conflicted with religious principles) (Fazio 1979; Manchester City Art Galleries 1987). Youth organizations, such as the boy scouts and the boys' brigade, were established to harness and improve the unruly passions of working-class city adolescents (Springhall 1977).

Rational recreation was enormously popular with many of the workers. For example, exhibitions of religious paintings, such as Holman Hunt's *Light of the World* (opposite), which shows a kindly haloed Christ with a lantern in his hand for Christians to follow, literally brought traffic to a standstill during its first exhibition in London. A late version of the work, painted between 1901 and 1904, toured the Empire and was viewed by over seven million people (Maas 1984). The touring exhibition was a forerunner of the spectacular leisure forms which some observers argue characterize leisure relations in mature industrial culture (Debord 1967; Chaney 1983). Similarly, organized games, sports and instruction were appreciated as a means of self-improvement by many workers who dreamed of upward mobility for themselves and their children (Gibbon 1934; Ewen 1976; Yeo 1976).

However, as Ewen (1976), Stedman-Jones (1977), Gray (1981) and other commentators have shown, there were also strong tendencies among some workers to resist the new training programmes and devise their own forms of rational recreation as a badge of class identity. Bourgeois-led programmes of rational recreation aimed to teach workers to be self-regulating and orderly. Some commentators have read it as an extension of the scientific management principles applied in the workplace (Andrew 1981; Rigauer 1981). Rational recreation is the corollary of the processes of commodification and homogenization described in the Introduction. All have the common effect of standardizing social life. This process of standardization is criticized by many writers as propagating alienation.

Alienation is of course one of the most enduring concepts produced by Marx (1964). He used it to denote the estrangement of individuals from themselves and from others. Marx's discussion focused on work experience. In Marxist sociology the will to labour is associated with self-discovery and species-making. Through our work activities we create ourselves and make our

William Holman Hunt, The Light of the World (1901–4)
(reproduced by permission of Keble College, Oxford)

own history. This generous interpretation of work associated the act of labour with creativity and the fulfilment of desire. For Marx, waged labour in capitalist society blocks creativity and strangles desire. It contributes to the alienation of the worker in two ways. In the first place, the tasks of waged labour are imposed upon the worker by the owner of capital or his or her management intermediaries. He or she is therefore forced to make a present of his or her energies and creativity to others. The result is that the process of labour is experienced as external to the worker; 'it does not belong to his essential being . . . he does not affirm himself, does not feel content but unhappy, does not freely develop his physical and mental energy but mortifies his body and ruins his mind' (Marx 1964: 110). The second point is that the products of the worker's labour do not finally belong to him or her but to someone else. The worker is forced to create value through the act of labour. However, this value is appropriated by the capitalist. The lives of workers and the products of these lives are, so to speak, robbed from them by the capitalist.

Although Marx's discussion of alienation seems to be narrowly focused upon work experience there are in fact clear implications for leisure experience. Marx understood labour to be the key to human fulfilment and happiness. What happens in work experience therefore affects the whole of human life. Thus, the experience of labour as external or self-denying finds its parallel in the experience of the consumption of leisure experience as external, coerced and manipulated. The spontaneous activity of human imagination seems to be sacrificed to a world of produced commodities and packaged experiences. Our leisure does not seem to be our own. Instead it is constructed for us by the captains of the leisure industry. We are reduced to the state of passive consumption – a state which Marx explicitly identifies with animal functions:

> The worker only feels himself freely active in his animal functions – eating, drinking, procreating, or at most in his dwelling and in dressing-up, etc.; and in his human functions he no longer feels himself to be anything but an animal. What is animal becomes human and what is human becomes animal. (Marx 1964: 111)

The reduction of leisure experience to 'mere animal activity' implies that there are cultural agencies in the leisure sphere of capitalist society which operate to repress and manipulate the worker. Marcuse (1964) argues that the standardization of work and leisure experience has created 'one-dimensional societies' in which 'pleasure' is equated with a donatory culture of amusement, with fee-paying activity, distraction and social control. This is of course fully implied by both the theory of the universal market and Fordism. However, the argument is most forcefully expressed in the Frankfurt School's culture industry thesis. It is to this controversial and influential Marxist theory that I now wish to turn.

The Culture Industry

The term 'culture industry' was coined by Adorno and Horkheimer (1944). It means the collection of entertainment industries dedicated to amusing the masses in their non-work time: film, jazz, pop music, television, magazines and radio. The culture industry is seen as a decisive new stage in the development of the universal market. It organizes subjects at the very moment when subjects are led to believe that they are truly free: in their 'non-work' time. One way in which this occurs is by feeding the masses unchallenging entertainment with overt and subliminal messages of an explicitly patriotic and conservative character. These messages relate that everything is for the best in society and that nothing fundamental needs to be criticized or changed. For example, in movies the cops always beat the robbers; in pop songs real love always finally triumphs; on television the corrupt are always exposed; everywhere fairness, decency and justice are portrayed as ultimately triumphing over adversity. Looked at in this way much popular entertainment is a grotesque parody of real life. It breeds complacency in the audience who move in a leisure–work cycle from their armchairs to their beds and out to work again secure in the belief that society is moving in the right direction and that things are not so bad after all. Furthermore it isolates social critics as misfits or dissidents. Existing leisure forms are presented as intrinsic social benefits and criticisms which fasten on the dehumanizing effects of leisure are cast aside as abnormal or unrealistic fancies.

Another important aspect of the culture industry thesis is identified by an associate of Adorno and Horkheimer: Siegfried Kracauer. He comments on the similarities between the rhythms of the body at work and in leisure:

> Everyone goes through the necessary motions at the conveyor belt, performs a partial function without knowing the entirety. Similar to the patterns in the stadium, the organization hovers above the masses as a monstrous figure whose originator withdraws from the eyes of its bearers, and who himself hardly reflects upon it. It is conceived according to rational principles which the Taylor system only takes to its final conclusion. The hands in the factory correspond to the legs of the Tiller Girls. (Kracauer 1975: 70)

Kracauer invokes the image of the metronomic society in which work, leisure, sleep and sex have their appointed time and place.[4] His work is one of the first contributions in the study of popular culture to attribute importance to bodily and spatial metaphors and symbols in managing mass conformity. The mechanical movements of the dancing Tiller Girls – a mass leisure craze in Weimar Germany – find their parallel in the mathematically precise organization of Fordism. Kracauer presents a mass psychology of bewitchment by which the masses 'voluntarily' comply with the system that brutalizes and enslaves them. The body at work is regimented to crave the same rhythms and synchrony in leisure. The Frankfurt School[5] authors offer the masses no escape. Marcuse (1964) submits that society has become 'one-dimensional' and that the masses are no longer able to distinguish personal freedom from manipulation.[6]

Not surprisingly the thesis has been much criticized. Hebdige (1979) argues that it misunderstands popular culture and leisure. The masses, he argues, are far from being the donkeys of the culture industry. Rather they have the capacity to neutralize, subvert and oppose codes of manipulation. Adorno and his associates are attacked for underestimating everyday acts of resistance and rebellion. The culture industry thesis of complete social control is dismissed as being over-pessimistic. Similarly Bernstein (1991) argues that the culture industry thesis is too crude. He calls for a more sensitive approach to the mass media which registers the symbolic dimensions of mass communication, identifies the schisms within mass culture and acknowledges the progressive possibilities of technology.

The Capitalist State

One obvious agency of social control which was neglected by the culture industry thesis was the capitalist state. Of course, it might be argued that the Frankfurt School analysis is predicated upon the idea of a capitalist state intent on regulating every nook and cranny of social life. On this reading, the culture industries can only function with the approval and support of the state apparatus. Be that as it may, there is no doubt that if the Frankfurt School writers did indeed hold this view they did very little to deliver it into print. Their work cannot be said to afford a theory of the role of the capitalist state in relation to culture and leisure.[7]

However, the concept of a regulative state mechanism overseeing social conduct is prominent in Braverman's (1974) thesis of the universal market. This was also Marx's view. As he put it in *The German Ideology* (1954: 80), the state is 'nothing more than the form of organisation which the bourgeois necessarily adopt both for internal and external purposes, for the mutual guarantee of their property and interests'. Nothing could be clearer than this. The classical Marxist view of the capitalist state is that it is simply the 'executive committee of the ruling class'.

It was the tragic French social philosopher Althusser (1971) who introduced one of the most important distinctions in the Marxist sociology of the state.[8] He argued that the capitalist state is divided into two segments or wings of operation: the *repressive state apparatus* and the *ideological state apparatus*. The former refers to the mechanisms of state control with access to the main battalions of physical force: the police, the judiciary, the prisons, the army. The *ideological state apparatus* refers to a more subtle sphere of state operations: the sphere of persuasion. It includes the education system, the ministries of government, the councils of sport, heritage, the arts and leisure and the civil service. This is, as it were, the government-sponsored persuasion industry. And what is its message? For Althusser it is basically the platitudinous message that the system is working, that is, things are slowly getting better; civil society is guaranteed by majestic laws of justice; leisure delivers happiness, freedom and life-satisfaction; and, above all, tampering with the system will only make things worse.

The work of Corrigan and Sayer (1985) is clearly the fruit of an engagement with the question of the organization of the subject which Althusser's work on the state poses.[9] It is also indebted to a less predictable source: the sociology of

Émile Durkheim. They quote Durkheim's (1958: 72) famous sentence approvingly: the state 'is above all, supremely, the organ of moral discipline.' The implication is that Durkheim recognized an ideological state apparatus in the regulation of morals, leisure and culture long before Althusser. Corrigan and Sayer build upon this idea with their focus upon the state as the key agency of moral regulation in capitalist society. By the term *moral regulation* they mean 'a project of normalizing, rendering natural, taken for granted, in a word "obvious", what are in fact ontological and epistemological premises of a particular and historical form of social order' (1985: 4). State moral regulation works directly through powers of licensing, moral leadership and policing. By these means certain forms of leisure activity are legitimated while others are classified as deviant. However, state moral regulation also works in more indirect ways. By establishing what might be called 'moral atmospheres' in which types of activity are presented as automatically 'healthy', 'uplifting', 'decent', 'proper' or what have you, certain forms of behaviour are classed as 'normal' whereas others are immediately classed as 'problematic'. I shall return to consider the question of moral regulation in greater detail later (pp. 42–5). At this point it is sufficient to emphasize that Corrigan and Sayer insist that the capitalist state is the primary agent of moral regulation.

The classical Marxist view of the state in capitalist society has, of course, been strenuously challenged. For example, Abercrombie et al. (1980, 1986) have been very critical of what they call 'the dominant ideology thesis'. This is the thesis that the capitalist class successfully imprints its values onto the masses. The aim is to win the consent of the oppressed while obscuring the engines of class manipulation so that the ruling moral order is accepted by 'voluntary' popular consent. For example, by presenting national values as the best possible values, or equating competitive individualism as having 'no alternative', the dominant class extends historically specific ways of behaving and organizing as the unchangeable state of nature. Abercrombie et al. argue that the main importance of dominant ideology in society is to secure the integration of the dominant class. Subordinates are not bound to the ideas of the ruling class. On the contrary, historically speaking, they have plainly been effective in challenging ruling class ideas.

One implication of Abercrombie et al.'s argument is that state moral regulation is much less successful in organizing the free time conduct of individuals than the work of Corrigan and Sayer would suggest. Abercrombie et al. maintain that cultural forms cannot be reduced to patterns of state domination in explaining moral orders and patterned types of activity. Hall and Jacques (1989) appear to move in the same direction with their *New Times* argument. According to them, the Marxist sociology of the state has tended to overestimate the homogenization and standardization of mass society. Advanced capitalist societies, they continue, are increasingly characterized by diversity, differentiation and fragmentation. This is linked to the shift in capital accumulation from 'Fordism', which defined the first two-thirds of the twentieth century, to 'flexible accumulation', which defines current conditions (see also Harvey 1989: 141–96). Hall and Jacques criticize interpreters who only comment on the economic dimensions of this change. The heart of the *New Times* argument is that cultural and moral relations have also been transformed. By extension, the problematic in Marxism has changed from a focus on state/class/ideology to culture/identity groups/negotiation. Many on the Left have seen this argument as flirting dangerously with the adventurism of postmodernism. They argue that a form of Marxism which acknowledges identity politics is fatally undermined. It becomes just another critical culture opposed to the logic of capitalist organization but unable to make the leap beyond it.

However, the roots of the Hall and Jacques argument lie deep in a well-established body of work concerned with the state, moral orders and the politics of consumption. This is, of course, the cultural studies approach to capitalist society associated with the publications of Hall et al. (1978, 1980), Hall and Jefferson (1975), Bennett and Mercer (1986), McRobbie (1978) and Fiske (1987). For a time this work was regarded as the leading critical position within leisure studies. Even now many authors contend that it is the best critical alternative to the traditional sociology of leisure (Tomlinson 1989). There are therefore two reasons for turning to a more detailed examination of this approach to leisure and society. First, it will provide depth to the Hall and Jacques *New Times* argument and perhaps help to show why the problematic of state/class/ideology is interpreted as too restrictive. Second, it will provide an account of what is arguably the most influential neo-Marxist approach to leisure under capitalism.

Cultural Studies

Although clearly located in the Marxist tradition, cultural studies is highly critical of many aspects of its roots. For example, the Frankfurt School culture industry thesis is criticized for being grossly monolithic. Where Adorno and his associates saw mass manipulation in leisure experience, cultural studies writers see multiple frontiers of resistance. Where Adorno et al. saw a society without opposition, cultural studies writers see vigorous and diverse forms of resistance and rebellion. Finally, where Adorno (1991) argued that radical change is not possible in existing conditions, cultural studies writers allude to the transcendence of existing social forms and agitate for class action to break the chains of capitalist domination.

The most systematic cultural studies treatment of leisure is to be found in the work of Clarke and Critcher (1985). Their approach is grounded in a Marxist reading of history. Capitalist society, they argue, is first and foremost class society. The capitalist class is defined by the ownership of capital and the endless search to accumulate profit; the working class is defined by its exclusion from the ownership of capital and its need to sell its labour power to survive. Leisure is theorized dualistically. On the one hand, it is presented as part of the universal market. The free time of the masses is subject to the processes of commodification and homogenization. On the other hand, leisure is presented as 'an arena for cultural contestation between dominant and subordinate groups' (Clarke and Critcher 1985: 227). Their argument pays due attention to the variety and diversity of popular culture. Objectively speaking the working class is uniform because its members share the experience of being excluded from capital ownership. However, within this objective uniformity several rich, particularistic cultural forms have emerged. For example, Clarke and Critcher recognize that class experience has been segmented along ethnic and regional lines. The resistance of youth groups differs in style from that of adult workers. Each oppressed group struggles to undo the rule of capital in its own way.

At first sight this argument seems to be in conflict with the conventional Marxist position that the working class is capable of acting as a class in itself to free itself from the shackles of capitalist domination. For the diversity and variety of cultures suggests the elimination of common ground. Clarke and Critcher reject this suggestion. For them the particularities of cultural experience are, in the final analysis, resolved by property relations. As they (1985: 220) put it, 'the primary antagonism is that between capital and labour'. Class is therefore seen as the bedrock for any accurate understanding of contemporary leisure experience. Cultural forms reflect and distort the class base but they are ultimately determined by it. As if to underline the point Clarke and Critcher (1985: 187–96) devote much of their analysis to dismissing various ends of class theses as fanciful. They round on commentators who claim that the decline of the manufacturing sector and the rise of the service sector in the economies of the West has divided the working class. The picture of a dwindling band of unskilled manual workers stubbornly attached to traditional community ties and forms of leisure as against a growing number of skilled manual and white-collar workers attached to privatization and middle-class forms is rejected by Clarke and Critcher as a myth. The essential point, they assert, is that both manual and non-manual class segments are part of the universal market which is controlled by capitalist imperatives. Diversity and variety within the system is therefore illusory since consumer choice is subject to the same framework of provisions (and privations) offered by the system. 'Our ability to choose between what is on offer is stressed,' write Clarke and Critcher (1985: 201); 'our ability to decide what should be offered is conveniently ignored.'

In analysing how normality in capitalist leisure relations is managed Clarke and Critcher give a starring role to hegemony. Hegemony is rather a slippery concept. The term was originally used by Gramsci (1971) to describe how one class achieves domination over another through ideological and political means. Following Williams (1973) and Hall et al. (1980), Clarke and Critcher argue that hegemony is a better tool to explain capitalist processes of control than the classical Marxist concept of dominant ideology. The latter relies on the crude base–superstructure distinction and treats the agencies of cultural control as a reflection of economic power. To put it bluntly, the dominant ideology thesis proposes that the class with the dominant economic power is also the class with the ruling ideas in society. Hegemony presents a more complicated picture. Where the dominant ideology thesis suggested that workers live in a state of false consciousness, hegemony suggests that lived experience is not illusory. The workers are aware of class manipulation and class control. The ideas of the ruling class are therefore not seen as all-pervasive. Rather there is continuing interplay and negotiation between the ruling and non-ruling cultures. Dominated cultures engage practically in resistance so that the ruling ideas are themselves in a state of permanent tension. According to Clarke and Critcher (1985: 227–9), hegemony best explains the processes of contestation and struggle which characterize the leisure relations under capitalism. 'Innovations in leisure,' they write, 'may test the limits of the dominant ideas about what are acceptable leisure meanings and experiences . . . there is "cultural work" to be done, legitimising and incorporating new forms, while marginalising and suppressing others' (Clarke and Critcher 1985: 227).

The cultural studies approach to leisure defines itself in opposition to the traditional sociology of leisure. The latter term is associated with the writings of Young and Wilmott (1973), Roberts (1978, 1981) and Parker (1983). These writers are held to associate leisure with freedom, choice, creativity and self-determination. They hold that the crucial variable for understanding leisure activity is work. They emphasize the humanizing potential of leisure experience. Against this, cultural studies argues that leisure choices are made in a context of structured inequality. The traditional sociology of leisure is criticized on several counts.

First, it is attacked for isolating the work–leisure nexus from the general context of social relations. Work and leisure cannot be studied as autonomous realms of experience. Rather they are bound up with the whole character of society. This opens up questions of culture and ideology which have tended to be ignored by traditional approaches.

Second, the traditional sociology of leisure is criticized for overestimating voluntarism in leisure choices. People do not have free choice in their leisure activities. Rather their choices are shaped by the character of society and its structures of power and domination. To insist that 'we' are free is to hold to an impoverished view of how the human subject is organized under capitalism.

This brings me to a third criticism. The traditional sociology of leisure has tended to rely on survey methods and quantitative data to formulate its main propositions. These methods produce an image of society as it is, not as it could be. We may note, *en passant*, that the image may not be very accurate for survey material is always selective and there are obvious problems in using partial material to make statements about the whole of leisure or the whole of society. However, the deeper point which emerges from cultural studies is that the survey method tends to impose meanings on respondents. Furnishing people with a series of questions and a range of prepared options to questions is a precondition of the survey. But it obviously limits the responses that people can make. In general, cultural studies writers have argued that ethnographic research provides a richer and more valuable method of discovering what is really going on in people's leisure. For at least people here may speak in their own words and make their own response-preferences.

Finally, the traditional sociology of leisure is scorned for showing no aspiration to transform society. In championing 'facts', 'objectivity' and 'science' it avoids the question of how society emerged and what society should be. In this way the traditional sociology of leisure becomes complicit with the structures of power which produce inequality in leisure and society.

The influence of the cultural studies approach in leisure climaxed in the 1970s and 1980s. Since that time it has come under increasing fire from critics. Five points are usually made. In the first place, the claim to be unique in studying leisure as part of an historically rooted structure of inequality is dismissed as wishful thinking. Other approaches also examine leisure as historically rooted and stratified by unequal power relations. The feminist approach to leisure and the figurational approach of the Elias school are most often mentioned as examples.

The second point is that the relation between culture and class is not satisfactorily worked out in the cultural studies approach. Cultural studies writers want to get away from the economism of classical Marxism. This is why they place such emphasis on the richness and diversity of cultural and leisure forms. However, at the same time they wish to retain classical Marxist concepts of social totality. Hence the insistence upon studying leisure as part of general social relations. The problem is that these general social relations are defined in orthodox Marxist fashion as ultimately determined by the class struggle. Given this definition it is not clear what autonomy for cultural and leisure forms the cultural studies approach recognizes in capitalist society. If culture is indeed finally understood as a reflection of the class base the objections to classical Marxism also apply to cultural studies. Namely, this approach to human relations is over-deterministic and fails to genuinely represent the variety and novelty of human forms.

A third criticism centres on the political commitment of cultural studies. To put it bluntly, can an approach which is so fervently committed to class struggle and intervention be trusted to produce an impartial view of leisure? Clarke and Critcher's (1985: 190) argument that 'class refuses to be buried – each announcement of its death has been premature' does suggest a blinkered approach to studying leisure and society. If the premise of all analysis is class struggle it is hard to see how the premise can be satisfactorily tested. Instead it is mechanically repeated to suit every eventuality.

The fourth point refers to the concept of hegemony. The theoretical formulation of leisure as a site of continuous struggle encumbers the study of leisure with an unfortunate responsibility to be relentlessly 'politically correct'. All too readily every move made by the leisure industry is interpreted as a sign of class manipulation. In some cases the interpretation is warranted. As Clarke and Critcher themselves note, the rational recreation movement with its ambition to 'civilize the roughs' fits very well with the model of capitalist hegemony. But when the concept is used without discretion, as it tends to be by students of cultural studies, the results can be embarrassing. For example, Tomlinson (1990: 28), intrepidly wandering through the streets of a northern England town, is amazed by the names of the shops: 'Crusts' (a breadshop), 'Blow' (a barbershop), 'Nosh' (a fastfood shop). Thunderstruck by witnessing the sinister capitalist hand of hegemony at work he rushes home and pens the observation that 'This is beyond doubt: spending has become intensively thematized' (1990: 28). The implication is that capitalism is responsible for this thematization. This is hardly news. But it is the inference that thematization is morally reprehensible and that the 'blame' for this must be laid at the door of the capitalist class which is more controversial. For it can legitimately be argued that thematization is a corollary of mass industrial culture and is not specific to capitalist forms. For example, in Durkheim's sociology thematization is analysed as an effect of the physical and moral density of populations. And this is just as convincing as Tomlinson's analysis of capitalist manipulation. Similarly, Willis (1990: 17–18), in a commentary on the increasing importance of leisure in social and political life, concludes that 'consumerism now has to be understood as an active, not a passive, process'. Again, one is struck most of all by the banality of the remark. It reflects the sense of anticlimax that one often feels after reading cultural studies work. Too often you expect 'the big conclusion'; what you get is a cliché or a trite observation. Clarke and Critcher are not exempt from the criticism. After 200 pages of analysis of leisure activity under capitalism they conclude that 'leisure is never wholly free nor totally determined activity' (1985: 227). Well, if it is not 'wholly free' or 'totally determined', what is it? This brings me to the fifth and final point.

Anyone who reads accounts of consumer society written by cultural studies authors will be impressed by the isolation of leisure experience from any connotation of play or fun. A stoney gaze is directed against rival accounts of leisure which emphasize the positive vitality and pleasure of everyday leisure (Cohen and Taylor 1992; Shields 1992; Chaney 1993). Instead the dogma of struggle and contestation is ritually repeated. So 'release' is piously turned into 'resistance'; and 'display' is primly interpreted as 'dissidence'. But these politically loaded propositions tend to be asserted rather than demonstrated.

These criticisms have led to doubts in many quarters about the power of the cultural studies approach to accurately explain leisure experience (Chaney 1994; Tester 1994). However, while I am in substantial agreement with these critics, it is perhaps important to stress that these doubts must not be permitted to blot out the achievements of cultural studies. I take these achievements to be threefold. To begin with, cultural studies has awakened interest in the structural dimensions of leisure experience. Cultural studies has made traditional views of leisure which align it with voluntarism, freedom and self-determination seem naïve and insupportable.[10] The second achievement is to turn attention back to what people actually experience in their leisure time and leisure space. Cultural studies may be legitimately criticized for perpetuating inflexible assumptions about the nature of experience in capitalist society (Rojek 1994). None the less, in highlighting how leisure meanings are imposed and challenged it situates research and theory at the level of people's perceptions and accounts. Finally, it has raised the question of the emancipatory potential of leisure. Cultural studies has been concerned not only with what leisure activity under capitalism is and what its historical roots are, but also with the crucial question of what leisure might be in non-capitalist forms of society.

Racism

References to race and racism in the work on leisure of cultural studies writers has been little more than perfunctory. Clarke and Critcher (1985: 152–3) deplore the paucity of primary research material on the subject. They confine themselves to a few generalities about the 'probable' specific 'contextualizations' of ethnic leisure patterns,[11] the unequal access to leisure resources of ethnic minorities and the racial prejudice of some segments of the traditional white working class. Race is recognized as a structural influence in the organization of leisure behaviour. However, in so far as it is dealt with at all racism is understood to be the expression of the commodification processes of capitalism. Incidentally, this is why I have situated the subjects of race and racism in this section of the book. Clarke and Critcher appear to be saying that racism is *produced* by capitalism.

However, this position is vulnerable to criticism on a number of counts. In the first place, it is by no means clear that race can be treated as a simple product of capitalism. Said (1978) notes the presence of racist stereotypes in the propaganda of Christian Crusaders. Similarly, Hughes (1993: 140–7) observes that the Muslim trade in African slaves was well established in the first millennium AD.[12] This work relates racism to the emergence of religious formations, ethnic identities and nation-states – all of which pre-date capitalism. If this is correct it follows that the overthrow of capitalist rule should not necessarily be theorized as coinciding with the elimination of racism. Racist divisions have different roots and to understand them the problematic of the capitalist mode of production is not sufficient.[13]

Second, Clarke and Critcher's position implies that race is a dependent variable of class. They understand the central division in society to be between the owners and controllers of the means of production and the propertyless. But it is far from clear that race can be subsumed under class in this way. The divisions within working-class ethnic minorities such as Sikhs, Afro-Caribbeans, Chinese, Hispanics and so forth suggest that it is not credible to entertain a politics of collective mobilization for these sections of society. Rather than speak of nascent class solidarity, what one sees here is the vigorous espousal of specific cultural characteristics and the development of a micro-politics of ethnic pride and self-determination.

Third, the leisure forms prevalent in these ethnic groupings are extremely diverse. They reflect a wide range of strategies of conciliation and reaction to the host (white) culture. If ethnic leisure forms do operate as foci of social integration by asserting and concentrating ethnic identities it is not easy to see how the common denominator of proletarianization can be squeezed out of them. In general, Clarke and Critcher's treatment of race and leisure bears out Miles'

(1993: 27) complaint that 'Marxist theory has experienced difficulties in attempting to comprehend and explain the expression and consequences of racism.'

Even so, within the camp of recent writers on culture and leisure there is at least one approach which places race and racism at the centre of analysis. Hebdige's (1979, 1987, 1988) work on subculture recasts the decisive confrontations and formations in postwar youth culture away from issues of class to issues of race. For Hebdige, postwar non-white immigration into Britain has been the key energizing force in popular culture and leisure. Afro-Caribbean and Asian forms of music, dress, cuisine, poetry and dance are presented as widening leisure choices and reviving traditional working-class culture. Black music clubs, drop-in centres and action groups are viewed as providing a counter-balance of community values which opposes the market-led values of white society. Hebdige is critical of commentators who have analysed this revival narrowly in terms of the intensification of white racism. He presents a more complex picture. Commenting on the formation of skinhead groups in the 1960s he writes:

> it was not only by congregating on the all-white football terraces but through consorting with West Indians at the local youth clubs and on the street corners, by copying *their* mannerisms, adopting *their* curses, dancing to *their* music that the skinheads 'magically recovered' the lost sense of working class community. (1979: 56; emphasis his)

Hebdige analyses the interplay between white and black cultural and leisure styles in terms of a complex 'conversation' of styles, dress, argots, contact networks and symbolic codes. Black culture and black leisure forms provided new standards of difference and otherness. When whites immersed themselves in these forms they created new identities and forms of leisure practice which set a critical distance from the inherited ambience and mores of white culture. They also bred new forms of possessiveness about black style. For example, Hebdige (1979: 58) reads the outburst of 'Paki-bashing' by skinheads in the 1970s not as evidence of a generalized resurgence of racism but as a 'displacement manoeuvre' in which the limited skinhead identification with one black group (the Afro-Caribbeans) was transformed into violence directed against a new black influx (the Asians).

But the process of adaptation and negotiation was not just a one-way street. Although Hebdige does not deal with the matter in any detail, the 1960s also witnessed the emergence of a black culture industry dedicated to promoting black consciousness and black culture. Black-controlled record companies like Tamala Motown and Trojan were initially pre-eminent. They provided a show-case of black artists who proved enormously successful with white and black audiences alike. But the black culture industry also branched out into black-owned and -controlled restaurant chains, fashion shops, night-clubs, literature, film and sports promotion. Black artists like James Brown, Marvin Gaye, Diana Ross, Jimi Hendrix, Muhammad Ali, James Baldwin, Sidney Poitier and later, Bob Marley, Magic Johnson, Daley Thompson, Whoopi

Goldberg and Michael Jackson emerged as role models for blacks and whites alike. In the 1960s and 1970s the boxing promoter Don King created a successful business empire by building a roster of black boxers and matching them at prestige venues. Similarly, Spike Lee's films of the 1980s raised awareness of black perspectives, black issues and black styles.

These developments were an important factor in promoting the ideology of multi-culturalism which is now widely espoused in metropolitan and national leisure and sport policies. In Britain state-funders of leisure activity like the Arts Council and the Sports Council have made special provision for raising multi-cultural awareness and activity. Of course this funding has been criticized for being nothing more than tokenism (Gilroy 1987; Cross and Keith 1993: 19). According to this line of criticism, blacks still suffer from fewer leisure and sport options and resources; they are still more likely to be living in deprived areas; and they suffer higher levels of unemployment. In the context of this structure of material deprivation the ideology of multi-culturalism is condemned as state-sponsored multi-racism. Yet despite the legitimate critical points regarding inequality in leisure opportunities, the inroads that multi-culturalism has made into the state agencies of leisure and sport planning and management are significant. It provides state recognition of the specificity of black leisure forms and it offers finance to develop this specificity. Instead of demanding monolithic assimilation into white culture, multi-culturalism insists on the right of blacks to have their own leisure spaces and resources. And this insistence is the basis for black activism at the level of national and local politics to engineer a shift in resources.

2

CAPITALISM: REPRODUCTION

One issue that must be confronted before examining feminist arguments on leisure is the connection between patriarchy and capitalism. To put the point concisely: male domination of women was not born with the commodity form of society – why then have I connected the two so directly in this chapter? The reason is that the majority of feminist accounts of leisure treat capitalism as the crystallization of patriarchy in the economic, political, legal and cultural spheres. The family is presented as a sort of prototypical capitalist factory in which the husband owns the means of production and the wife is the oppressed creator of unpaid surplus value (Wimbush and Talbot 1988; Green et al. 1987; Henderson and Bialeschki 1992). There are also important parallels between orthodox feminism and the Marxist critique of capitalism. Both work with a dichotomous model of society. For Marxists the key dichotomy is between the capitalist class and the proletariat; for feminists the key dichotomy is between men and women. Similarly, the feminist and Marxist arguments posit a universal oppressed subject. For Marxists it is the proletariat; for feminists it is women. Finally both traditions endorse political activism as a strategy of liberation. By breaking the grip of capital, organized activity can break the mechanisms which make objects out of people and brutalize human relations. It might be argued that all of these features – the dichotomous model of society, the notion of a universal oppressed subject and emancipatory politics – reflect the mark of modernism rather than capitalism. There are rather complicated technical questions here which it is not appropriate to try to tackle in a book of this type, which, after all, aspires to do no more than provide a critical introduction to theorizing leisure. To my mind the crunch issue is that both Marxism and orthodox feminism play down the ambiguities of commodification in favour of a utopian model of society in which these ambiguities are eliminated. Since capitalism is the commodity society *nonpareil*, it makes sense to consider orthodox feminism in the context of capitalism rather than modernism. The question of what modernism is will be taken up in more detail in the next section of the book. So much for preliminaries, let us now turn to some of the leading arguments made by feminist writers on leisure.

Feminists argue that the study of leisure, culture and society has been dominated by a 'male-stream' of perspectives (Deem 1986; Bella 1989; Hargreaves 1989). The traditional sociology of leisure is criticized for ignoring the existence of women. Additionally, it is held to posit a classless, deracialized, degendered 'individual'. Questions of gender construction and the gendered management of 'free' time activity are ignored. The critical sociology of leisure fares little better in most feminist accounts. It is attacked for prioritizing the politics of production over the politics of reproduction. We labour and experience not merely as 'workers' but crucially as gendered subjects, that is, as men and women. Feminists attack the critical male-stream in leisure studies for blotting out gender and dreaming of a revolution of 'free' workers rather than a revolution of free men and women. They treat gender as an aspect of being which is distorted by capitalist domination but which is distinct from class. Thus, feminists argue that capitalism has produced 'a common world' of women's experience regardless of the social position of individual women in the hierarchy of social stratification.

The feminist sociology of leisure argues that women's experience of leisure is structured by various male exclusionary strategies. These strategies limit both the quantity and quality of women's leisure experience. For example, women in capitalist society are valued primarily for their reproductive function. This means that they tend to be confined to the home. Since housework does not produce the surplus value in the same direct way as factory/office work it has tended to be labelled as non-work. In some classifications of leisure, household chores, bodily maintenance, child-care and shopping are defined as part of the leisure spectrum, that is, as non-work activity (Barrett 1980; Wearing and Wearing 1988). What constitutes women's leisure is therefore by no means clear. It is subjected to various informal pressures calling for 'responsible', 'caring' behaviour. These pressures are not so pronounced in male leisure experience. Thus for most married husbands going out to watch a film or to have a drink with work-mates is a 'natural' continuation of the workplace. For married women the same leisure choices require far more planning to ensure that the children are properly looked after.

The restraints on women's leisure are not specific to the stage of family life in the life-cycle. Rather they act consistently on women from birth until death. McRobbie (1978) and Griffin (1985) noted that domestic responsibilities were commonplace among young girls – but not so with young boys. Most girls help with domestic chores such as washing-up, cleaning and cooking. These responsibilities impinge upon their 'free' time activities. Griffin (1985) argues that even when girls do get out of the house they find leisure spaces in the exterior dominated by men. For example, youth clubs are dominated by boys and pubs are filled with men and boys. Hanging about on the streets and parks is something that boys do. Girls are only present in these leisure spaces by the consent of their male partners. Evening or weekend paid labour for young girls suffers from the same condition as paid labour for all women in the labour force – namely it is much lower *pro rata* than male labour. All of these forces coalesce to produce strong pressures to make the home, or more precisely the girl's bedroom, the focal leisure space for the leisure experience of young girls. The time spent in external society is time spent subject to the more powerful male gaze.

With marriage and family life the leisure privations of women increase. Children cut into women's leisure space and time more sharply than into the leisure space and time of men. Child care dominates the life-world of mothers. It prevents them from going out or working unless adequate care provision is organized. Men are not under the same social pressures. Equal child care for men represents a conscious personal choice, a decision to sacrifice 'freedom' and 'self-determination' – for women child care is an extension of social expectations. Children again re-emphasize the dependence of women upon the home as the primary leisure space. After they have cooked, cleaned, shopped, helped the children with their homework, looked after the bills, prepared supper snacks, received calls from their mothers and mothers-in-law, the home is where they put their feet up! It is not just that mothers generally have less leisure than fathers, whole areas of growth, opportunities for enriching identity by improving personal knowledge and confidence seem almost surgically removed by society.

Children do not simply limit what mothers can achieve in their 'free' time, they also limit career opportunities. By interrupting women's paid labour experience or terminating it, children sharply underline the reliance of mothers upon the income of their husbands or state support. This can have disastrous consequences for women after retirement age. As Deem (1986: 130) notes, it is at this stage in the life-cycle that the economic effects of interrupted work patterns translate into lower pension entitlements (because pension contributions have been suspended by the requirements of child care). It is also at this stage that many women are deprived of the financial support of their husbands, because male life expectancy is lower than female life expectancy. For many women, then, old age rubs salt into the wounds of restricted career and leisure opportunities in working life by rewarding them with an unstable source of income.

Feminist Methodology

One of the strongest claims made by feminists is that feminist methodology enables them to study questions of leisure more accurately than other approaches (Wimbush and Talbot 1988; Henderson and Bialeschki 1992). Among the arguments most commonly made to support this claim is that feminist methodology enables researchers to study dimensions of power relating to sexual inequality which are either invisible or understated in non-feminist research. Male-dominated research is criticized for making a fetish of scientific method and hierarchical relationships in research. Non-feminist research, it is argued, treats people as objects and therefore fails to understand real experience (Stanley and Wise 1992). Non-feminist approaches are also taken to task for being morally unacceptable. To study power and inequality in leisure without making any commitment to change conditions is seen as being complicit with the structures of power that produce inequality. Against this feminism treats emancipation as the object of research. 'Feminism,' declare Henderson and Bialeschki (1992: 63), 'is both an ideology – a set of beliefs and values about women and gender relations – and a social-political movement for change.'

Hammersley (1992) has taken issue with these arguments. In a truculent assessment of feminist methodology he concludes that feminism does not constitute a coherent alternative to non-feminist approaches. In his view the arguments which feminists make against positivist method and in favour of non-hierarchical research relationships are not unique to feminism. Parallels are easily found in research devised and conducted by men. The feminist commitment to emancipation, he continues, interferes with objectivity and produces biased findings. For Hammersley gender is simply one important variable among many important variables. In criticizing the blinkered approach of feminists he cites the work of black feminist researchers who criticize white feminists for making the variable of race invisible.

Ann Game (1991) has also criticized the work of Oakley (1974) and Stanley and Wise (1992). This work, argues Game, was concerned to produce feminist research by and for women. It was highly critical of hierarchical subject–object relations within male research. But can the subject–object opposition which is implicit in all research be eliminated by feminist recognition of gender power and inequality? For Game the feminist research of Oakley, Stanley and Wise has produced new relationships of power between feminist researchers and the subjects of their research. 'The very idea of representing women,' she maintains, 'even if in the form of "letting them speak", is to constitute women as object. To claim that "they" are subject is to avert the question of authorship and the constitution of a "feminist self" via an other' (Game 1991: 31).

Hammersley's criticism provoked a salvo of counter-criticism from feminists. Ramazanoglu (1992) contends that he is naïve to seek refuge in the notion of 'scientific value-neutrality'. Feminism rejects the positivist illusion of a 'pure' science of society. Instead it treats the empowerment of women as integral to feminist practice. Male researchers may not like this. But by treating it as a defect they lose sight of feminism's main virtue: realism. For her part, Gelsthorpe (1992) takes issue with Hammersley's argument that feminism privileges gender as the key factor in explaining social relations. Rather than speak of 'feminism', she avows, it is more accurate to speak of 'feminisms'. While some of these support Hammersley's argument about the privileging of gender, others produce explanations of social life which explore the complex articulation of gender inequality with variables of class, ethnicity, locality and so on.

Gelsthorpe's position is replicated in feminist research into leisure, notably in the work of Deem (1986), Wearing (1992) and Harrington et al. (1992). However, the most influential feminist position within leisure studies to date has undoubtedly been the one which emphasizes the importance of gender over other variables. While I want to come to 'post-feminist' arguments later in the chapter, my object at this stage of the discussion is to examine the writings that claim that women inhabit a common world of leisure experience.

A 'Common World' of Women's Leisure?

A prominent theme in feminist research on leisure is that women inhabit a 'common world' of experience. This 'common world' is home-centred in the sense that women's leisure experience is concentrated in the home. But it is also home-centred in the sense that women's work opportunities in the labour market tend to reflect the qualities which are said to characterize the home sphere: caring, listening, helping, supporting, cleaning, home-making, design, decorating and so forth (Bialeschki and Henderson 1986). Because of this women are denied real equality in the external world of the market.

Yet there are dangers involved in accepting the 'common world' view at face value. Much research shows that differences in status, class and type of household affect women's subjective experience of leisure (Glyptis et al. 1987; Bolla et al. 1991). Similarly, by concentrating on women's powerlessness the important role that women have played historically in enriching public leisure space and creating 'rounded personalities' as an important social goal is obscured. The involvement of women in the development of public education, social work, the planning of metropolitan space, the protection of nature, and many other areas of modern life not only 'softened' male values but also provided an alternative set of values for assessing how personal and public life ought to be organized (Hayden 1981; Rojek 1993a: 51–96).

Emphasis on a 'common world' view of women's leisure can also lead to exaggerated expectations about strategies for change. For example, Talbot (1988: 174) reviews the various options open for women to combat male domination. She notes that women's participation in mixed-sex organizations can have unfortunate consequences. Women who set out to change male values are often incorporated into the male world of competition, aggression and the denial of feelings. Women-only groups, Talbot concludes, have the advantage of raising women's self-esteem as well as providing women with experiences of authority and responsibility denied in mixed-sex organizations. However, 'women-only' groups appear to be politically limited by sectarian characteristics which prevent them from successfully changing society 'as a whole'. In particular they appear to leave no avenues open for men who also believe that male values of competition, aggression and the denial of feelings damage private and public life. Furthermore, it is by no means obvious that groups organized along the line of sexual membership will overcome the divisions of class, race and locality that beset human relations elsewhere in society. Women are clearly divided along lines of stratification too and these divisions interfere with communication, mutual understanding and solidarity (Ramazanoglu 1989; Harrington et al. 1992).

Despite the inherent difficulties with the concept, there is little doubt that the concept of 'the common world of women' has been pivotal in feminist approaches to leisure. The reasons why have to do with feminist methodology. The commitment of feminists to be both a movement of action and a way of understanding is predicated upon emancipatory politics. This politics is predicated on the view that women alone are vulnerable to the rule of men. However, women who organize and act together are in a position not only to challenge the rule of men but also to articulate alternative forms of identity, association, organization and practice. This notion of emancipatory politics is heavily dependent upon the assumption that there is a tyranny to escape from.

To describe this order as 'men' or 'male rule' is over-simplistic. As many feminists acknowledge, men are not naturally bound to adopt sexist attitudes. They can be changed by feminist arguments. Indeed a growing body of pro-feminist writing by men demonstrates a male rejection of male sexist attitudes (Seidler 1989, 1992; Rutherford 1992). The order of tyranny which feminists seek to overthrow is patriarchy. As Wimbush and Talbot (1988: xvi) put it:

> Patriarchal relations, like class relations, are culturally reproduced, even magnified within leisure and recreation. They are legitimated and sustained by a complexity of ideological and material forces which help to shape our social institutions – the family unit, the media, the education system, the legal system and so on. The policies, provisions and professional practice promulgated by the institutions of leisure and sport are an integral part of this framework.

Patriarchy, then, is theorized as an integral moral and political order which excludes women from some social forms and types of experience.

However, many sociologists argue that patriarchy is not an accurate way to classify the current balance of power between the sexes. 'Women,' observes Turner (1984: 154), 'still experience sexism in everyday life, but this is a defunct patriarchalism, an interpersonal strategy of dominance on the part of men who find their traditional sources of power increasingly open to doubt.' Borrowing from the race relations theory of Banton (1967), Turner (1984: 154–6) suggests that a distinction should be made between patriarchy and patrism. Patriarchy is based in the systematic exclusion of women from the public sphere by a complex system of legal relations, political organizations and economic arrangements. Patrism involves discriminatory, prejudicial and paternalistic beliefs and practices of men towards women but it has no systematic support in legal or political terms. Women continue to be disadvantaged in work relations, taxation arrangements and banking facilities but, argues Turner (1984: 155–6), 'such inequalities are under attack and are generally regarded as discriminatory and incompatible with existing democratic arrangements.' While patriarchy accurately described relations between the sexes in early capitalism it has been replaced by patrism, which suggests that a more ambiguous, less polarized balance of power now exists between men and women.[1]

Turner's argument may be critical of some forms of feminist argument but it is quite unambiguous in insisting that feminism as an approach to social life is necessary. We live in societies in which sexist attitudes have obviously not 'withered away'. If patrism suggests that anti-sexist movements have punctured patriarchy it stops well short of implying an end to sexism. On the contrary, the concept of patrism recognizes that sexist attitudes are a part of everyday life and that they must be constantly interrogated and challenged.

Post-feminism?

Feminism has succeeded in making gender central in the study of leisure. Any work on leisure published since the mid-1980s which fails to mention gender is correctly attacked for its partiality and lack of realism (Deem 1986: 8–18). Feminist theories have been fundamental to contemporary theories of leisure because the feminist movement has problematized the relationship between ideology, gender and choice. The universal freedom which the traditional sociology of leisure tended to associate with non-(paid)work activity seems absurd when set against the feminist analysis of the production and reproduction of sexual ideologies and leisure options between the sexes in male-dominated societies. 'Although leisure is generally perceived in terms of hedonism, pleasure and freedom,' write Woodward et al. (1989: 144), 'in practice norms about femininity, respectability and motherhood operate as powerful constraints on women's licence to engage in leisure activities.'

One question which has perhaps not been examined deeply enough in feminist research is: how do women exploit these constraints *with men*? Undoubtedly feminist research has been successful in showing how womens/girls' leisure groups operate 'beyond the male gaze'. Among the effects claimed for these groups are the raising of consciousness, the development of confidence and the opening up of feminist identities (Dixey and Talbot 1982; Wimbush 1986). However, when it comes to examining leisure relations between the sexes the assumption in some quarters seems to be that women's leisure consists of uniform repression. Thus women's leisure is described in terms of self-denial and self-mutilation (Wimbush and Talbot 1988; Henderson and Bialeschki 1992). What is missing from these accounts is any sense that women might enjoy their leisure with men. Recently critics from within feminism have questioned if it is correct to picture women as losers in a zero-sum power game where men always win (Bella 1989; Game 1991; Wearing 1992).

For Wearing (1992) the balance of power between the sexes involves struggle, resistance, negotiation, subversion, power shifts and pleasure as well as pain and frustration. Her approach allows for ambiguity in relations between the sexes and variety in the forms of leisure identities that women develop. 'Each actor', she writes, 'constructs her subjectivity at the interface of discourses which may be contradictory, and in relationship to the forces of power present in a particular site and at a particular point in time. Individual subjectivity can be a resistance to dominant stereotypes; differences within women and between women are possible' (Wearing 1992: 327).

Wearing's concepts of subjectivity and power seem to be different from the same concepts found in the work of feminist authors like Deem (1986), Talbot (1988) and Henderson and Bialeschki (1992). Wearing sees subjectivity as fluid, often playful and ironic, and conscious of its own ambiguities. These characteristics are absent from the concept as it is used in the work of the other feminist writers mentioned. For them subjectivity is definite, focused, unambiguous and won through struggle. Turning to the concept of power, Wearing rejects the idea that subjectivity is finally defined by an over-determining structure of patriarchy. She gives prominence to the multiplicity of power structures in society and the slippages between them. This line of argument is not evident in the work of the feminist writers mentioned. Instead they emphasize that the main problem with the sociology of leisure is precisely that the over-determining power structure of patriarchy has been made invisible by male writers. Their work assumes a functional relationship between the structure of patriarchy and the system of leisure options and choices between the sexes.

Do these differences reflect a rift in feminism and the emergence of post-feminist positions?[2] Certainly the work of Bella, Game and Wearing rejects traditional feminist notions of the common world of women and the inalienable superiority of feminist research. It allows for heterogeneity and ambiguity in forms of women's leisure relations with women and men. It considers playfulness, contradiction and irony to be integral to feminism. It is suspicious of attempts to define the essence of sexual identity or to attribute iron-like functions to social structures. In the work of Deem (1986), Wimbush and Talbot (1988) and Henderson and Bialeschki (1992) feminism is treated as a garrison from which women must attack the brutality, injustice and delusions of male rule. For Wearing and Game feminism is an orientation to social life which is acutely sensitive to gender inequalities and committed to challenging them, but, crucially, they recognize that men as well as women are caught up in systems of self-deception and self-mutilation.

PART 2
MODERNITY AND LEISURE

3
MODERNITY 1: THE ROOTS OF ORDER

In the Introduction I noted that discussions of leisure organized against the backcloth of modernity tend to emphasize two sets of contrasting forces: order and control and disorder and fragmentation. For the sake of simplicity I propose to name these two sets Modernity 1 and Modernity 2. In this chapter I shall examine how the key ideas relating to leisure relate to Modernity 1. In the next chapter I shall move on to consider some of the mechanisms of control which shape leisure under Modernity 1. The two chapters following this will discuss the meaning of Modernity 2, explore some of the distinctive mechanisms of de-differentiation associated with it and show how Modernity 2 and these mechanisms relate to leisure. Although the two sets are considered separately here it is important to realize that this is solely for the purposes of analysis. In fact Modernity 1 and Modernity 2 are interdependent.

Functionalism, Positivism and Pluralism

It is difficult to write about Modernity 1 and leisure. Modernity 1 refers to the general transformation of personality, economy and society which has its roots in the Renaissance and the Enlightenment but which crystallized with the industrial revolution. By confining the discussion to leisure the idea that modernity is only relevant to so-called 'free time' practice might germinate in the reader's mind. Nothing could be further from the truth. As many commentators have argued, to fully understand modernity a general theory of society is necessary (Berman 1982; Frisby 1985). However, this proposition cannot be fully examined in a book of this type which is devoted to exploring but one part of society, namely leisure. To solve the problem I have elected to concentrate upon those writers and ideas who/which in my view best exemplify the mark of Modernity 1 in leisure studies.

A variety of labels have been used to describe these ideas: functionalism, pluralism and positivism. None is quite satisfactory because each has a specialized meaning in the discipline from which it emerged. Functionalism emerged from biology and sociology and states that society is an organism which requires people and organizations to perform essential functions in maintaining social order. For example, the health of society requires that some people must maintain a clear system of law, so the judiciary and the police emerge to perform this function. Similarly, the health of society demands that people work, so a system of labour training, allocation and reward develops to perform this function. Leisure here is seen as one of the functions that must be fulfilled if society is to remain in good order. If leisure activity contributes to the disorder of society it follows that this type of activity must be corrected since it disturbs the harmony of the social system.[1]

Positivism emerged from natural science and philosophy. It holds that science can only deal with observable processes and conscious experience. The positivist aims to record observations about objects and processes and to build general laws from this material. Positivism therefore tends to place ultimate weight on quantitative data. A typical positivist project in the study of leisure might involve recording what television programmes families from different social strata watch and building general theorems of leisure and stratification from this data. Or it might consist in a statistical survey of the uses of public recreation facilities according to pre-selected criteria, for example class, sex, race, locality.[2]

Pluralism emerged from political economy. It argues that power in society is shared out between a variety of interest groups. In the short term it is quite possible to show that one interest group is more successful than the others in getting its way. However, pluralism holds that there is no long-term tendency for any single group to dominate the decision-making process. For pluralists society is basically democratic. The main impetus in political life is to provide channels of articulation for the diverse groups that make up society. Pluralism holds no commitment to transform society.[3]

Functionalism, positivism and pluralism have been very influential in our understanding of ourselves and our societies. However, they have also been ferociously criticized. It is not possible here to give anything more than a flavour of the general points which critics make. The most important criticism is that facts cannot be expressed in social life without values interposing themselves (Kolakowski 1972; MacIntyre 1981). Hence the attempts to produce 'factual' accounts of society are always problematic. In particular, they are vulnerable to the charge that what is identified as 'factual' or 'crucial' simply reflects the values of the dominant group in society. But there is also the wider problem that facts – like societies and individuals – change. For example, it used to be believed that automobile exhaust fumes posed no major threat to the environment. Now we are conscious that leaded petrol creates serious pollution and is a major contributor to global warming. Similarly, it used to be thought that the consumption of fatty foods posed no threat to the health of individuals. However, we now know that low-fibre diets are associated with heart disease and cancer. Unfortunately social knowledge does not work smoothly. So that when a change in our knowledge about social life occurs it does not always follow that this change results in concomitant changes in people's behaviour. Thus the discredited 'facts' of one period may still have a powerful influence on people's behaviour despite the weight of accumulated evidence stacked against them.

A second general criticism is that functionalism, positivism and pluralism produce a view of society which is too formal. They do not help us to understand the real variety of human experience. Instead they over-exaggerate the importance of established and observable patterns of behaviour. For example, in leisure studies there has been little interest in deviant forms of leisure. By deviant forms of leisure I mean activities which break the law, for example illegal drug-taking, joy-riding, trespassing, animal-baiting and illegal sexual activity. We know that deviant leisure activity is crucial in organizing identity and forms of association for large numbers of people. Yet this spectrum of behaviour is, as it were, largely marginalized in public life. That is, it is not considered as part of the orderly life which regulates daily behaviour.

A third point is that the approaches in question have not been sufficiently comparative or developmental in their approach to the study of human behaviour. So 'laws' which are formulated from the observation of behaviour in one society at one time are extended to apply to all societies in all times. For example, the functionalist proposition that leisure functions to recuperate the jaded energies of workers ignores the fact that leisure forms have developed *within* the workplace as an ordinary part of work culture (Moorhouse 1989). It also underestimates the extent to which some forms of leisure might be experienced as boring and oppressive.

Despite these criticisms the three research traditions in question have a powerful position within leisure studies. The reason for this are twofold: they appear to give objective and impartial answers to questions which can be tested; and they are adaptable as tools in the formulation of leisure policy. The fact that they also give clout to hard-pressed academics and researchers working in universities and research centres where questions of leisure are often seen as marginal or unimportant is also significant. In what follows I will describe in a general way how these traditions have influenced our understanding of leisure. I will then move on to discuss five contrasting theories of the relation of leisure to order under Modernity 1.

Order

Modernity 1 defines leisure as occupying an observable space and time in society and having an observable function. Thus Dumazedier (1974: 71) writes:

> I . . . reserve the word leisure for the time whose content is oriented towards self-fulfilment as an ultimate end. This time is granted to the individual by society, when he has complied with his occupational, family, socio-spiritual and socio-political obligations.

Dumazedier defines the function of leisure from the standpoint of the individual. This is also the common-sense way of proceeding. However, there is of course another way of defining leisure and that is from the standpoint of society. Here leisure is seen as a subsystem within the social system which contributes certain functions which are necessary to the stability of the whole social system. These functions include relaxation, exercise, innovation, education and preservation. Typically leisure is seen as a dependent variable of the subsystem of work. As Olszweska and Roberts (1989: 2) put it:

> Societies create leisure only in so far as their economies produce in excess of more 'basic' requirements. And the growth of leisure in the modern world continues to rest on the relentless application of science and technology. . . . The more committed and successful they are as workers, the greater will be any group's leisure opportunities. Leisure can never replace either work or the values that underlie economic success without undermining its own vitality.

What both of these definitions have in common is the conviction that leisure is a necessary element of the modern social order. That is, its functions contribute to the well-being of the individual and society. This proposition is supported with a number of assumptions. In the first place, leisure is seen as a civilizing influence and an ultimate moral value. As Kaplan (1984: 61) puts it, 'the primary value of mankind in industrial societies is leisure.' Modernity 1 associates leisure with progress – a vital part of 'the good society' – and life-satisfaction. As we saw above, this produces blindspots in what can be examined as leisure under Modernity 1. More specifically, Modernity 1 tends to marginalize 'deviant', 'abnormal' or 'hidden' forms of leisure with the result that doubts must be raised concerning its accuracy and completeness.

A second assumption is that there are legitimate spaces and times in modern societies where leisure occurs. Concerning leisure space these include theatres, cinemas, parks, sports grounds, public walkways, protected monuments and sites of nature. As for leisure time, Modernity 1 identifies holidays, weekends and evenings as times in which leisure is concentrated.[4] There are important political implications about these time and space divisions. Once leisure time and leisure space have been created they must be policed and defended. This is of course the basis for all manner of conflicts, notably from social actors who reject the basis for the definition and hence object to policing. For example, the leisure-user may contest the management of leisure provided by the leisure-supplier as has happened in the organization of public parks in the USA or the management of public monuments such as Stonehenge in Britain (Gold 1980; Rojek 1988).

A third assumption is that certain forms of identity, association and practice are appropriate in leisure time and leisure space while others are not. Sometimes these forms can be bluntly codified as is the case with licensing laws relating to lewd behaviour or the consumption of alcohol in public places. However, it is more general under Modernity 1 for these distinctions to rest upon 'understandings', 'manners', 'mores' and other standards associated with the term 'civilized behaviour'.

In summary, then, Modernity 1 regards leisure to be a legitimate and progressive feature of civilized social life. It identifies leisure with social integration, with enhancing the well-being of society. To this end leisure time and leisure space are allocated where leisure identities, associations and practices can develop. Finally, it installs and maintains a formal and informal system of policing which aims to ensure that leisure practice is orderly and decent.

What produces social order? The question is relevant because as soon as one looks at history it is obvious that many standards of order are relative. For example, in the ancient societies of Greece and Rome vast surpluses of leisure space and time were created for the ruling classes. However, this surplus rested upon a system of slavery which was typically regarded to be a 'normal' and 'just' part of the social order. Similarly in the nineteenth century legal means were used to outlaw forms of animal mistreatment in the leisure industry such as dog-fighting, the immolation of cats and bear-baiting which had hitherto been accepted as 'normal' (Ritvo 1987).

There are many competing explanations of the historical construction of social order. Five in particular have claims upon our time: conservative theory, moral regulation theory, the Protestant ethic thesis, conspicuous consumption theory and the theory of the civilizing process. Each of these developed as general theories of social change. However, they have a particular resonance for the question of how Modernity 1 orders leisure in everyday life.

Conservative Theory

Conservative theory reproduces many of the assumptions of positivism, functionalism and pluralism. Order is conceived in much the same terms as Adam Smith thought of 'the invisible hand' in the eighteenth century. That is, individuals are seen as pursuing their self-interest within the limits of the law and, through this, society providentially pursues the collective good. In the long run no individual or group is seen as having the capacity to dominate society. Life in society is regarded as akin to an open race in which the best finally win through. What is the place of leisure in this social order?

'Leisure,' writes Kaplan (1975: 26),

> is a relatively self-determined activity experience that falls into one's economically free-time roles; that is seen as leisure by participants; that is psychologically pleasant in anticipation and recollection; that potentially covers the whole range of commitment and intensity; that contains characteristic norms and constraints; and that provides opportunities for recreation, personal growth, and service to others.

Most of the key conservative assumptions and beliefs are reproduced in this definition. Leisure is equated with individual choice and self-determination. It is regarded as the antithesis of work. It is associated with personal growth and social harmony. It is held to be bound by rules which establish the limits of civilized behaviour. And it is regarded to be inherently progressive.

The close identification of leisure with creativity and social integration translates into the isolation of leisure services as an implement for social improvement. For example, Kraus (1987: 15–17) lists six benefits for society in funding effective leisure and recreation services:

(1) *Social cohesion and adjustment.* There is an enlargement of personal skills

and therefore the growth of satisfying social conditions. Leisure and recreation are held to increase social tolerance, develop personal happiness, cater to 'natural' needs of companionship and competition and develop a spirit of co-operation. They are identified as a social good because they promote order and stability.

(2) *Self-realization*. The creativity and satisfaction which is often denied in the work sphere is said to be liberated in the leisure sphere. Leisure is viewed as enriching personal skills and producing happier people. By increasing personal happiness the stock of social happiness is increased and social life becomes more pleasant and satisfying.

(3) *Community renewal and restoration*. The cohesive values of leisure and recreation can restore pride and excitement into run-down inner-city areas. By turning redundant industrial buildings into heritage centres leisure and recreation conserve and educate. The benefit to society is an increase in tolerance and enjoyment in the inhabitants of the social community.

(4) *Citizenship and responsibility*. Participation in leisure and recreation is associated with neutralizing anti-social behaviour. It is said to breed 'wholesome attitudes' and 'habits of positive social conduct'. Equally it is believed to increase the stake of the individual in the maintenance of social harmony.

(5) *Personal health*. There is a long tradition of identifying leisure and recreation with the development of physical and social health. 'All of the internal systems are benefited by physical and emotional release', contends Kraus (1987: 17). 'On a moderate and continuing basis . . . [leisure] supplies that form of exercise and mental stimulation which supplements and complements the normal course of daily life.'

(6) *Personal involvement and commitment*. The ideals of the group and society are seen as strengthened by voluntary, pleasurable free time activity. By playing together we add to our experiences and problem-solving skills. Leisure and 'recreational activity', declares Kraus (1987: 17), 'is a positive experience. It in no way causes the degeneration of the individual.'

Kraus clearly perceives leisure to be an unequivocal benefit for society. He sees it both as an implement to correct negative social tendencies and an essential foundation of the good society. Similar views can be found in the work of Dower et al. (1981) and Collins and Strelitz (1982). All see leisure policy as a way of formalizing progressive tendencies in social life and, through this, increasing the general stock of human happiness.

But there are problems with the view of leisure espoused by these conservative writers. Above all, what is missing in their work is any real appreciation of the viability of difference or otherness. Leisure forms built around hedonism, drug experience, anti-possessiveness and mindlessness tend to be dismissed as being of temporary significance. However, for many commentators it is precisely these forms of 'free time' experience that have become prominent in contemporary society. For example, Godbey (1989: 75) refers to *anti-leisure*, by which he means 'activity which is undertaken compulsively, as a means to an end, from a perception of necessity, with a high degree of externally imposed constraints, with considerable anxiety, with a high degree of time-consciousness, with a minimum of personal autonomy, and which avoids self-actualization, authentication and finitude.'

Similarly, there is insufficient discussion of the ends of leisure policy. To talk abstractly about increasing the happiness of people and the stability of society can be very misleading. For example, the *Kraft durch Freude* ('Strength through Joy') movement in Nazi Germany organized cheap package holidays, walking tours, weekend excursions, theatre and music events. At a time of mass unemployment when many German workers had a lot of superfluous 'free' time, the 'Strength through Joy' movement was immensely popular. However, it was also one of the main transmission belts of Nazi political and racist propaganda (Bessel 1987).

The failure of conservative theorists to adequately come to terms with these matters considerably weakens their claim to speak authoritatively on leisure in society today. However, this failure has created a space which has been rapidly occupied by more critical, reflexive and challenging types of theory.

Moral Regulation Theory

Economic regulation theory developed in the late 1970s and 1980s (Aglietta 1979; Lipietz 1987). The seminal work is generally agreed to have been Gramsci's (1971) 'Americanism and Fordism'. Here Gramsci comments that the revolution in production associated with the assembly-line mass-production techniques and the high-wage strategy practised by the Ford Motor Car company necessarily translates into a revolutionary transformation in the consumption of the working class. The regulation school develops Gramsci's argument by proposing that every form of capitalist production requires a complementary form of consumption.[5] The collective term for the two forms is *regime of accumulation*. The maintenance of this regime requires a set of non-economic institutions called a *mode of regulation*. Among the institutions involved are schools, universities, hospitals, the welfare system and mass advertising. The co-ordination of the mode of regulation is regarded as the responsibility of the state. For the regulation school, advanced capitalism requires an interventionist state to manage aggregate demand and create the right moral and political framework for the maintenance of order. In this view mass consumption is not part of some humanist programme of Modernity 1 designed to bring a higher standard of living to workers. On the contrary it is a technical requirement of the general regime of accumulation which takes as its ultimate end the production of profit, not the needs of human beings.

Although economic regulation theory has not been extensively developed in leisure studies it has left its mark on the sociology of culture. Since in many of these accounts leisure is seen as subsumed by culture, there are important implications of this work for understanding leisure. One of the most interesting and relevant recent attempts to develop regulation theory into a social history of moral behaviour and state formation is the work of Corrigan and Sayer (1985). They argue that moral regulation attempts to 'normalize' historically and socially specific forms of conduct as universal. Where moral regulation is successful subjects accept certain forms of identity, practice and association as 'natural' or 'inevitable' and reject other forms as 'deviant' or 'impossible'.[6] Strategically speaking, then, moral regulation is concerned with constructing normality. It operates through a variety of mechanisms. The voluntary sector often plays an important role in criticizing standards and launching programmes of self-improvement. For example, between 1870 and 1940 the rational recreation movement in Britain and the USA attempted to exert a 'civilizing influence' over the lower orders in society. However, the central regulating mechanism is always the state. It codifies programmes developed through voluntary initiatives and is the ultimate force in constructing and legitimating normality. Corrigan and Sayer provide a rich historical analysis of the various state agencies which are used to organize subjectivity. In essence they can be reduced to three types: physical force; taxation and licensing; and moral example. Let us look at each in more detail.

(1) *Physical force*. Weber (1970) identified the monopoly over the legitimate use of physical force as one of the defining characteristics of the modern state. The police, the standing army and the judiciary possess the means to outlaw and prevent the expression of certain human capacities. For example, in the early nineteenth century the state attacked several traditional common rights over land-use, hunting (notably the British game laws), irregular work habits and combinations among labour. The purpose was of course to create a disciplined, docile workforce. Central to this was the necessity to destroy the worker's independent means of subsistence and to undermine traditional community rights, for these conflicted with the capitalist ideal of an atomized workforce with no alternative but to throw itself upon the mercy of the market.

(2) *Taxation and licensing*. Although physical force could be brutally effective it had certain obvious disadvantages. For one thing it bred resentment. Sweeping away traditional rights generated a strong sense of injustice. This conflicted with the ethical authority of capitalist society. This authority insisted that capitalism is the best possible form of society because it administers order by allowing each individual to pursue his or her private interest within the limits of agreed laws and agreed notions of justice. As capitalism developed, therefore, physical attacks on folk forms of leisure tended to becomes less frequent. They were replaced by taxation and licensing. For example, Harvey (1985: 101) notes that in Paris under the Second Empire street singers and entertainers who were suspected of popularizing socialist sentiments had to be licensed and their songs officially approved by the state. Literature and art which was deemed to be incommensurate with official standards was likewise marginalized. Similarly a combination of licensing and taxation laws were enacted in Britain, France and America to control the public consumption of liquor and drugs and to ensure that the sabbath was held sacred (Cunningham 1980; Dingle 1980; Wigley 1980; Berridge and

Edwards 1987). Laws were also created to regulate standards of public decency (Mort 1987; Newburn 1992). Through these means the state aimed to achieve voluntary regulation and thus to avoid the criticism of dictatorship.

(3) *Moral example.* This refers to the manipulation of sentiments and symbols which aim to emphasize civilized collective bonds. For example, the creation of national holidays celebrating a heroic figure in the life of the nation or a famous victory in battle aim to concentrate sentiments of collective solidarity. Other examples include national spectacles likes marches, parades, coronations, sporting fixtures and festivals of culture. Smoodin's (1993: 91–2) work suggests that cartoons, newsreels and comic-strips act as subliminal shapers of our moral consciousness in our leisure time. Similarly in the early 1990s government figures in the UK and the USA attempted to launch 'a back to basics' campaign which celebrated 'traditional family values'. The effect is twofold. In the words of Corrigan and Sayer (1985: 196) it operates to 'constitute and regulate a field of social vision which is both unitary (minimizing difference within the nation) and Manichaean (opening up a regulative and rhetorical space for those who are "alien" to what is claimed to be "the (national) way of life"'.[7] Moral example also includes the state enshrinement of approved programmes of self-improvement. For example, by providing financial support and public leisure space for activities which it values, the state directly manipulates 'free time' behaviour. In this way certain forms of leisure identity, practice and association are imprinted upon the collective mind as 'normal' while others – especially those which celebrate the values of peripheral cultures – are marginalized.

Like Foucault (1975, 1981), Corrigan and Sayer regard the development of the modern order of things to be a movement from external constraint to self-discipline. Of course external constraint never vanishes as a method of regulating minds and bodies. However, the crux of the modern order is self-discipline. By 'voluntarily' keeping ourselves in order, morally and socially, the moral and social order of modernity is cemented.

The analytical advantages of moral regulation theory are that it clearly ties personal conduct to social structures; it demonstrates that leisure time and space are constructed by social forces and that the personal is political. Although Corrigan and Sayer draw heavily on British experience their argument is relevant to Western society as a whole. So similar programmes of state moral cleansing and policing can be identified in Europe, Australia and the USA. In the latter two cases the policies of white state culture with regard to the aboriginal people and the African slaves, respectively, provide clear examples of how the state sought to marginalize cultures and destroy forms of identity, practice and association of which it disapproved.[8]

The main disadvantages of moral regulation theory are twofold. First, it tends to underestimate the degree to which identity, practice and association in leisure are negotiated and bargained. The subjects of moral regulation are not lumps of plasticine to be moulded at will but creative actors who can contest and disrupt the agencies of rule. Thus, for example, Cunningham (1980) and Gray (1981) argue that moral regulation provoked a reaction in the subjects of regulation which challenged the authority of the moral values which underpinned the regulating bodies. Popular leisure forms celebrating the life of the people emerged to counterpose official values and to make the moral order of modern society more ambiguous and elastic than accounts of moral regulation might suggest. It is therefore perhaps too rash for a writer like Thompson (1963: 443) to conclude that 'the disciplinarians lost a few legislative skirmishes [but] they won the battle of the Industrial Revolution.' Modernity 1 never achieved the finished, unchallenged order of things to which it so ardently aspired. Modernity 2 was always waiting in the wings behind every legislative movement and every moral edict to bluntly reveal the fundamental disorder of things. The second disadvantage is that moral regulation theory renders the role of the state as the pre-eminent influence in ordering social life. It is presented as the focal point for understanding how leisure activity emerges and operates. Other relations of power tend to be undervalued.

The Protestant Ethic Thesis

Modernity 1 values work as the central life interest and regards leisure to be a necessary but secondary part of life. One of the neatest and most influential explanations of how this came about is provided by Weber (1976) in his Protestant ethic thesis. According to Weber (1976: 67), the attitude to life in traditional society was 'comfortable and leisurely'. The number of business hours was moderate – often less than five or six per day. People worked to earn enough to lead a respectable life and, in good times, to save a little for a rainy day. Competition was not intense or cut-throat. Work was typically punctuated by 'a long daily visit to the tavern, with often plenty to drink, and a congenial circle of friends' (Weber 1976: 67). Leisure was woven into the fabric of everyday life. It was not space and time to be challenged or struggled for, rather it was seen as an immemorial feature of life. But, continues Weber (1976: 67), 'at some time this leisureliness was suddenly destroyed.' How did this happen?

Weber's answer points to the rise of the Puritan tradition which emphasized self-control, thrift, work and modesty and condemned hedonism, luxury, idleness and vanity. Puritans were called 'by God' to serve His greater glory. Other religions identified the same calling but only under Puritanism did it lead to the emergence of the acquisitive character type. Why was this? Weber takes the doctrine of Calvinism as an example to illustrate his argument. Calvinism, he argues, is identified by three major features. First, God is identified as the creator of the cosmos. God is seen as the centre of things and humans as God's creatures. Second, the Creator is invested with properties that are beyond human comprehension. We may come to know aspects of the divinity but His essence will always be a profound mystery to us. Third, the doctrine believes in predestination, that is, the belief that some are chosen by God before they are born to receive eternal grace. Predestination is seen by Calvinists as part of God's implacable will. Nothing that we can do in this life will alter His divine judgement.

Weber takes this third feature to be the root of the development of the acquisitive character. The doctrine of predestination, he argues, leaves individuals in a wretched state of inner turmoil. They live in a state of mystery about the only question which makes their lives meaningful: namely 'Do I belong to the ranks of the chosen?' The psychological way of bearing this burden, continues Weber, is to demonstrate to those around you that you are one of those chosen by God. This involves strictly following the letter of God's laws. Life must be spent 'not in leisure and enjoyment, but only in activity [which] serves to increase the glory of God' (Weber 1976: 157). You must show to others that you are one of the chosen by hard work and abjuring the enjoyment of wealth with its temptations of idleness, pleasure, vanity and enjoyment for enjoyment's sake.

> Waste of time is the first and in principle the deadliest of sins. The span of human life is infinitely short and precious . . . Loss of time through sociability, idle talk, luxury, even more sleep than is necessary for health, six to eight hours, is worthy of absolute moral condemnation. (Weber, 1976: 157–8)

Puritanism made a virtue of asceticism. Leisure was not banished from everyday life since it was recognized that a modicum of leisure is necessary for physical efficiency and social well-being.

> But, as a means for spontaneous expression of undisciplined impulses, it was under suspicion; and in so far as it became purely a means of enjoyment, or awakened pride, raw instincts or the irrational gambling instinct, it was of course strictly condemned. Impulsive enjoyment of life, which leads away both from work in a calling and from religion, was as such the enemy of rational asceticism. (Weber, 1976: 167)

Puritan habits produced an accumulation of wealth. They demonstrated that ceaseless work and rigorous self-discipline is capable of producing real material improvement in the conditions of one's life. As such they were widely emulated and became transformed into the work ethic which became the foundation of Modernity 1 influencing all aspects of life. As Weber (1976: 181) puts it:

> The Puritan wanted to work in a calling; we are forced to do so. For when asceticism was carried out of monastic cells into everyday life, and began to dominate worldly morality, it did its part in building the tremendous cosmos of the modern economic order. This order is now bound to the technical and economic conditions of machine production which today determine the lives of all individuals who are born into this mechanism, not only those directly concerned with economic acquisition, with irresistible force.

Weber shows how a life of leisureliness was turned into a life of regimentation in which work and leisure are divided. The Protestant ethic thesis demonstrates how the development of self-control, calculation, surveillance and regimentation became the foundation of the modern social order. It shows how 'the rational ethos' of modernity was an unintended consequence of ascetic religion. By using Weber's thesis as a background context it is possible to explain the routinization of leisure behaviour as well as the psychology of guilt and anxiety which surrounds the 'wasteful' use of leisure time.

The Protestant ethic thesis has been criticized on a number of counts (Marshall 1982; Poggi 1983). Two points in particular are regularly made. First, Weber is criticized for exaggerating the uniqueness of Protestantism. The beliefs of other religions, notably Catholicism, were equally compatible with the development of capitalism. In isolating Puritanism, Weber is castigated for producing a misleading account of the rise of capitalism. Second, Weber's description of leisure as ascetic and secondary in importance to work marginalizes the significance of hedonistic and ostentatious forms of leisure. Other commentators, notably Veblen (1925), argue that hedonism and ostentation are central to understanding the modern order of things. By prioritizing asceticism and modesty the Protestant ethic thesis is attacked for ignoring crucial features of the modern social order.

Conspicuous Consumption Theory

Display and show are central in understanding order under Modernity 1. Everyday life is influenced by the politics of emulation. We see an outfit in a fashion magazine and we wish to copy it; we watch a television programme about luxury travel and we wish to experience it. Modern society perpetuates a psychology of emulation. This is associated with a generalized sense of dissatisfaction in our leisure because we are always troubled with the thought that our free time experience is not as full or exciting as it could be. All of this was penetratingly analysed by Veblen (1925), writing at the turn of the century. Veblen (1925: 46) defines leisure as the 'non-productive consumption of time'. He argues that taste and fashion in modern society are dictated by a leisure class. The key feature of this class is ownership of capital. They signal their abstention from the mundane world of labour by cultivating conspicuous consumption. Veblen regarded conspicuous consumption as inherently wasteful. He describes the leisure class as exulting in lavish conspicuous consumption to demonstrate their pecuniary power. They signal their exemption from labour by steeping themselves in dead languages, occult sciences, the detailed proprieties of polite behaviour and equipage, elite sports and elite husbandry. Moreover, by employing a 'vicarious leisure class' of servants, maids, grooms, groundstaff and the like they both install intermediaries between themselves and external society and further symbolize their exemption from labour.

Veblen's discussion of the repertoire of social behaviour which the leisure class uses to represent their privileged status is exceptionally rich. It ranges over canons of taste, dress, architecture, the conservation of archaic traits, notions of beauty and the function of sport. Sometimes his reading of the activities of the leisure class seems to be eccentric. For example, in describing the history and social significance of the corset he argues that its popularity among women of the leisure class is fundamentally a matter of symbolizing pecuniary advantage. The corset interferes with movement and it reduces the vitality of the wearer. No worker could afford to be so obviously constrained. For Veblen (1925: 107) these features 'go to show that the person so affected is incapable of useful effort and must therefore be supported in idleness by her "owner". She is useless and expensive, and she is consequently valuable as evidence of pecuniary strength.' His sympathies here are very clearly on the side of women. The leisure class, he argues, is a fusion of patriarchy and pecuniary might. It oppresses women by confining them to a wholly subordinate role.

However, while it is legitimate to read Veblen as one of the first male contributors to the feminist cause, the manifest purpose of his analysis is to expose the moral bankruptcy of mature industrial culture. Throughout, he pointedly contrasts the fecklessness, superficiality and waste of social relations in his own day with the thrift, sobriety and controlled industry that inspired the industrial revolution. The motivation to produce useful commodities and services which add to the real stock of wealth in society has ceded place to possessing wealth and social standing without expending effort.

Veblen's thesis has been the subject of criticism. Riesman (1960), in a broadly sympathetic assessment, none the less chides Veblen for exaggerating the importance of pecuniary values in the organization of everyday life. Riesman accuses Veblen of neglecting the significance of spiritual and religious values and therefore of producing a one-sided theory of human motivation. Similarly, MacCannell (1976) and Williams (1982) question Veblen's emphasis on a dominant leisure class which sets the trends for the rest of society. Veblen's thesis is rebuked for overstating dominant class integration and underestimating the power of subordinate classes to construct their own leisure forms.

These are serious criticisms. But they should not be allowed to obscure Veblen's achievement in constructing an immensely compelling account of the semiotics of leisure. Few authors since have matched his understanding of the symbolic power of luxury, ostentation and grand acts of display in mature industrial culture.

An exception is perhaps Erving Goffman (1967, 1971, 1974), who in the postwar years produced an extraordinarily rich and subtle analysis of the symbolic rituals of urban-industrial society. Unlike Veblen, Goffman is not concerned with producing a theory of leisure. However, his varied writings on social roles, frames of interaction, social ritual and spatial allocation constantly alight upon matters of 'free time' behaviour. Here I wish to concentrate upon his (1967) discussion of 'action spaces' and to explore how it relates to leisure activity as conspicuous consumption.

According to Goffman, modern society has evolved specialized spaces where conspicuous role display and reversal, preening and symbolically exciting situations are concentrated. He defines action spaces quite formally as spaces in which 'activities that are consequential [and] problematic [are] undertaken for what is felt to be their own sake' (Goffman 1967: 185). Examples include pool halls, casinos, discos, amusement parks, sports arenas and game arcades. Action spaces provide the opportunity for what Goffman calls 'fancy milling' and 'vicarious experience'. By the term 'fancy milling' Goffman means relatively open social contact with others in a setting dedicated to conspicuous consumption or the mere acquisition of pleasure. As he explains in more detail:

Adults in our society can obtain a taste of social mobility by consuming valued products, by enjoying costly and modish entertainment, by spending time in luxurious settings and by mingling with prestigious persons – all the more if these occur at the same time and in the presence of many witnesses. This is the action of consumption. Further, mere presence in a large, tightly packed gathering of revelling persons can bring not only the excitement that crowds generate, but also the uncertainty of not quite knowing what might happen next, the possibility of flirtations, which can themselves lead to relationship formation, and the lively experience of being an elbow away from someone who does manage to find real action in the crowd. (Goffman 1967: 197–8)

Fancy milling involves symbolically relaxed participation with others and opening oneself up to acceptable risks and uncertainties. Vicarious experience in the sense of projecting oneself into the role display pattern and apparent life situation of others is certainly compatible with fancy milling. Indeed it is clear from Goffman's account that the potential for vicarious experience is one of the attractions of the action place. However, vicarious experience is also crucially atomized experience. That is, it does not require participation with others. The distinction is important in Goffman's sociology of action places because he suggests that the most ubiquitous and immediate purveyors of vicarious experience in modern society are the mass media. Cinema, film, fiction, comics and theatre are places in which

practical gambles, character contests and serious action are depicted. They may entail make-belief, biography, or a view of someone else's currently ongoing fateful activity. . . . Everywhere opportunity is provided for us to identify with real or fictive persons engaging in fatefulness of various kinds, and to participate vicariously in these situations. (Goffman 1967: 262)

Action places permit the individual to engage in flamboyant behaviour and to experience the adventure denied to him or her in 'serious' life. Goffman (1967: 268) suggests that they are part of a central division in the organization of the modern life-world:

On one side are the safe and silent places, the home, the well-regulated role in business, industry and the professions; on the other are all those activities that generate expression, requiring the individual to lay himself on the line and place himself in jeopardy during a passing moment. It is from this contrast that we fashion nearly all of our commercial fantasies. It is from this contrast that delinquents, criminals, hustlers and sportsmen draw their self-respect.

In belonging to the 'other' side action places are part of the dreamworld of modernity.[9] Gambling halls, discos, sports arenas, cinemas and the like allow us to identify with the apparently more exciting lives led by others. Here we can momentarily engage in conspicuous acts of projection and release. However, this charmed experience is essentially temporary. Were it to become permanent, Goffman suggests, everyday social life would become impossible. Action places therefore ultimately reaffirm the paramount reality of 'the silent world' of safety and security.

Goffman's sociology is concerned with the appearance of things. For him signs and symbols regulate conduct. His work points to a semiotics of social life – a decoding and deciphering of the surfaces. But it shows little interest in determining or positing underlying structures or investigating power relations. It is as if Goffman calls upon the sociologist to be an alert consumer, observing and recording the quirks of everyday relations but stopping well short of trying to build an explanatory theory. He invariably discusses leisure from the standpoint of the consumer. There is no sustained attempt to investigate how the leisure industry operates to supply or shape leisure needs. Leisure itself is too narrowly associated with consumption. There is not enough in this perspective about production, innovation or challenge in leisure conduct. Order is assumed too readily. And when disorder and abnormality are considered, as they are in Goffman's discussion of asylums (1959), spoiled identity (1963) and frame-breaking behaviour (1974), it is not their challenge to or criticism of paramount reality that preoccupies Goffman but rather the techniques of their accommodation to the status quo.

The Theory of the Civilizing Process

The theory of the civilizing process was created by Norbert Elias (1978, 1982). His associates have made notable contributions in developing the theory, especially in respect of understanding the roots of aggressive masculine behaviour in sport (Dunning et al. 1988) and the sociology of food and manners (Mennell 1985). Essentially these writers see social order as a structured yet unplanned process. For them it is a consequence of the chains of interdependence which link people together in society. These chains refer to the intertwining that has arisen through the innumerable intentional actions of groups and individuals over time and space. For people to be intertwined it is of course not necessary for them to be *equally* intertwined. The theory allows for some individuals and groups to have greater power chances than others and to exercise these chance to pursue their will. But the theory avoids the *zero-sum* models of power that one often finds in other sociological attempts to explain social order. In these models power is conceived of as something which one actor uses to force the compliance of others. These models wrongly support the inference that some actors are omnipotent while others are powerless. Notions of mutuality and even reciprocity of power tend to be ignored. In contrast, the theory of the civilizing process assumes that everyone is empowered and constrained by the web of chained interdependencies which make social life possible. This is a useful antidote to the cruder models of power which one often finds in some classical Marxist or militant feminist models. Here the power of the ruling class or male hierarchy is often presented in zero-sum terms. There is little appreciation that even the most powerful actors in society are caught up in the web of naked and tacit assumptions and connections which enmeshes them and frequently pushes and pulls them in directions which are against their will.

The theory of the civilizing process identifies a special place for leisure. As we have seen, the theory explains order in terms of the growing connections which link people together. It is perhaps easiest to think of these connections in terms of the division of labour. However, it is important to remember that Elias also has in mind the full range of emotions that bind us together in ties of compliance or antagonism. These connections mean that it is quite unusual for a person to get his or her own way irrespective of others.[10] Quite apart from the obvious threat of the direct intervention of the police in the case of illegal or violent action, there is the more subtle intervention of standards of shame and repugnance to consider. These militate against aggressive outbursts. Perhaps one sign of their power in ordinary life is the extravagant, ritualistic violence with which they are overturned when ordinary life is dislocated. The numbing horror of the 'ethnic cleansing programmes' and mass rapes conducted in the civil war in former Yugoslavia during the early 1990s is but one of the most recent and ghastly examples. For most people in advanced industrial society aggression is regulated. We may feel strong dislike and even hatred for someone else but in general these feelings do not spill over into acts of physical violence. Yet only a very naïve person would deny that aggressive feelings and violent tensions course through the very veins of modern life. According to Elias and Dunning (1986) two of the most important mechanisms for releasing these tensions in a relatively harmless way are sport and leisure:

> While excitement is severely curbed in the pursuit of what one usually regards as the serious business of life, . . . many leisure pursuits provide an imaginary setting which is meant to elicit excitement of some kind imitating that procured by real life situations, yet without its dangers and risks. Films, dances, paintings, card-games, horse-races, operas and detective-stories and football matches; these and other leisure pursuits belong in this category. (Elias and Dunning, 1986: 42)

Elias and Dunning believe that much leisure and sport consists of *mimetic* activity. That is, it enables us to abandon the restraints on our emotions in relatively controlled and enjoyable ways. The passion of the sports field or a Hollywood thriller may be less intense than the passion of a battlefield but it is also safer. Sport and leisure, then, enable us to project our passionate feelings onto players whom we identify with or to release them by participating as players ourselves. The traditional sociology of leisure has associated leisure with rest and relaxation. Far from this being the case, contend Elias and Dunning, leisure demands the arousal of passions and tension balances between aggression and restraint.

Another way in which Elias and Dunning break with traditional approaches to leisure and sport is to question the polarizations between routine and escape, necessity and freedom. These polarizations recur again and again in the literature. For example functionalist sociologists present work as a realm of deprivation and leisure as a realm of fulfilment. Feminists present women's leisure as controlled by the necessities of patriarchy and contrast this with men's leisure, which is seen as free and self-determining. Against this, Elias and Dunning present a more varied and ambivalent picture. Many work activities, they point out, are enjoyed and associated with pleasure, while leisure time can often be associated with emptiness or boredom. Similarly the picture of ever more routinized and regimented forms of leisure which Marxist writers on consumer capitalism often portray is rejected. According to Elias and Dunning (1986: 69), leisure activities

> can all be, and usually are, routinized up to a point, but they can also be de-routinized from time to time. . . . At the same time, they all have this in common with the mimetic class of activities: they can provide heightened enjoyment provided one is able to cater for them in a non-routine manner.

This highlights another important feature of Elias and Dunning's approach – the strong emphasis they place upon seeing social life as a *process*. The theory of the civilizing process is regularly criticized for implying that the West has reached a pinnacle or end-point of civilization; in fact the exact opposite is the case (Dunning 1992). That is, the theory does not see civilization as finished business. 'De-civilizing movements' are quite compatible with the theory. By extension the theory does not attribute rigid unchangeable functions to leisure and sport. The probability is that tension balances will always be involved in these activities because the length of interdependency chains in modern society make tension an inevitable part of ordinary life. However, it is quite possible for the tension balance in leisure and sport to shift from the relatively controlled and pleasurable arousal of passions into a dangerous and life-threatening situation. The theory regards leisure, sport and social life in general to be an unfinished processes. Indeed Elias (1978: 221–63) reserved his greatest scorn for those sociologists who take the opposite view and present society as a fixed social system in which the specialized parts discharge their functions in rigid, unchangeable fashion.

The publication of the English-language edition of Elias's two volumes on the civilizing process in 1978 and 1982, respectively, was widely celebrated as a significant event. It injected into the Anglo-American mainstream a classic work which had very unfortunately been cloaked in obscurity.[11] However, acclaim was matched by criticism which attacked the theory for its alleged evolutionism, historical inaccuracies and Western triumphalism. These criticisms are by now well known and they have been dealt with very thoroughly in the literature (see, for example, Rojek 1985: 169–72; Dunning 1992). Here I prefer to comment on the theory of leisure associated with the work of Elias and Dunning.

The first thing to note is that this work displays what I take to be a healthy distaste for positivist and functionalist thought. Elias and Dunning do not automatically associate leisure with 'the good life'; nor do they believe that leisure time and leisure space necessarily correlate with the experience of freedom, choice, spontaneity and self-determination; nor do they think of leisure and sport in terms of inevitable, unchangeable functions. Furthermore, their entire approach runs counter to the positivist and functionalist practice of investigating leisure in connection with an isolated, controlled variable (usually work experience). Instead they are solidly, even militantly, sociological in their approach – insisting on the necessity of studying leisure in connection with the total field of interdependencies, or 'the figurations', in which personal experience occurs.

However, there are problems with the approach. In the first place, by prioritizing the civilizing process other analytically significant processes in explaining leisure tend to get pushed to the sidelines. This is especially true of processes of commercialization and patrism (Clarke 1992; Hargeaves 1992). This connects up with a more general criticism made by several writers that the theory of the civilizing process is unduly empiricist (Bauman 1979; Smith 1984; Jary and Horne 1987). That is, the theory tends to be preoccupied with the intrinsic logic of the civilizing process so that contrary examples and processes are either neglected or ignored.

Furthermore, no attempt is made to speculate on social forms and leisure forms which have greater emancipatory potential for actors, players and spectators. Indeed, the whole question of alternative social forms and 'imagined otherness' does not have a very high profile in the figurational approach. This leads some commentators to allege that figurational sociology is guilty of political quietism. The comparative silence of Elias and his followers on the question of the reconstruction of society is viewed as colluding with the prevailing social order of things.

A related point is that the theory tends to suggest that mimetic leisure forms have replaced aggressive or violent forms. Aggressive outbursts are analytically portrayed as aberrations or deviations from the normality of relatively controlled leisure practices. To be sure, in contrast to this, Dunning and his associates (1988) have argued that football hooliganism will remain a problem as long as class inequality remains a feature of society. None the less, given the strong emphasis in their discussion on the 'binding', 'interweaving' effects of lengthening chains of interdependency, this insistence on removing class inequality reads like a *non sequitur*. The whole thrust of the theory is that mimetic forms of leisure enable class, racial and other forms of aggression to be played out in a controlled and relatively harmless way. One can sympathize with those critics who therefore believe that the theory of the civilizing process seems to rule out the possibility of an alternative order of things, for the theory seems to be a casebook demonstration of how a society rooted in stratified inequality has created safety valves through leisure, sport and other areas of social life which ensure that the order of oppression can remain intact.

A further criticism arises from Elias and Dunning's (1986) characterization that we live in 'unexciting societies'. Mennell (1989: 141) remarks that the authors were being ironical in the use of this term. However, it is quite consistent with their view that the civilizing process increases thresholds of repugnance against aggressive outbursts and produces sport and leisure as outlets for pent-up emotions. The problem with this is that it underestimates the excitement of ordinary life in the metropolis. The assault of stimuli and the confusion of the senses that one experiences in walking along any big city street is frequently very stimulating. The failure of organized sport and leisure to achieve comparable levels of arousal perhaps explains the experience of anti-climax that we often feel in our 'free' time experience.

Despite the repeated emphasis which exponents of the civilizing process place upon 'concrete research' and 'testability' it remains a thesis which has never been adequately tested.[12] For example, there is no doubt that physical aggression today is more controlled and disciplined than in the Middle Ages. We do not spit at the dinner table or use the tablecloth to wipe our nose; nor do we torture and butcher our enemies.[13] Of course there are still examples of intense and violent acts of physical barbarity. However, these aggressive outbursts are notable both for their relative isolation from the standards of 'civilized' life and the disapproval which they generate from the international community and its organs of representation such as the United Nations.[14]

Nevertheless, there is a danger of being over-complacent about our attachment to 'civilized' standards. Freud (1939), of course, noted that civilization is founded upon the repression of instinctual gratification. He contended that, psychologically speaking, 'what we call our civilization is largely responsible for our misery' (1939: 23). Freud's work holds open the possibility that the civilizing process increases the sum of human unhappiness by generating mental discontent and illness. This is not a proposition which Elias's work necessarily discounts, but at best one can say that it is hugely underdeveloped.[15]

Finally, although figurational sociology is intensely critical of positivism it holds fast to a scientific model of sociology. The propositions of the civilizing process are tested ultimately against the known 'facts' of human development. But the question of what a 'fact' is in the social sciences is far from being a simple thing. As MacIntyre (1981: 79–108) argues, the social sciences are based not upon facts but upon generalizations. Further, the generalizations achieved by social science are of a very low-level type. They coexist with recognized counter-examples and the recognition of these counter-examples does not necessarily weaken the standing of the generalizations. For example, the theory of the civilizing process has been attacked by many commentators on the grounds that it is historically incorrect. That is, these critics allege that aggression has not been 'dampened down' in Western societies but merely sublimated; and further that, in some ways, new forms of warfare and mental-emotional violence are more lethal than anything in the past (Curtis 1986; Mestrovic 1993). Whether one agrees with these critics is, for the moment, neither here nor there. The important point is that they show that the generalizations made by figurational sociology are not of the same order as in physics and chemistry. Although their exponents present them as factual statements of reality there is still widespread dispute about their accuracy.

It is important to acknowledge clearly that most figurational sociologists would find unobjectionable the observation that their propositions are not of the same order as the propositions of physics and chemistry. As Elias himself never tired of asserting, sociological explanation is not at the same level of development as the more established physical sciences. It is therefore facile to compare social and natural science in respect of their comparative explanatory and predictive power. None the less it is striking that, when pressed, figurational sociologists strenuously insist that their work is more 'objectively adequate' than rival theories. By the term 'objectively adequate' is meant that propositions of figurational sociology correspond more closely to the observable facts of sport and leisure behaviour than competing theories in the field.

Now, few words in the English language carry the same weight as 'objectivity'. By insisting on superior 'object adequacy' figurational sociologists imply that forms of sociology which are concerned with impressions and experience are less valuable. This is a questionable matter, and I will attempt to show why in detail later in the book, when I discuss phenomenological approaches and postmodernism (see pp. 104–28). The point to be made here is that in claiming to be objectively adequate figurational sociologists fail to be sufficiently reflexive about their own methods.

As is perhaps well known, figurational sociology contrasts 'involved' (value-laden) positions in social life with 'detached' (objective/value-neutral) positions. The figurational approach is presented to the public as a sustained exercise in 'detached' scientific research. But the concept of 'detachment' is not satisfactory. For one thing, figurational sociology offers no code of practice or disciplined method to achieve detachment. At best it is referred to as 'a state of mind' or perhaps more commonly as 'a spirit of enquiry'. This of course causes major analytical problems for anyone interested in pinning down detachment as a method of sociological enquiry. Despite the suspicion that figurational sociology shows towards 'impressionistic' forms of analysis, its treatment of detachment is itself somewhat imprecise. In lieu of objective criteria to determine 'involved' from 'detached' propositions, figurational sociology leaves itself open to the charge that its theorems and methods are themselves impressionistic instead of 'objectively adequate' accounts (Rojek 1986, 1992).

Another difficulty is that the concept of detachment is itself theoretically loaded. That is, it expresses a certain way of approaching social matters and determining 'facts'. For example, Dunning (1992: 254–5) contrasts the detached approach of figurational sociology to the study of sexual repression in sport with the 'involved', 'passionate' and 'committed' position of feminist writers such as Jennifer Hargreaves (1992). Again he associates figurational sociology with superior 'objectively adequate' activity. 'Our view of sociology,' he writes, '[is of] a subject primarily concerned with adding to the social fund of knowledge – in the hope that such knowledge will be of practical value, if not now, then in the longer term' (1992: 254). What this ignores is that *all* sociological theories are to some extent value-laden (MacIntyre 1981: 79). To oppose the generalizations of figurational sociology with those of other positions such as feminism on the grounds that the former are more 'objective' and 'detached' might therefore in some circles seem to be gratuitous. Problems of 'detachment' in the study of social life all depend on where you start from. And most of the key contributors to the theory of the civilizing process start from the position of being white, middle-class, lifelong academic males.

Nevertheless, despite these criticisms there is much that is of value in the figurational approach. For example, it works on the scale of grand social theory which is both rare and courageous in these days of post-structuralist and postmodernist scepticism about 'the universal subject'. Although it explores immediate social issues in terms of long-term processes of development it insists that the future is relatively open-ended. In stark contrast to those critics who complain of its alleged evolutionism, figurational sociology does not maintain that human behaviour is determined or fixed. Its suspicion of politicized sociology has consistently enabled it to take a more rounded view of social developments. There is also an underlying humility in the approach which tends to get lost in its trenchant and uncompromising identification with scientific activity.[16] Figurational sociologists do not maintain that they have all of the answers. Rather they see their work as one small step in the process of gaining reliable knowledge about social life. This modesty can of course be pointedly contrasted with the hubris found in many functionalist, neo-Marxist and feminist contributions to the study of leisure and sport.

Conclusion

In the name of 'progress', Modernity 1 sought to control both nature and society. This involved prioritizing certain personality types and spaces in the social and geographical landscape and annexing others. The ideology of Modernity 1 identified normality with white, Christian, work-centred and propertied attitudes. 'Let me indicate two or three conditions essential to success,' said the self-made millionaire Andrew Carnegie (1903: 4, 5, 8, 12, 16, 17, 18) in an address to young men:

> Do not rest content for a moment in your thoughts as head-clerk, or foreman, or general manager in any concern, no matter how extensive. Say each to yourself. 'My place is at the top'. . . . You must not drink liquor to excess. Better if you do not touch it at all – much better. . . . Nothing is more essential to young business men than untarnished credit, credit begotten of confidence in their prudence, principles and stability of character. . . . One false axiom you will often hear, which I wish to guard you against: 'Obey orders if you break owners.' Don't you do it. This is no rule for you to follow. Always break orders to save owners. . . . There is one sure mark of the coming partner, the future millionaire; his revenues always exceed his expenditures. He begins to save early, almost as soon as he begins to earn. No matter how little it may be possible to save, save that little. . . . There is always a boom in brains, cultivate that crop, for if you grow any amount of that commodity, here is your best market and you cannot overstock it, and the more brains you have to sell, the higher price you can exact . . . lastly, be not impatient for, as Emerson says, 'no-one can cheat you out of ultimate success but yourselves.'

Carnegie's preconditions for success involve prioritizing individual interest over collective interest, promoting the spirit of competition and asceticism, developing absolute self-discipline, turning work into the central life interest, and policing pleasure. Modernity 1 called upon individuals to commit themselves to a particular kind of self-making. The self was organized as a machine to accumulate value from leisure as well as work, and to consume commodities and 'civilized' experience. The corollary of this process of self-making was an empiricist, rationalist, atomistic, calculating egoistic outlook.

This is a monolithic world-view and it inevitably generated criticism. Campbell (1987: 181) notes the significance of Romanticism with its 'philosophy of "dynamic organicism" with the metaphor of growth substituted for that of the machine, and the values of change, diversity, individuality and imagination, for those of uniformitarianism, universalism and rationalism.' But although it generated intense and continuous interest, especially among young people, Romanticism in the nineteenth and early twentieth century was secondary to the rationalist, empiricist, egoistic outlook exemplified by Carnegie's words above. Into this narrow vessel millions of lives were poured and a dominant 'natural', 'common-sensical' order of things developed. Leisure, with its time-worn associations with pleasure and freedom, was welcomed as the reward for work. But an excess of leisure was feared as undermining society. Leisure was always treated as secondary. The Romantic argument that it is only through leisure that we truly enrich ourselves and society was treated as a threat to society precisely because it encouraged a disrespect for the inflexible, time-tabled existence favoured by the ruling order. Modernity 1 treated the subject of organizing leisure with the same sober spirit of rationalism that it applied to every other part of life. Leisure time and space was materially and symbolically divided from work time and space. The seaside resort, the spa, the music hall and other leisure spaces offered 'an escape from formality' (Walvin 1992: 217).

Kasson (1978: 106–7) argues that at the turn of the nineteenth century a pivotal change occurred from an economy organized around production to one organized around consumption and leisure. The development of department stores as luxury shopping outlets in the last quarter of the nineteenth century created new displays of commodities for consumption and new forms of leisure experience (Chaney 1983, 1993; Saisselin 1985). Similarly the introduction of package tour holidays which occurred over the same period made travel to the great symbols of Victorian refined leisure – Greece, Rome and the Holy Land – possible for the non-leisure class. Indeed, as Pemble (1987) shows, greater accessibility to these leisure spaces promoted outbursts of rage from the leisure class who despaired that their havens of retreat were about to be over-run with pleasure tourists from the middle and artisan orders.

The turn of the century was therefore a time when leisure and consumption assumed greater prominence in the organization of everyday life. The key values of early capitalism, argues Kasson, namely hard work, punctuality, thrift, sobriety and self-control, were oriented to an economy based on productivity. The shift towards a society where consumption and leisure were more prominent inevitably changed the way in which people responded to the key values of earlier times. As Kasson (1978: 107) puts it:

> the old genteel injunctions lost their force. The rewards promised for those who conformed to such strictures – upward mobility, family security, social respectability – grew less compelling as new agencies emerged that offered far more immediate gratification . . . popular amusements prospered not by promising the attainment of ultimate rewards but by providing instant pleasures and momentary release from work demands and social prescriptions.

Kasson himself questions the degree to which the new popular amusements delivered the escape experience which they promised. Indeed, he comes down finally in favour of a version of regulation theory. The new leisure forms and consumption experiences, he argues (1978: 109), ultimately protected existing society. The fantasy experience they produced resulted in passive acceptance of the cycle of production and consumption rather than a genuine apprehension of radically new social possibilities. Paradoxically, the spirit of egalitarianism fostered in the new leisure spaces ultimately functioned to reconcile leisure-users to the inequalities of society at large.

The argument that leisure under Modernity 1 operates to imprison the individual and reinforce conformity is, of course, very familiar. We have already encountered it in the discussion of the Marxist and feminist critiques of leisure under capitalism (see pp. 28–30) and we shall return to it in Chapters 5 and 6 which examine leisure and Modernity 2. At this stage in the discussion it is perhaps important to note that Modernity 1 fully recognized that the order which it buttressed limited some human capacities. However, it submitted that this was a price worth paying for the security of society. The mechanisms of regulation were seen, in short, as enabling liberty and development by guaranteeing stability and predictability. To assess the validity of this argument it is necessary to examine the mechanisms of regulating leisure under Modernity 1 in more detail. The next chapter is devoted to this task.

4

MECHANISMS OF REGULATION

Modernity 1 might be thought of as a grid which is imposed upon life. Time and space cease to be carefree. Each is schooled in a rigid discipline of order. Special times for work, special times for play; segmented space for serious activity, segmented space for the less serious side of life – the life of leisure. All of this is imprinted upon the heart, mind and soul of the individual. Typically this is accomplished not through the use of force but through, as it were, 'voluntary' contract.

How is voluntary contract engineered? Foucault (1975, 1981) wrote of 'carceral networks' of power in society. By this he meant webs of control which both empower and regulate behaviour. In Foucault's sociology the idea of carceral networks is indissoluble from the idea of the individual. The forms of speech, writing, received ideas and law, the forms of *discourse,* associated with carceral networks are also the forms by which we recognize the individual as a separate subject possessing specific needs and rights. This is a complicated idea which requires further elaboration. For Foucault the individual is, so to speak, 'written before he or she is born'. Our characteristics are not simply biologically determined, they are moulded by social discourse. The case of sexuality illustrates this very clearly. The debate on sexuality is divided between essentialist and constructionist positions. Putting it simply, the essentialist case is that sexuality is determined by nature. We are born with heterosexual or homosexual desire. The constructionist case argues that sexuality is shaped by language. Weeks (1991: 2–3), who in many respects is critical of Foucault's work, none the less expresses the nucleus of the constructionist case very well when he writes:

> 'Sexuality' as we know it has been constructed and shaped as a set of organised meanings and activities in and through language: the preaching and practices of religions, the codifications of experts such as doctors and psychologists, the prescriptions of planners, educationists, architects, social workers. . . . Sexuality is as much about language as it is about sexual organs.

Foucault's sociology is ultimately about the organization of subjects. He conceives carceral networks and discursive fields as parasitic and all-enveloping. His sociology aims to map the discursive fields and carceral networks which 'produce' the individual and 'normalize' behaviour and to trace movements in the development of these fields. 'The question', observed Foucault (1988: 13–14) of his own approach, 'is to determine what the subject must be, what his condition must be, what status he must have, what position he must occupy in the real or the imaginary, in order to become a legitimate subject of any given type of understanding.' In pursuing this task Foucault (1982) identifies three types of power:

(1) *Institutional power*, which refers to ethnic, social and religious forms of domination. Here the individual is generally constrained to behave in normally approved ways by powerful edicts, injunctions and rituals.
(2) *Economic power*, which refers to the operations of the class system. Here the individual is relatively powerless if he or she lacks capital and is condemned to selling labour power on the market to the highest bidder.
(3) *Subjective power*, which refers to personal struggles against subjectivity and submission. Here, one might say, the individual struggles against the discourses organized around the self.

According to Foucault, all three forms of struggle are evident in contemporary society. However, he also maintains that there has been an historical tendency for the first two types to be replaced by the third. That is, politics is moving away from collectivist movements and considerations to what might be called an identity politics centred on what is done to selves and how selves act. In Foucault's work, then, it is possible to trace an arc of historical movement from external regulation, external discipline to self-regulation and self-discipline. This position exists in some tension with approaches like Marxism or feminism which attempt to explain society exclusively in the context of relations of production or reproduction. As Foucault (1982: 213) put it, each of the three levels of power 'entertain[s] complex and circular relations with other forms'. To prioritize one is logically inadmissible and practically misleading.

In what ways is the concept of carceral networks relevant to the study of leisure? Although traditional and radical approaches to leisure differ in their analysis of leisure they show remarkable similarity in their underlying philosophy of leisure. For example, both functionalist and neo-Marxist positions associate leisure with freedom. For functionalists, current leisure practice already achieves freedom; against this neo-Marxists maintain that the class system and commodification make genuine freedom impossible under capitalism. However, they insist that the communist transformation of society will produce a realm of freedom in which individuals can freely and fully develop their natural capacities within the limits of common law. Foucault's approach is more subversive. His emphasis on discourse and carceral networks logically means that control and regulation are integral to concepts of leisure and freedom. Western civilization 'naturally' imposes prohibitions upon what 'healthy' individuals can do in their leisure. The question of what impression we make on others gnaws at us; we fret about using our free time wisely; we worry about drinking too much, or becoming too set in our ways. Foucault's sociology denies the possibility of leisure as a 'realm of freedom'.[1]

Foucault's sociology presents carceral networks as simultaneously a source of regulation and empowerment. It does not look forward to utopia, but neither does it discount the importance of utopian ideas in the organization of everyday life. It pitches analysis at the level of micro-politics – the level of the habitual, the mundane, the 'natural' – rather than the level of macro-politics – the level of the universal, the structural, the irrepressible. Foucault has no truck with the so-called 'deeply rooted historical processes', such as the class struggle, patriarchy or the civilizing process.

In what follows I want to explore how the micro-politics of leisure is organized under Modernity 1 by examining some concepts which relate directly to understanding how leisure is structured: work, bureaucracy, the nation, the family, habitus, citizenship and the body. The aim is not to present these concepts as something above or outside the individual. On the contrary, the aim is to show how these concepts are mediated and realized through the conduct of the individual to reinforce order. The discussion begins with what Foucault himself took to be one of the most important facts about human beings: our bodies.

The Body

Turner (1984, 1992) has argued that one of the most serious defects in modern social theory has been the neglect of the body. The criticism is particularly relevant for leisure theory. Much of our leisure time is devoted to maintaining our bodies, improving them, displaying them, scenting them and decorating them. Similarly, much of the leisure industry revolves around dressing our bodies, increasing our attraction, preserving our youthfulness and cosmeticizing our less appealing physical characteristics. Yet leisure theory has been notably silent about the body and its place in the organization of leisure.[2]

Organizing bodies is a central preoccupation of Modernity 1. It created the atomized individual ruled by the dictates of the life-cycle. Several commentators on leisure have used Foucault's metaphor of 'the gaze' to explain orderly leisure behaviour (Urry 1990a; Game 1991). The gaze is not an easy term to define. The basic idea is that our behaviour is regulated by the gaze of others and by the gaze of our own self-reflection. The eye controls order so that, at a glance, we can determine what the appropriate ways of behaving are for a given situation. The gaze is a social product, a construction of signs. In Foucault's sociology it is associated with the disciplinary society – visual culture and the power of the eye are mechanisms for ordering things. The gaze is a 'naturalistic' characteristic of everyday life in that it enables us to differentiate leisure time and leisure space from non-leisure time and non-leisure space. However, it is also exploited by the leisure industry, which designs leisure settings to conform to the requirements of the eye of leisure. Game's (1991: 181–3) analysis of plans to redevelop Bondi Beach in Sydney shows powerfully that leisure entrepreneurs have a clear conception of how leisure sights ought to look. She demonstrates how they impose their conception, their gaze, upon leisure-users so that the design of the leisure object itself acts as control upon physical, social and moral behaviour. Similarly, Findlay's (1992) discussion of leisure and recreation spaces like Disneyland, Sun City Arizona and the Seattle World's Fair of 1962 illustrates how designers used landscaping techniques to control leisure behaviour. According to Findlay (1992: 296–303), these 'magic lands' operate with a standard repertoire of design codes which structures the tourist gaze. The main features of this repertoire are as follows.

(1) *Essentialism*. Magic kingdoms aim to represent the essence of the surrounding metropolis. They operate as sacred landmarks in the mental maps of tourists. They refine one's sense of meaning and place by shutting out the extraneous, chaotic elements of metropolitan life and reducing visual and functional forms to a few key images.

(2) *Pride*. Magic kingdoms are structured to intensify respect and pride. They become places to see. The reverence which they generate is the reverence of the extraordinary, the out-of-the-way, the monumental distillation of national culture.[3] By encouraging the sense of pride in the extraordinary through landscaping and design the architects of magic kingdoms seek to pattern leisure behaviour. They also create the means for reproducing this behaviour by a system of visual representation which frames the tourist's anticipation and recollection. 'People linger over such a gaze,' writes Urry (1990a: 3), 'which is then normally visually objectified or captured through photographs, postcards, films, models and so on. These enable the gaze to be endlessly reproduced and recaptured.'

(3) *Promise*. Magic kingdoms uphold the promise of a better life. High-quality design, workmanship maintenance and service are built into the design plan for the sites. The object is to harmonize and edify leisure behaviour. The sites celebrated Americans' increasing leisure time and affluence. But they also sought to convey the impression of being situated on the threshold of the future. The citing of these sites in California was quite deliberate. 'Magic kingdoms,' comments Findlay (1992: 299), 'implied that the urban West constituted not only a frontier of continuing migration but also a frontier of the twenty-first century.' They are the spatial corollaries of expansionism and growth.[4]

Another way of exploring the eye of power in relation to leisure is to consider the individual life-cycle. The problem of the physical ageing and death of its members is something that all societies face. But they do not deal with it in uniform ways. Modernity 1 frames the physical process of ageing in a social life-cycle. The individual's biological cycle of birth, sexual maturity and death translates into a segmented series of social powers and responsibilities. Kelly (1987: 66–90) produces a life course model of leisure which identifies discrete stages of growth: infancy (0–12 months); childhood (1–11); early adolescence (12–15); late adolescence (16–18/20); youth (19/21–29); early maturity (30–44); maturity (45–retirement); retirement–disabling event; disability–death. In each of these stages leisure assumes different salience in our lives. For example, according to Kelly (1987: 79–80), leisure orientations in youth are dominated by acquisition and asserting independence; leisure dominates life; and the individual seeks to form a stable family unit. Kelly contrasts this with early maturity, which he characterizes as a period of 'stability and accomplishment'; leisure here tends to be home- and family-centred; accomplishments at work translate into higher leisure expenditure.

There are many variations on this model in the literature. However, the basic idea of stages in physical development corresponding with typical leisure forms and practices is common. It is supported by the social institutions of the family, education system and advertising. Each combines to produce powerful social images of lifestyle at different stages in the life-cycle. These influence leisure behaviour in complicated ways. For example, Chaney (1992) presents ageing in terms of a status passage. One of the crucial stages in this process is retirement, when individuals withdraw from paid employment and enter full-time leisure. Chaney is interested in how the leisure industry prepares the individual for this stage. He takes the case of representations of holidays as an example. Holidays for the aged, he argues, are part of the ritualized process of ageing. The tourist industry caters for the aged as a niche market. Their tourist brochures emphasize company and care – items which are vital for people who may be widowed and physically frail. Individuality is permitted but only within the parameters of communalism and 'conservative hedonism'. Unlike earlier stages in the life-cycle, they present the holiday not as a break with home-life but as a continuation of it. The brochures emphasize that all of the comforts of home will be at the fingertips of the pensioned vacationer. 'The imagined community of one's peers', writes Chaney (1992: 17) 'is therefore both a form of *rites de passage* as well as a utopian alternative to an implied loss of autonomy.' What seems to be an individual choice made in response to the physical process of ageing turns out to be a highly codified, socially organized process.

Another way of exploring how the body is organized in leisure under Modernity 1 refers to women's bodies. The leisure industry predominantly treats women as the objects of male fantasy and desire. Women need to look right and smell right. The female body is therefore thoroughly valorized. Certain parts signify high erotic value. 'In our culture,' observes Perry (1992: 131), 'the breast is defined as the quintessence of female sexuality, symbolic in its externality of both the pornographic and erogenous possibilities of female flesh. . . . For women in twentieth-century America, breasts often emblematize their femininity and their success or failure as sex objects and hence women.' Hair, lips, waists, bottoms and legs also carry high erotic value. The great emphasis which consumer culture places upon the female looking right produces anxiety in women who believe they don't or can't have the right appearance. In the nineteenth century the corset offered women the idealized feminine form of a narrow waist, prominent breasts and curvaceous hips. However, it also led to the mutilation of the female body with perpetual shortness of breath, listlessness and damage to internal organs emerging as new female complaints (Sennett 1977: 187; Ewen and Ewen 1982: 139–42).

In the postwar period fears about the mutilating effect of consumer culture upon the female body have centred on anorexia nervosa. This reflects the rise in incidence of the disease since 1945, especially among women from middle- and upper-class backgrounds. A strong theme in feminist accounts of the disease is that anorexia arises from consumer culture's taboo against fatness. Western culture associates fat bodies with indiscipline and indulgence; by contrast, thin bodies symbolize asceticism and self-control. Sufferers starve themselves in order to comply with the requirements of the male gaze (Boskind-Lodhal 1976; MacLeod 1981). Other commentators have taken issue with this interpretation (Bruch 1977; Turner 1992: 214–27). They argue that feminist analysis cannot satisfactorily explain why some women become anorexic while others show no sign of the disease. Although these critics do not deny the importance of the male gaze, narcissism and the idealization of the female body, they place much greater emphasis upon certain forms of moral management within the middle-class household in diagnosing the reasons for the illness. Bruch's (1977) clinical work argues that over-dependence in daughters upon parents and an excessive stress on cleanliness and obedience are common features in the case-histories of anorexic patients. Her conclusion is that these factors inhibit individualization by preventing transition to the external world. The anorexic literally shrinks from life. Bruch's solution is to expose the restricting factors which inhibit the development of personality and to support the empowerment of the patient.

Leisure as a symbol of personal merit and health is also evident in fashion. The new body-styles and informal dress codes of the 1980s and 1990s emphasized 'the leisure look'. As Wilson (1985: 42) observes:

> The leisure for which the woman in a track suit, leotards, leg warmers is costumed is actually both display and 'work'. You have to have already become 'fit' in order to participate adequately in the public ritual of the jogging track or the aerobics class. The bright uniform acts out a lifestyle, as does the elaborate make-up, the artificially flushed-cheek and the kohl-enlarged eyes of health-made-erotic. The natural signs of exertion on the other hand such as sweat and glistening forehead must be rigorously concealed. The correct costume of the fitness freak has its own obsessional details.

Consumer culture emphasizes body maintenance and hedonistic lifestyle. It requires the body to be shaped and influenced by the images of advertising and the media. The body becomes both a battlefield in which the individual struggles to combat deterioriation and decay and a monitor of pleasure and self-expression (Featherstone 1982: 18).

The Family

The family is the ideological centre of leisure under Modernity 1. Samuel Smiles (1859) – the self-appointed nineteenth-century conscience of the bourgeoisie – described the family as 'the crystal of society'. Elsewhere Smiles (1894: 32) remarked that

> it is in the order of nature that domestic life should be preparatory to social, and that the mind and character should first be formed in the home. There the individuals who afterwards form society are dealt with in detail and fashioned one by one. From the family they enter life, and advance from boyhood to citizenship. Thus the home may be regarded as the most influential school of civilization.[5]

Much functionalist sociology is predicated on the assumption that the family is the prime unit of analysis in leisure. By the term 'family' is meant a legally binding, heterosexual, lifelong adult union and legally recognized dependent children (Roberts 1981; Parker 1983; Kelly 1987). Leisure management responsibilities are seen as split along gender lines. The father is typically seen as the motivating force in outside pursuits while the mother assumes the role of domestic leisure manager. Conflict resolution is seen as being confined within the home. The family contributes to society through taxation and consumption activity but normal family life is autonomous and self-regulating.

This ideology of family life has been subject to intense criticism. To begin with, although there is much evidence that marriage remains a popular institution, it is equally clear that the incidence of divorce and one-parent families is growing. In Britain one in three marriages now end in divorce and 21 per cent of live births occur outside marriage (Barrett and McIntosh 1982; Clark 1991). Similar levels of divorce and illegitimate birth can be found in the USA, Canada, Australia and North-Western Europe. In addition, the media exposure of child abuse, spouse-battering, marital rape and the impact of feminism and gay and lesbian activism have combined to call into question whether the family is the best institution of child-support and child-rearing.

Another criticism is that the ideology of nuclear family life is a massive distortion of reality. It ignores the huge unequal division of labour between husbands and wives within the home. Also it ignores the fact that women in most families have to engage in paid labour as well as domestic unpaid labour in order to maintain family standards of living (Barrett 1980).

A third line of criticism has centred upon the diversity of stable family forms. Laslett (1965) identified five factors which create variation in family life:

(1) *Organizational*: relating to the division of labour within and outside the home. For example, the growth of commuter marriages in which partners live apart during the week and rejoin on weekends and vacations.
(2) *Cultural*: relating to different ethnic, religious, class, political and child-rearing traditions.
(3) *Class*: relating to different access to resources of capital and time.
(4) *Life course*: relating to changes in the family unit which arise through the mortality of either the husband or wife or the departure and marriage of children.
(5) *Cohort*: relating to changes in the density of populations, the ratio of men to women, young people to old and so forth.

This list corresponds with a variety of 'non-traditional' family forms: never-married singlehood, voluntary child-free unions, step-families, open marriages/open families, same-sex families and multi-adult households. Similarly, both Weeks (1991) and Plummer (1992) argue that fulfilling and enriching adult partnerships outside heterosexual family life have long been a normal part of daily life in Western society. The ideology of family life, they continue, is grossly at odds with experience and tangible reality. As Weeks (1991: 152) concludes, it is perhaps most useful today to see the family as 'a variable set of relationships between men and women, adults and children, shaped and structured by uneven power relations, whose unity is historical and ideological rather than natural'. In leisure studies the logical and practical requirement of this argument is that researchers and planners open themselves up to the variety of family forms and produce a more relevant connection between leisure-suppliers and leisure-users.

Religion

Religion has traditionally played an important part in the organization of normality in society. In primitive society it functions to support order and control deviance (Douglas 1966; Levy-Bruhl 1966). It also legitimates ceremonies of release and rituals designed to arouse collective effervescence, transport and ecstasy (Lewis 1988). As Beckford (1989: 167) observes, religion is rooted in ideas of orderliness, normative guidelines for action and the ultimate basis for meaning. However, Modernity 1 is associated with the waning of organized religion. Durkheim (1915) argued that increased geographical mobility, structural differentiation, pluralization and the growth of scientific knowledge produced a decline in religious belief. At the same time he believed that industrial society was producing new sources of social and moral solidarity which were replacing religious belief. He placed 'the cult of the individual' at the head of the list. By this term Durkheim meant scientific beliefs in the sanctity of individual rights and capacities. For Durkheim these rights and capacities went hand-in-hand with duties and responsibilities. Modernity required that individuals should obey the law, respect the state and conform to the constraints of civil society. In return it permitted individuals more mobility, freedom and moral space than any other social order known hitherto.

Secularization refers to the decline in the social significance of religious institutions and practices. Wilson, who is one of the strongest advocates of the secularization thesis, directly relates this decline to the new structural shapes associated with Modernity 1:

> Instead of work activity, family life, education, religious practice, the operation of law and custom and recreation, all being part of each other and affecting everyone in more or less self-sufficient close-knit small communities, as occurred in large measure in all pre-modern societies, we have highly specialized places, times, resources, and personnel involved in each of these areas of social life. (Wilson, 1976: 40)

It is often argued that leisure institutions and practices have filled the vacuum left by the decline of religion. Durkheim (1915) himself speculated that the establishment of a new calendar of state leisure ceremonies and national recreation and sporting events could fulfil the role of generating collective effervescence, release and pleasure in secular society. The rational recreation movement which emerged in the 1860s was in part an attempt to morally elevate the 'deserving' working class through leisure (Borzello 1987). Similarly, the development of national and international sports fixtures at the end of the nineteenth century has been associated with the emergence of a new secular religion (Hargreaves 1986). The sense of purpose and authenticity that religion used to provide is now provided by leisure. Burns (1973: 54) expresses the functional switch particularly clearly:

> Organized leisure can be construed as contemporary society's response to the enduring need to ritualize the unfamiliar and disconnected, the unattainable and the threatening. . . . The structures of leisure exist to serve as repositories of meaning and value for everyday life.

MacCannell (1976) takes tourism as an archetypal case of the search for authenticity in contemporary society. The tourist, he argues, is preoccupied in leisure with the search for real things in a society saturated with artifice.

> The rhetoric of tourism is full of manifestations of the importance of the authenticity of the relationship between tourists and what they see: this is a *typical* native house; this is the *very* place the leader fell; this is the *actual* pen used to sign the law; this is the *original* manuscript; this is an *authentic* Tlingit fish club; this is a *real* piece of the *true* Crown of Thorns. (MacCannell 1976: 14; emphasis his)

Like the medieval pilgrim clutching his or her piece of the cross or sorrowfully trudging along Christ's footsteps to the crucifixion (Jusserand 1888), the modern tourist is preoccupied with separating real experience from artificial experience. The irony, as MacCannell (1976: 14) goes on to note, is that 'the level of authentication can be very low.' He develops the notion of 'staged authenticity' to refer to manufactured, calculated, distorted presentations of 'reality' which are offered as real presence. MacCannell's work bluntly emphasizes the *produced* character of our ideas of 'nature', 'normality', 'freedom' and 'truth'. The search for authenticity through leisure activity in a secular society is as intoxicating as the search for God in a pre-scientific society: but not necessarily as constant or fulfilling.

Habitus

Modernity 1 treats leisure as a segmented part of the social structure. That is, leisure forms are theorized as distinct from the rest of life and they are invested with determinate functions. This is, of course, consistent with the general view of leisure espoused under Modernity 1. Bourdieu's (1984) concept of 'habitus' is useful in capturing how segmented behaviour is generated. Habitus refers to an imprinted generative schema. The term 'generative' means a motivating or propelling force in social behaviour. The term 'schema' means a distinctive pattern or system of social conduct. For Bourdieu the socialization process imprints generative schemata onto the individual. We learn systems of speech, deportment, style and value from our families and local communities. Bourdieu argues that these systems thoroughly organize the individual. At the most basic level they teach us ways of blowing our nose, walking and gesticulating. However, they also structure our conscious and unconscious responses to, *inter alia*, questions of sex, race and morality. The origin of these systems is the habitual way of doing things and viewing the world that prevails in the social positions occupied by our families and local communities – hence the root of the term 'habitus'.[6]

By recognizing that different families and communities occupy different social positions Bourdieu identifies a differentiated quality to habitus. For example, the habitus for the children of a surgeon will be different from the habitus for the children of a docker. The difference stems from both the material, economic level of capital in each home and also the cultural capital. The term 'cultural capital' refers to the knowledge of and skills in the discursive realm relating to society, the arts, leisure, sport, science, politics and all the other elements recognized as 'culture' in society at large. Bourdieu does not invite us to regard the cultural capital in a doctor's home as being totally superior to that which obtains in the home of a docker. His interest is in how society evaluates this cultural capital through visible and tacit systems of reward and punishment.

This raises another important concept in Bourdieu's sociology: distinction. Habitus is essentially a classifying tool which helps us relate to the external physical and social world. However, just as it enables us to classify the world, it is a marker of behaviour which allows to be classified by others. Habitus is closely tied to Bourdieu's conception of distinction. Indeed distinction might be defined as the social evaluation of habitus. According to Bourdieu, schemata of social evaluation are structured along class lines. He identifies three class lines in contemporary society: legitimate, middle-brow and popular. Each level is associated with a generic habitus. Thus they enable us to classify the behaviour of others and compare it with the mores and values that prevail in our own habitus. According to Bourdieu, the three classes compete for power. In leisure relations this is expressed in the struggle to dominate access to leisure goods and services. For example, by attaching the badge of distinction to certain leisure activities, each class seeks to increase its stock of cultural capital and hence real power.

Here Bourdieu's analysis is very like Veblen's (1925) thought on the leisure class. Both writers fasten upon the symbolic expression of leisure pursuits. Both regard leisure activity as a way of accumulating or losing distinction. For example, a traditional leisure pursuit of the upper classes in Britain is fox-hunting. Traditionally, to participate in this activity has been to display distinction. However, recently fox-hunting has been widely censured as a cruel and evil pursuit. In many circles it is dismissed as a barbaric activity. Hence participation in it is now more equivocal.[7] Another example refers to the growth of heritage centres like disused coal-mines, water-mills, factories and sites of traditional craft production which now survive as places of leisure. In this case paid labour, which in Veblen's sociology is labelled as an activity with low distinction, is relabelled as an activity possessing high distinction. Dying crafts have been preserved by the struggle of groups intent on maintaining their traditional way of life. The examples illustrate another aspect of Bourdieu's thought on leisure which is that different classes and strata in society regularly engage in a relabelling process with regard to leisure. Rather like financial currency, cultural capital is subject to inflationary and deflationary pressures. Leisure activity can be exploited as the focus for battles of distinction between competing strata.

Bourdieu's concept has been criticized for being over-deterministic. It suggests that the individual simply reflects the conditions in which he or she is born. The individual is therefore deprived of any will or power to shape his or her own existence (Jenkins 1992: 79–80). Against this Bourdieu (1990: 116) argues that the criticism of determinism misses the flexibility which is integral to his concept of habitus. It is essential to his view that habitus is seen as an influence on social behaviour which is itself in process.[8] Thus circumstances change how habitus operates. One of the main circumstances is the competition between the different social levels. These can expose the effects of a specific habitus and assign them a negative or positive value. Rather like Popper (1962), Bourdieu seems to offer free discussion in 'the open society' as the guarantee that habitus avoids having a determining effect on social behaviour.

However, as Habermas (1971, 1979) and other commentators have pointed out, the notions of 'free discussion' and 'the open society' are rather problematic. They ignore the role of the unconscious in shaping the contours of everyday life and they marginalize the distorting effect of ideology which is quite capable of presenting organized compliance as freedom and openness. Furthermore, while the concept of habitus undoubtedly clearly conveys how many 'personal' or 'individual' aspects of our behaviour are socially conditioned, it is a matter of debate whether the concept deals with this matter with greater originality or clarity than subcultural analysis. American delinquency theory in the 1950s and 1960s presented a powerful view of subcultural formation and segmented behaviour which anticipates much of Bourdieu's work on subculture. Moreover, its treatment of the place of crime and deviance in the leisure practice of certain delinquent subcultures is in some ways more suggestive and valuable than Bourdieu's concept. For it implies that leisure activity is an important testing-ground for opposing the values of 'straight society' (see in particular Cohen 1955; Cloward and Ohlin 1960; Suttles 1968).

Bureaucracy

Weber (1970: 214, 215) argued that bureaucratic organization involves precision, speed, impersonality, unambiguity, methodical training, specialization and agreed rules of conduct. The aim of bureaucracy is to produce co-ordinated, calculable action. By standardizing the basic elements of interaction, predictability and efficiency are increased. Weber argued that bureaucracy is, technically speaking, the most efficient form of organization known in human society.

Weber distinguished bureaucratic rule from charismatic and traditional forms of rule. Charismatic forms of rule refer to cases in which people invest an individual with special powers or gifts and on this basis pay obeisance to him or her. An example from the contemporary field of leisure might be the respect or strong emotions which fans show to a film or pop star. Traditional rule refers to cases in which order is maintained by time-honoured practice and established habit. An example from leisure might be traditional rituals, festivals or processions which occur on holidays and feast-days. For Weber these three forms are co-existent although, at the same time, he recognizes a demonstrable historical tendency for bureaucratic forms to replace charismatic and traditional forms.

At the heart of Weber's discussion is the idea that the bureaucratization of society increases calculation, measurement and control. This is evident in leisure practice at the level of both the body and society. With regard to the body, the influence of bureaucracy is evident in leisure activities such as dieting, grooming and exercise. These activities regulate, standardize and discipline behaviour. At the level of society, the influence of bureaucracy is evident in the differentiation between work time and leisure time, work space and leisure space. The creation of purpose-built leisure spaces in which leisure time can be invested was a product of Modernity 1. In the second half of the nineteenth century a variety of new leisure spaces emerged: seaside resorts, parks, boarding houses, winter gardens, promenades, pavilions, pubs, music halls, country cottages and holiday homes (King 1980). These new spaces were produced in part through working-class agitation. However, they were also the result of the surpluses generated by capitalism and the commitment of the state to increase standards of public health, education and recreation. But bureaucracy also standardizes 'free' time behaviour and this brings me to my second point.

The bureaucratization of society contributes to a decline in spontaneity, contrast and passion. 'No-one today,' complains Horkheimer (1974: 25), 'learns to devote his leisure to anything but the much praised "concrete reality", that is, to accomplishments that are very much like work: doing amateur repairs, driving an auto, sitting at machines; even the idea of an old age free of toil no longer awakens any great yearning.' The division of leisure is seen here as sapping the quality of experience. In our 'free' time, implies Horkheimer, we succumb to the programmatic order of instrumental rationality and routine which defines the bureaucratic order of the whole society.

The third point refers to the displacement of bureaucratic ends with bureaucratic means. Merton (1940), in a famous essay, observed that bureaucratic organization tends to breed an excessive conformity in the bureaucratic personality. This is often expressed in rigidities of behaviour, a punctilious attention to formalized procedures and the rituals of behaviour. In Merton's view, conformity to rules may interfere with the achievement of the purposes of the organization and contribute to the mindless veneration for red tape. Merton's argument can be extended to leisure practice. For example, rituals of exercise can be more important than the exercise itself; the insistence of taking leisure at a particular time and in a particular place may also demonstrate traits of Merton's obsessional bureaucratic personality.

Nationalism

Leisure has traditionally had strong connections with nationalism. In the six-teenth and seventeenth centuries certain leisure accomplishments and pastimes, such as horsemanship, hunting, coursing, hawking, fowling, fishing, archery, fencing, travel, dancing, music, bowling, tennis, the playhouse and the cockpit were accepted marks of the gentleman (Vale 1977). Similarly, in the nineteenth century the public schools used organized sport and leisure to inculcate self-discipline and 'manliness'. Games were the main device for the training of a boy's character. Through them, wrote Mangan (1985: 18), 'the public schoolboy supposedly learnt *inter alia* the basic tools of imperial com-mand: courage, endurance, assertion, control and self-control.' Manliness and gentlemanly behaviour became the model of masculinity. Veblen (1925: 179–80) identified the cultivation of sport and manly pursuits with the leisure class. He identified both with the 'survival of the predatory temperament and habits' typical of the old warrior class (1925: 179).

However, it would be a mistake to identify these characteristics too closely with the dominant class. Sport and leisure events have been used by industri-alizing elites to instil discipline into the nation and to symbolize national unity (Hargreaves 1986: 220). The invention of royal ceremonial occasions, fes-tivals and processions which occurred in Britain at the end of the nineteenth century used leisure events to organize stability and national unity. 'The invariable real focus for such exercises,' writes Nairn (1988: 282), 'was the Nation . . . people grew convinced in a short time that such contrived harking back was the real thing. That there actually was a throbbing "thousand years of continuity" behind each wave of the Lord Chamberlain's wand.' One exam-ple of the success of this experiment in social engineering can be found in the growth of popular patriotism. Summerfield (1986) demonstrates that between 1870 and 1914 the music halls transformed the popular song from an instru-ment of social criticism into a vehicle of jingoism and conformity. The music hall turns eschewed political controversy and presented the British Empire as noble and kind, Anglo-Saxon culture as superior and the colonies as willing and grateful subservients.

In Nazi Germany the 'Strength through Joy' movement, which was referred to in the previous chapter, used workers' outings, holidays, camps and treks to raise nationalist consciousness. The discipline of the body was a constant fea-ture of Nazi propaganda. The male body was to be turned into a machine through drill, exercise and sport. In the Nazi case this self-discipline assumed a pathological form so that the desire for a life of leisure and the celebration of hedonism were stigmatized as illnesses. 'The core of all fascist propaganda,' comments Theweleit (1988: 7), 'is a battle against everything that constitutes enjoyment and pleasure. Pleasure, with its hybridizing qualities, has the dis-solving effect of a chemical enzyme on the armoured body. Attitudes of asceticism, renunciation, and self-control are effective defenses.'

Sport and leisure, then, operate as ways of organizing subjects through nationalist identification and strengthening the grid-like order of Modernity 1.

Of course, this is not a one-way process. Organized sport and leisure can also be a focus for challenging the ruling order and there is some evidence that the development of sport and physical recreation among women between 1870 and 1914 exposed the complicities of male power (McRone 1988). Similarly in the 1960s and 1970s international athletics became a focus for black consciousness. Nevertheless, there is an important sense in which free time was used after 1870 by the state to extend the rule of nationalism, to organize obedient subjects. Through the fictive community of 'the Nation' working together and playing together a discrete political and moral economy is produced and reproduced.[9] It is one which automatically and 'naturally' prioritizes one voice and excludes other voices. 'To speak the name – and language – of the nation,' write Corrigan and Sayer (1985: 195), 'both denies the particularity of what is being said (and who is saying it) and defines alternatives and challenges as sectional, selfish [and] partial.'

Citizenship

Nationalism is always ultimately exclusionary. In defining who 'we' are, subtle and sometimes brutal distinctions are made with the anonymous mass of 'others'. This leads to obvious difficulties when legal attempts are made to codify universal citizenship rights. According to Marshall (1977), there are three major dimensions to citizenship:

(1) *Civil*. This refers to equality before the law, personal liberty, the right to own property and freedom of speech. Civil rights assumes the independence of the judiciary and the law from sectional interests.
(2) *Political*. This refers to universal rights of suffrage, access to parliamentary institutions, electoral rights, regular elections and secret voting. In the twentieth century attempts have been made to extend political citizenship to universal rights of welfare entitlement, education and the minimum wage.
(3) *Social*. These refer to universal rights of economic and social well-being.

Capitalism is a system which holds out formal political equality for all while at the same time actively generating vast inequality in the economic and social spheres. In Marshall's terms there is a disjunction between the civil and political dimensions of citizenship and the social dimension. In the case of leisure the disjuncture is very evident in the contrast between the commodities on offer in the 'free' leisure market and the stratified inequality of access to the market associated with gender, race and class. 'The leisure society' embraces some as active participants but condemns the majority to the status of non-participants. Through advertising and the mass media we are bombarded with invitations to travel, to see the world, to relax, to have fun, but we are sharply aware that we lack the resources to fully participate in the life of leisure that seems to be at our fingertips.

Another issue relating to citizenship rights refers to the management of open spaces and heritage sites. The state undertakes to manage these resources 'for the nation'. In doing so it lays down statutory powers to control access, use and conduct. This can raise problems with groups who wish to employ these common spaces and sites in ways which conflict with the state's management policy. Campaigns for open access to inland spaces of outstanding natural beauty or coastal paths highlight the partial and contentious nature of citizenship claims on leisure resources. Two good examples refer to the access dispute regarding the monument of Stonehenge in Britain and the 1993 Indian Supreme Court ruling on the pollution hazard posed to the Taj Mahal.

The dispute over access to the site of Stonehenge has simmered in British public life since the early 1980s. This ancient monument is managed by the state for the benefit of the nation. Access to the site is limited by barriers and the state manages the car park and the refreshment shops on the slip road which leads to the monument. Throughout the 1980s and early 1990s Stonehenge has been the focus of civil disobedience. Groups of travelling people and hippies have claimed the right to worship at the site on the summer solstice. They insist that Stonehenge has religious significance for them and they claim the right to use the monument freely as part of their religious celebrations. Their claim has been resisted by the state, which has used police to control processions to the site and to debar the travellers from entering the inner area. The conflict has led to several outbursts of aggression between the police and the travellers.

As I have argued at greater length elsewhere (Rojek 1988), the battle for Stonehenge raises important questions of citizenship rights and the state's management of leisure resources. Three points must be made. In the first place, the formal equality of access to sites recognized by the law is not translated into practice. The state defines a minimal set of uses for the site and tends to stigmatize and obstruct groups who define the use-value of the site in different terms. Second, the state tends to apply secular, bureaucratic distinctions in site management. One of the main complaints of the travellers to Stonehenge is that the state management of the site has contributed to the disenchantment of the monument. The erection of barricades and the construction of the car park and refreshment area are deplored for violating the mystical integrity of the site and turning Stonehenge into just another tourist attraction. The state might respond that these facilities are in place to service the needs of 'normal' visitors. But this raises questions about the definition of 'normality' and the managerial remit of the state in controlling 'our' heritage. Third, the conflicts have highlighted the social and moral values which come into play in managing public leisure resources. While the public provision of leisure is often associated with progress, the battle for Stonehenge shows the problems involved in using 'freedom' and 'choice' as universalistic concepts in thinking about leisure. For the state clearly applies a low trust evaluation on the travellers which is based upon judgements about the travellers' lifestyle and the threat that this lifestyle poses to the site. Although state policy on leisure is often legitimated on the grounds that it benefits all of us this case shows very clearly how it actually marginalizes and scapegoats the citizenship rights of certain groups.

Turning now to the case of the Indian Supreme Court ruling of 1993, this arose after complaints from the heritage and tourist lobby of a pollution hazard to the Taj Mahal – the country's most cherished historic monument and biggest tourist draw. The ruling ordered that more than 200 factories in the local township of Agra must be closed with the loss of more than 200,000 jobs.[10] Opponents of the ruling claim that the closures will push many families to starvation levels and they criticize the government's apparent desire to appease foreign tourists instead of attending to the employment needs of Indian citizens.[11] The Taj dispute is interesting because it clearly illustrates the collision between local, national and global citizenship rights in the management of some outstanding heritage sites. At the local level the consideration of jobs is quite understandable. 'There is no justice in letting human beings starve to death just to save a stone monument,' one Agra iron foundry worker is quoted as saying (*Guardian*, 15 November 1993). However, at the national level the site represents a key symbol of the Indian leisure industry and a large foreign currency earner to boot. The corrosion of the monument would leave the government open to international charges of state vandalism. Finally, at the global level the Taj is valued as a part of world heritage. The threat of pollution posed to it by local industrial activity is therefore not simply a matter of Indian politics but rather it raises issues of global preservationism and responsibility. The example illustrates the global dynamics of citizenship issues with regard to leisure. It shows how national leisure policies must be increasingly sensitive to international opinion. I shall return to this point later in the book in the course of discussing the concept of the 'risk society' (pp. 152–6).

Escape

Intimations and ideologies of escape, the promise of life beyond duty and routine, nostalgia for simpler times/truer feelings – these sentiments abound wherever leisure is referred to under Modernity 1. Doubtless they reflect older, utopian longings for the good life, the life of movement and free contemplation decorated with 'garlands of repose', as O'Loughlin (1978) has it. As we saw above, these longings were often expressed in the form of religious beliefs in the paradise of the after-life – that massive cultural transference of freedom, choice and flexibility from the back-cloth of this-worldly cares, troubles and responsibilities to a perfect future.

With the onslaught of Modernity 1 the secular embodiment of these sentiments became more urgent, more gross. The reason for this is, of course, the fecundity of industrialization, the vast surplus of commodities and time generated by capitalism. Not everyone shared in this surplus. We know only too well that access to commodities and time was stratified along lines of gender, race and class. All the same, historians leave us in no doubt that one of the most typical responses to nineteenth-century consumer capitalism was sheer

wonderment at the wealth generated and the variety of new experiences on tap
in the rapidly expanding metropolis (Hobsbawm 1975, 1987; Schivelbusch
1988, 1992; Williams 1982).[12] This was also the time when the fundamentals of
Modernity 1 were set in place and the grid-like structure through which life
was meant to be led was imposed upon populations. Central to this structure
was, of course, the wise and industrious use of time. To accurately gauge how
deep this ran in popular consciousness we only have to consult the common-
sense and practical advice books devoured by the status-conscious middle
class. As the *Young Woman's Guide to Domestic Happiness* (1834: 44–5) put it:

> To make a proper use of that short and uncertain time allotted us for our mortal pil-
> grimage, is a proof of wisdom; to use it with economy, and dispose of it with care,
> the province of prudence and discretion. . . . By being *constantly and usefully
> employed*, the destroyer of mortal happiness will have but few opportunities of
> making his baneful attacks, and by regularly filling up your precious moments, you
> will be less exposed to dangers, and in a manner guarded against the numberless
> snares and errors in which idleness would perpetually involve you. (emphasis in the
> original)

Among the amusements which the *Young Woman's Guide* recommended were
needlework, family conversation, flower arranging and reading fiction.[13]

In the context of a strong and invasive work ethic one can easily see that
dreams of escape were especially vivid and compelling. Under Modernity 1
these dreams were harnessed and mobilized in a variety of ways. Advertising
created a symbolic universe of escape and fulfilment. 'The idea of a *free world*',
comments Ewen (1976: 191) neatly, 'characterized by *goods* established itself as
a pacific social ethic' (emphasis in the original). Escape messages were supported by the transport revolution. The mass-produced automobile increased
personal mobility and enabled the worker to enjoy the illusion of control.
Escaping the factory and the city was simply a matter of putting your foot on
the accelerator (Flink 1975; Bayley 1986). The motor-car also intensified the
impression of having the world at your fingertips. All of this seems to confirm
the ideology espoused by the marketing departments of Ford, General Motors
and other leading automobile manufacturers that the automobile necessarily
delivered freedom and choice. The modernist architect Le Corbusier (1929)
shared the view that the automobile is unequivocally a progressive force in
human history. His design for 'the cities of tomorrow' advocated the replacement of ancient, narrow winding streets in European cities with rapid
transport, multi-lane highways. The demolition of all pre-modernist buildings went hand-in-hand with Le Corbusier's general philosophy. It was not
until the late 1960s that an ecological counter-ideology emerged which focused
on the destructive effects of the automobile on the environment. Similarly, the
rise of the cinema reinforced the general sense of mobility with a constant
stream of images of escape and adventure (Richards 1984).

Urban planning also incorporated leisure as an essential principle of design
and healthy life. Le Corbusier (1929) – who has some claim to be regarded as
the most influential modernist architect of the twentieth century – based his
architecture on a social design for living which assumed that daily life could be

segmented into eight hours of work, eight hours of leisure and eight hours of sleep. Similarly, Walter Gropius, the high priest of Bauhaus style, argued that symbols of leisure and escape should be an essential part of modern architecture. Writing on the virtues of high-rise developments, he (quoted in Isaacs 1991: 160) maintained that 'with high-rise apartments there are wide spaces with light and air and areas for children's play and where nature can enter . . . roofs can become gardens. . . . Another possible advantage of high-rise buildings are community facilities and services . . . opportunities for informal social contact . . . a new form of urban living.'

Many of these ideas crystallized in the late 1950s and 1960s with the rise of post-industrial society theory. Riesman (1964: 158–79), who is generally recognized to have coined the term, noted that the average working week an America had declined to forty hours in 1958 as opposed to seventy hours in 1920. Work was apparently diminishing in importance as the central life interest. Leisure was emerging as the focus of lifestyle and consumption. The mechanization of production promised to banish drudgery in the workplace. The argument was advanced and refined by a number of writers including Kerr et al. (1973), Bell (1974), Touraine (1974) and Toffler (1981). Kerr et al. (1973) wrote of 'the logic of industrialization' which compelled industrial nations to generate more leisure, more opportunities in education, better welfare services and higher standards of living. In their view more leisure for everyone is an inevitable effect of industrial progress.

From today's standpoint these arguments inevitably appear to be wildly optimistic. Structural changes in the post-1960s economy have created an excess capacity of free time. However, this has not translated into more leisure for all. Instead two parallel and interrelated processes appear to have been triggered into motion. On the one hand, an underclass of part-time and unemployed workers has been created. They are rich in free time but they lack the economic resources to participate fully in the leisure opportunities offered by advanced consumer capitalism. On the other hand, those who remain in work are subject to more demands on their time. Harriman (1982) ironically terms them 'the harried leisure class'. For while they are relatively rich in economic resources they lack the free time to develop leisure experience except in short, concentrated bursts, such as annual vacations or the odd night out at the theatre or concert hall. What was missing in post-industrial society theory was a realistic assessment of the social and political impediments to egalitarian leisure policies. Notions of escape were therefore exaggerated.

Conclusion

The main twentieth-century line of criticism relating to pleasure and enjoyment under Modernity 1 has argued that the social structure is capable of only generating abstract happiness or the particular, momentary happiness of the monadic individual. The symbolic universe of consumer culture stimulates the individual with messages promising escape and self-realization. But the pursuit of these objects is ultimately unfulfilling since no individual can possess the infinity of commodities which the market offers and the objects of consumption are themselves subject to constant and unpredictable change. In addition, possession itself involves struggle and the organized repression both of one's own instinctual need for gratification and the capacity to consume of others. For Marcuse (1988) and other critics in the Frankfurt School, self-mutilation, antagonism and surplus repression are the defining characteristics of Modernity 1. Market organization divorces individuals from their true needs by requiring them to be competitive and acquisitive. Under Modernity 1, contends Marcuse (1988: 166, 183, 190):

> Enjoyment and truth, happiness and the essential relations of individuals are disjunctions. . . . Acts intending enjoyment do not achieve the fulfilment of their own intention; even when they fulfil themselves, they remain untrue. . . . Pleasure in the abasement of another as well as self-abasement under a stronger will, pleasure in the manifold surrogates for sexuality, in meaningless sacrifices . . . are false pleasures because the drives and needs that fulfil themselves in them make men less free, blinder, and more wretched than they have to be. They are drives and needs of individuals who are raised in an antagonistic society.

For Marcuse the solution is to bring the administration of society in line with the real needs of its members. He reasoned that when the limits placed upon personal and societal growth have been removed the nature of the needs and wants will themselves change. The individual will no longer be forced to subsist between a 'particular interest and a hypostasized general interest that suppresses the individuals. In his relation to an authentic general interest, the individual would relate to truth; the demands and decisions of the whole would then preserve the individual interest and eventually promote his happiness' (Marcuse 1988: 193). This solution calls upon the individual to participate in dismantling the mechanisms of control and turn over the administration of society to the association of free producers. It also assumes that individuals in industrial society have universal pent-up real needs which will be released by the rational transformation of society.

But if we follow the logic of Foucault's account of carceral networks Marcuse's demand for social transformation appears unrealistic. Practically, Foucault's sociology raises the question of whether the 'association of free producers' can agree on binding definitions of social responsibility and personal freedom. Since the scale of society requires some form of representative government there is an obvious danger that the interests of the representatives will become disjoined from the interests and needs of the electorate. Theoretically, Foucault's account of carceral networks also raises the problem of whether it is legitimate to see society as constructed around a single contradiction. The 'association of free producers' also inevitably consists of men and women, people with regional and ethnic affiliations, members of sexual minorities, representatives of particular moral positions and political interests. It does not follow that the antagonisms and identities associated with these divisions can be subsumed under the contradiction between capital and labour. If this is allowed, there are obvious difficulties with the proposition that the decisions of the association of free producers will promote the interest and happiness of the individual.

Foucault's discussion points to a fatal contortion in Modernity 1, a knot which strangles the elegant rational uniformity of the grid-like structure of order. The modernist ambition to construct a universe of segmented order is opposed on the grounds that, in practice, it produces a nest of irrationality and disorder. Foucault is, of course, not alone in expressing this view. Nietzsche's philosophy exposed the megalomania of Modernity 1 and called for the tangled order of things to be cleared so as to enable, at the very least, honest relations. Similarly, Weber's sociology walked the tightrope between maintaining the necessity of rational rule to uphold justice and order and acknowledging the hopeless contradictions of rational rule. Modernity 1 celebrated leisure as a playground of escape; yet at the same time it smelted and burnished the reality chains which permanently thwarted the will to escape. One unintended consequence of installing mechanisms of regulation was to narrowly limit the human life-world.[14] Reaction, conflict and an encroaching general sense of *disorder* were the inevitable consequences of Modernity 1's will-to-power. The next chapter examines these themes at greater length in the context of a discussion of leisure and Modernity 2.

5
MODERNITY 2: THE DISORDER OF THINGS

Berman (1982) argues that modernity consists of a unified mode of experiencing space and time, the self and others and life's opportunities and perils. 'But,' he goes on to note, 'it is a paradoxical unity, a unity of disunity: it pours us all into a maelstrom of perpetual disintegration and renewal, of struggle and contradiction, of ambiguity and anguish' (1982: 15). For Berman, Modernity 1's grand ambition of producing an enveloping rational order of things is sheer folly. This is because, in his view, constant change, not stable order, is the defining characteristic of modern life. To ignore this is to pose the wrong questions about the nature of our existence and, of course, to provide the wrong answers.

Berman's argument produces two important conclusions. First, that there is a discrepancy between the leading theories of modern life and popular experience. The divisions between base and superstructure, state and society, men and women, time and space, which many conservative and critical authors apply to make sense of modern society are not coherently or uniformly present in the everyday experience of ordinary men and women. The popular experience of modern life is of seething, ambiguous, irrepressible change. Second, Berman's argument concludes that the rich and deeply rooted traditions of social thought which have highlighted the significance of change and transformation in popular experience have been marginalized. Berman himself retrieves the insights of Goethe, the young Marx, Baudelaire, Dostoevsky and Mandelstam to support his case. The reason for marginalization is not difficult to find. Modernity 2 emphasizes change, flux, de-differentiation and metamorphosis. This is hardly the stuff to buttress the rising political parties and social sciences in the late nineteenth and twentieth centuries in their quest to manage society. This quest is often expressed in the philosophy of establishing a 'pure science' of 'the laws of motion of society'.[1] To be sure, the rational bias of Modernity 1 emphasized the harmony and ascendancy of science.

Modernity 2 has a more poetic emphasis upon phenomenology and experience. Nowhere is this clearer than in the work of Baudelaire. As we have seen (pp. 5–6), he defined modernity as 'the ephemeral, the fugitive, the contingent (1964: 13).' He contrasted this pointedly with what he saw as the bloated ambitions which abound in modern life: the ambitions for an eternal, scientific and immutable order. 'The transitory, fugitive element,' writes Baudelaire (1964: 13) with terrible prophetic power, given the bloodbaths that were to occur in the twentieth century, 'whose metamorphoses are so rapid, must on no account be despised or dispensed with. By neglecting it, you cannot fail to tumble into the abyss of an abstract and indeterminate beauty.'[2] Baudelaire emphasized the restless, episodic, incidental features of modern experience. Like Nietzsche and Simmel who followed him, he was absorbed with the contradictory aspects of daily existence.

Apollo and Dionysus

In struggling to encapsulate the contradictory exuberance and also the mediocrity of modernity, Nietzsche drew on the Greek gods of Apollo and Dionysus. In Greek tragedy Apollo is the god of music and poetry. He is associated with structure, order and self-discipline. Dionysus is the god of wine. He is associated with sensuality, abandon and intoxication. Greek tragedy sought to reconcile these principles in dramatic form. By displaying the contradictions between Apollo and Dionysus in the theatre it supplied binding metaphors for the conduct of everyday life.

Modern life, argues Nietzsche, also struggles to reconcile the conflicting impulses symbolized by Apollo and Dionysus. However, the modern attempt at synthesis is not typically expressed in the heights of drama but more blandly in the nettled monotony of everyday life. Apollonian culture has achieved material abundance and superficial order. But it has done so at a ghastly cost to human life. Under Apollonian culture the individual is isolated from others by the specialized character of his or her activities and the legal and symbolic ties of his or her possessions. The fundamental Dionysian impulse for union, contact and affirmation is denied. However, precisely because of its fundamental nature it can never be ignored. Dionysus teaches us to love life because death is inevitable. To close off experience is to welcome death. 'Yes to life beyond death and change,' declares Nietzsche (1979: 4–5), '*true* life as collective continuation of life through procreation and the mysteries of sexuality. . . . Affirmation of life even in its strangest and sternest problems, the will to life rejoicing in its own inexhaustibility . . . that is what I called Dionysian' (emphasis his). For Nietzsche, Apollonian culture permits us a degree of freedom, but it is the timid freedom of respectable leisure. 'They climb the hill like animals,' he complains of *pleasure tourists*, 'stupid and perspiring, no-one has told them there are beautiful views on the way' (1983: 360). The relish of the passions and the contact with beauty which are so essential for personal and social health and creativity are blocked by the habitual requirements of civil society. Modern life echoes with the sigh of self-denial. We are dully aware of Dionysus' call to open ourselves to experience, to embrace the pain and joy of life and to act guiltlessly, but instead we meekly surrender to the conventions of respectable society.

Nietzsche is often presented as the philosopher *nonpareil* of nihilism. Certainly, in many places in his work he demands that we coldly acknowledge that we live in a world of illusions where even the quest for truth is ultimately a delusion (Frisby 1985: 8). However, in sharp contrast to the popular view,

Nietzsche's advocacy of the Dionysian impulse shows him to be the philosopher *par excellence* of affirmation. For Nietzsche the denial of experience withers the flesh, decomposes the mind and deadens the soul. We are constantly driven to discover what Apollonian culture hides from us. Indeed this culture could not exist without our willing embrace of the forbidden, the buried, the repressed. Dionysus encourages us to regard the accumulation of experience as life's main purpose.

For critics, Nietzsche's uncompromising celebration of our freedom, of the capacity to experience everything, is potent evidence of the immorality of his philosophy. Nietzsche's answer is found in *Thus Spake Zarathustra* (1973), in which he outlines his concept of the *Übermensch*, the superman. Nietzsche's (1973: 3) much misunderstood discussion begins with the proposition that 'man is something to be overcome'. Although he frequently proclaims 'the end of man/end of history' thesis it would be a mistake to take him literally. He was, of course, one of the master rhetoricians of the nineteenth century. Nowhere are his gifts better displayed than in the sprawling and often wildly inconsistent utterances of *Zarathustra*. Here Nietzsche appears to consign all of modern culture to the flames – human achievement, human endeavour, human compassion, are dismissed as if they amount to nothing. However, what Nietzsche is actually asserting is not the end of man or history, rather he is calling for an end to the hesitancy, neutrality, repression and guilt that typify modern personal and social relations. By 'overcoming man' humanity is not replaced, but released and elevated. 'We want to become who we are,' insists Nietzsche (1994: 335) 'the new, the unique, the incomparable, those who give themselves their own laws, those who create themselves.' Nietzsche's concept of the *Übermensch* envisaged the superman as the self-creator, the transfigurer of existence. But at the same time he equated creation and transfiguration with control. His supermen were not to live lawlessly: on the contrary, part of their strength came from following the ordinance of their own self-made laws. The steel of the *Übermensch* is forged through the struggle with the passions and the white heat of genuine self-knowledge. This is in fact quite a virtuous model of human behaviour, quite antithetical to the Nazi philosophy of *Macht* with which it has often been unfortunately associated.

Nietzsche's significance in defining the character of Modernity 2 can be distilled into four propositions:

(1) *The rational order of Modernity 1 is an illusion.* The grid-like structure which it imposes upon us is not inevitable or necessarily the best of all possible worlds. In fact, Nietzsche believes that this Apollonian culture is the source of drudgery, paralysis and torpor in human relations. It obstructs the accumulation of experience, and, for Nietzsche, experience is life's blood.

(2) *Change is inevitable and must be positively embraced.* Unlike the Apollonian aldermen of Modernity 1 who believed that they were conscientiously laying the foundation of permanent order, Nietzsche emphasized the convulsive, restless and ephemeral character of modern life. These tendencies manufacture anxiety and nervousness. However, he believes that it is only by embracing them that we can hope to gain release and elevation.

(3) *Modernity 2 relishes the Dionysian spirit of affirmation.* Nietzsche was appalled by the timidity and self-denial of Modernity 1. He identified greatness with the philosophy of *amor fati*. By this term he meant a continuous, positive spirit of affirmation. One must learn to confront the good and evil parts of one's personality just as one must seize the opportunities and suffer the frustrations and sadness of the times. On this reading self-denial is a kind of death. Instead Nietzsche urges humankind to pursue a questing curiosity and a lack of guilt about one's desires. But the backcloth to this philosophy of emancipation is the notion of the nobility of the *Übermensch*.

(4) *Modernity 2 celebrates the unavoidability of division and fragmentation.* The vibrant, endless character of change under Modernity 2 means that separation, disintegration, differentiation and de-differentiation are inevitable. Nietzsche's philosophy is sceptical of the concept of social totality, which he associates with a form of literary decadence (Frisby 1985: 33). Instead he emphasizes fragmentation, decomposition, innovation and flux.

Apart from a rather perfunctory reference in the work of Kelly (1987: 51), Nietzsche's work has largely been ignored by students of leisure. Perhaps this is understandable. Nietzsche's style is aphoristic. Nowhere does he present his readers with a systematic account of leisure. Furthermore a superficial reading of his work might conclude that his affirmation of Dionysian culture supports the orgy and ecstatic experience as ideal leisure forms. A sceptic might wonder how society can possibly work under these generous conditions.[3] However, Nietzsche's philosophical method and his general critique of Modernity 1 do have direct relevance to leisure studies. Three points relating to pleasure, deviance and process must be made.

(1) *Pleasure.* Nietzsche's dismissal of Modernity 1 is based on the argument that the present is a form of organized mortification. The personality structures which Modernity 1 requires to maintain social order macerate the human body, numb the mind and murder the soul. Current leisure forms offer only timid freedoms and weak choices. According to Nietzsche, the capacity for arousal and pleasure associated with the passions is denied because the passions are themselves reined in by the requirements of respectable society. The result is the production of pleasure-seeking individuals who are incapable of finding pleasure and the reproduction of a society which values the accumulation of pleasure as one of the highest social goals but which also legally and morally inhibits goal achievement.

(2) *Deviance.* Nietzsche's insistence that human beings have free will inevitably problematizes moral and civil law. Rather than seeing them as the reflection of 'rationality', Nietzsche sees them as the gross expression of power. To understand free will it is necessary to examine not only what the law allows but also what it forbids. For Nietzsche, the forbidden, the hidden and the repressed must be affirmed, since only then can the evil passions which animate them be transcended. Instead of affirmation Modernity 1 practises neglect; instead of knowledge of right and wrong it administers sanctimonious platitudes. The deviant is either imprisoned or driven underground – but never listened to or understood. This is reflected in the academic study of

leisure: leisure studies has no worthwhile tradition of investigating deviant leisure forms; indeed it is no exaggeration to claim that, throughout its history, it has effectively ignored the subject of deviance.[4]

(3) *Process*. Nietzsche is violently dismissive of approaches to the study of social life which invoke fixed principles or the concept of social totalities. 'The whole no longer lives,' he thunders, 'it is compounded, calculated, artificial, an artefact' (1980: 27). He goes on to contend that theories which preach 'equal rights for all' or 'freedom of the individual' inevitably lead to 'paralysis', 'drudgery', 'torpor', 'enmity' and 'chaos'. For they reduce humans to the lowest common denominator and ignore the convulsive, vibrant characteristics which identify processes of change in modern society. Nietzsche's philosophy is therefore sharply opposed to any social approach that posits a collective subject – such as 'the working class', 'women' or 'oppressed ethnic minorities'. His account of fragmentation, division, differentiation and de-differentiation in modern life rules out any possibility of a collective subject being 'born', 'maturing' or 'gaining knowledge'. As such his philosophy obviously challenges the major traditional and radical approaches in leisure studies such as functionalist sociology, cultural studies and feminism. It ridicules the ideas of progress and emancipation which these traditions posit for their respective collective subjects – the abstract individual, the working class and women. 'All "purposes," "aims," "meaning",' concludes Nietzsche (1968: 356), 'are only modes of experience and metamorphoses of one will that is inherent in all events: the will to power.' Thus he attacks all social positions identified with collective 'needs', 'aspirations' and 'desires' and which apply these collective concepts to demonstrate their superior moral power.

Circulation and Repetition

Modernity 1 is geared to the accumulation of value. Even if we follow Kasson (1978) and allow that a shift in the dynamics of the system occurred at the turn of the century from an economy organized around production to one organized around consumption, it is clear that the ultimate aim of the productionist and consumerist stages is the same: profit-making. This aim involved the vast circulation of commodities, information, bodies and symbols – so vast that Modernity 1 thought nothing of trying to construct the entire world in its own image. Advertising, marketing, packaging and design were all used to make the commodity stand out. Their effect was not merely to inform but also to stimulate consumption by glamorizing it. Marx, who is the acknowledged progenitor of this sober way of analysing society, certainly recognized that processes of circulation must accompany processes of production. However, he treated them as in every way subordinate to the production of value. As he put it in the third volume of *Capital*:

> The process of circulation is a phase of the total process of reproduction. But no value is produced in the process of circulation, and therefore, no surplus value. Only changes of form of the same mass of value take place. In fact, nothing occurs

there outside the metamorphosis of commodities, and this has nothing to do as such either with the creation or change of values. (Marx, 1977, III: 279)

'The metamorphosis of commodities' is a sufficiently broad term to include the effect of advertising and marketing in creating a symbolic universe of sign values. Implicitly at least, Marx distinguishes between the sign form of commodities and the commodity form. However, the commodity form is consistently presented as subsuming the sign form. Any transformation in values produced through packaging and selling the good is seen as a mere apparition.

Benjamin (1970), whose work is also very concerned with circulation and apparitions of value, takes the discussion a stage further with his concept of 'mechanical reproduction'. Benjamin argues that the mass-production processes of capitalist manufacture throw questions of originality and authenticity into permanent doubt. We are surrounded by reproduced objects which violate our sense of reality and authenticity. By the term 'reproduced object', Benjamin simply means any consumer item that is mass-produced, according to a standardized design and marketed for a global market. According to Benjamin, capitalist manufacture has entered a phase of development in which it is possible to reproduce anything. The camera shows us images of the Taj Mahal and the Statue of Liberty before we have actually visited them. Images of unique objects are reproduced on clothes, wallets, mugs and other mass-produced items.

According to Benjamin, this technical development consigns cultural relations into a state of permanent crisis. Benjamin still worked with a distinction between high and low culture. While he saw both as enmeshed in a common crisis he maintained that they registered this crisis in slightly different ways. High or elite culture presents itself as authoritative. Its relics and rituals are distant from the level of everyday life. To participate in this culture one must dislocate the routines of ordinary existence. 'Unapproachability,' wrote Benjamin (1970: 245), 'is . . . a major quality of the cult image. True to its nature, it remains "distant however close it may be".' For Benjamin, the logical and practical corollary of unapproachability is the journey. He meant this both literally and symbolically. Thus, Benjamin's sociology assumes that participation in high culture carries with it the responsibility of leaving one's home and travelling some distance. But equally it is one's duty to make an inner journey – one which often requires considerable preparation and learning – in order to meet high culture on equal terms.

The critical effect of mechanical reproduction is to detonate the authority of high culture by making its relics and rituals more accessible. Surrounded by images, treatments and distortions of the unique object we are no longer able to distinguish between the original and facsimile, the authentic and the artificial. The result is that high culture loses its authority and the disciplinary boundaries between high and low, truth and fiction, evaporate. As to low or mass culture, Benjamin sees a tendency to level all experiences and commodities to a state of equivalence. Nothing which is mass-produced can be individual or separate. In tuning our lifestyles to consumption and leisure as a method of expressing our individuality we negate the possibility of real individuality. Instead our consumption and leisure experience is composed of mass-reproduced items and standardized accessories which can be found anywhere. On this reading, leisure in mass culture is not about a search for authenticity or fulfilment; instead it consists of distraction activity. What one is distracting oneself from is the realization that originality, uniqueness and spontaneity are dead.

Modernity 1 presents consumer culture as essentially democractic. That is, the immense circulation and mass-reproduction of commodities are seen as widening consumer choice and producing new escape experience. Marx and Benjamin reject this view. For them leisure experience under consumer culture is alienating because the individual is divorced from the fruits of his or her production and isolated from authentic experience by the juggernaut of consumer culture which appears to be beyond control. The glittering show windows of consumer culture which are meant to expand and intensify consumer experience of freedom and choice simply reinforce the consumer's sense of homelessness and powerlessness.

The Carnivalesque

The concept of the carnival is most closely associated with the work of Bakhtin (1984) on folk humour and ritual in the Middle Ages and the Renaissance. During this period carnival festivities, with their complex pageants, processions and rituals, were the central leisure event in society. 'The carnivalesque' refers to the spirit of carnival – a spirit which was sharply distinct from the serious, official, ecclesiastical, feudal and political ceremonials and forms of protocol which dominated life during the rest of the year. According to Bakhtin (1984: 10), 'carnival celebrated temporary liberation from the prevailing truth and from the established order; it marked the suspension of all hierarchical rank, privileges, norms and prohibitions.' The dogma and pomposity of official culture was made into an object of comedy. Death, punishment and all that was terrifying was grotesquely caricatured. Carnival imagery bluntly emphasized the body and bodily processes. For Bakhtin the rituals and iconography symbolized the collective life of the people – the social body – and their ties with Mother Earth. Carnival, he argues, is both a utopian reaction against the norms of individualism associated with the growth of the market and a licensed release from the hierarchical order of 'high' culture.

With the rise of market society and the insistence that modernity should be different from other societies in producing the rational order of time and space, the carnivalesque was marginalized and repressed. Carnivals, fairs and popular games were seen politically as sites of obstruction to the encroaching powers of capital and the state. From the 'moral cleansing' campaigns of the seventeenth century to the rational recreation programmes of the nineteenth

century, historians of leisure and popular culture have traced a curve of social
control over the popular pastimes and traditional rights of the people. Of
course the attempt to extend social control often had the effect of politicizing
popular culture by turning rituals into resistance. For example, Poole's (1983)
account of the police arrests at the Oldham wakes in 1864 shows that there was
resistance from both the merry-makers and the local press. The arrests turned
the question of the limits of state power into a political issue. Similarly, the
1833 Factory Act designated only Christmas Day and Good Friday, together
with eight half-days, as holidays. However, as Thompson (1967) and Bailey
(1987) demonstrate, many workers continued to insist on their traditional holiday rights, notably with respect to New Year's Day and Easter Monday.

Popular leisure events were not, of course, eliminated by the policies of capital and the state. Golby and Purdue (1984: 83) speak of the 'repackaging' of
traditional leisure events. From the beginning of the nineteenth century popular culture became increasingly subject to commercialization. The effect was
to transform traditional practices of playing and spectating into activities
requiring a cash transaction. The professionalization of sport and the licensing policies of the state on the consumption of liquor and public gatherings
reinforced this tendency. In addition, as we saw in Chapter 3, in the closing
decades of the nineteenth century the state invented a series of 'traditional' ceremonies centred on the monarchy which aimed to combine the popular with
the 'Nation' (Cannadine 1983).

The carnivalesque was not so much uprooted by Modernity 1 as pruned and
replanted at the margins of society. Addison (1953) shows the fairs in London
during the nineteenth century being steadily pushed out of the centre and
into the suburbs. Similarly Walvin (1992) charts the rise of new centres of
'carnival' on the coastal periphery in the development of seaside resorts dedicated to health and amusement. The association of health with pleasure did
not offend the utilitarianism and calculating parsimony of the middle classes.
However, well before the end of the century there were already grumbles from
the middle class that some resorts were becoming too gaudy.

In the USA a similar pattern of confining the carnivalesque to the periphery
of society is evident. The most colossal and garish popular entertainment complex in the country – Coney Island – was literally situated on the edge of
society. It consisted of three great amusement parks, Steeplechase (1897), Luna
Park (1903) and Dreamland (1904), which offered the people a variety of cheap,
tawdry and sensational sideshows. But by the 1920s the parks were already in
decline, victims of the explosion of rival popular amusements and the criticism
of middle-class reformers who argued that 'Coney represented a loss of deference to older genteel standards, a vulgar and disorderly pursuit of sensation
rather than the cultivation of sensibility' (Kasson 1978: 108). Kasson goes on
to conclude that the sexual symbolism and vulgar exuberance of the parks has
been sanitized by the technological perfectionism of 'solidly middle-class'
amusement parks such as California's Disneyland and Florida's Disney World.

Bogdan's (1988) fascinating history of the freak show indicates that, between
the late 1870s and right up to the 1930s, the display of people with physical,

mental and behavioural anomalies was a staple part of American popular culture. Whatever one feels about the ethics of the situation it is clear that the freak show was an important focus of the carnivalesque at this time. People went to them to be shocked and to witness minds and bodies which seemed to elongate, stretch and in other ways distort the terms of 'normal' human existence. Bogdan dates the demise of the freak show to the 1920s. He puts it down to the effect of the Great Depression, competition from other forms of popular entertainment and organized protests from the medical profession.

What explains the strong fascination in popular culture with the carnivalesque despite all of the efforts of rational recreationists to repress it? The answer perhaps lies in the basic categories which Modernity 1 used as the foundation of order. According to Stallybrass and White (1986: 191), Modernity 1

> continuously defined and re-defined itself through the exclusion of what it marked out as 'low' – as dirty, repulsive, noisy, contaminating. Yet that very act of exclusion was constitutive of its identity. . . . Disgust always bears the imprint of desire. These low domains apparently expelled as 'Other' return as the object of nostalgia, longing and desire.

In other words, by demonizing lewdness, lust, greed and vulgarity Modernity 1 multiplied their glamour. By banishing the carnivalesque from the household or instead tolerating it only in a pallid form, Modernity 1 transformed it into an object of wrenching speculation and curiosity. Respectable society – perhaps essentially, but not totally, aware of the repression to which it subjected itself – was secretly fascinated with bodies and minds which were *not* 'respectable' and 'self-disciplined'. This is reflected in the hallucinatory image of the harlot in the culture of Modernity 1. As Theweleit (1987) shows, the rationalization of society withdrew respectable women from public places. The typical paterfamilias of the nineteenth century insisted that the street was a dangerous place for his women-folk. They were therefore confined to the home where they were required to be modest, passive, deferential, kind, clean and loving. In calling them 'white women' Theweleit emphasizes the idealized feminine purity which these women were required to represent. But the absence of unchaperoned respectable women from the streets intensified modernist fantasies about the women that remained in public view. Theweleit describes these women as the 'red women' of modernist mythology. They were seen as undisciplined, sexually experienced and above all available. In the image of the harlot the culture of Modernity 1 created a fantasy-type at once both thrilling and threatening. She potently signified free licence, sexual abandonment, amorality and the laughter of the carnival, now subdued or lost in the arid acres of rationalized society; but she also signified disease, defilement and death. Hence the guilt, self-recrimination and hatred of women that men often spoke of (and still speak of) after spending their leisure time with 'ladies of the night' (McHugh 1980).

In seeking to capture the vacillation between tension and release that accompanies leisure activity, Shields (1991, 1992) uses the term 'liminal zones'.

By this he means 'thresholds of controlled and legitimated breaks from the routines of everyday, proper behaviour' (1992: 7). Examples include leisure spaces such as deserts, wilderness, forests and the sea which represent areas where one can 'be oneself'. They represent this because they appear to be 'free spaces' beyond the control of civilized order. Although Shields concentrates on liminal spaces, the idea can be extended to liminal identities, practices and forms of association. The prostitute is an example of a key liminal identity in the mythology of modernist culture. In being with her, men dreamt of being themselves because they were not with their legally defined spouses and they could therefore act in ways which might be outlawed by the conventions of respectable marriage. But, as Shields points out, liminal zones can never be areas of either genuine freedom or genuine control. In them, he continues, 'rather than the complete suspension of morality one finds the lifting of the curtain of morals followed by embarrassed or guilty returns to moral codes' (1992: 8). And so the attempt to escape perishes because it depends upon the very conventions which make everyday life possible. By searching for the total sexual encounter, the orgy of freedom and self-expression, the unbridled carnivalesque and the other 'real' experiences which lie beyond of civil society, we collide with the antinomies of our desire.

Dreamworlds of Consumption

Marx's thesis that processes of circulation are subordinate to processes of production has been widely challenged. Williams (1982), McCracken and Pollay (1981) and Ewen and Ewen (1982) argue that the symbolic universe of goods sells more than goods and services; it sells a way of understanding the world. Advertising and other branches of the mass media present commodities as the focal point of desire. They generate accessible and convenient dreamworlds of consumption which invite the individual 'into a fabulous world of pleasure, comfort and amusement' (Williams 1982: 66).

In retailing, the department store was the first attempt to create an hallucinatory dreamworld of light, luxury and exotica (Chaney 1983; Saisselin 1985). However, through the development of shopping arcades, shopping malls and the greater sophistication of advertising campaigns, the dreamworld of consumption became an ordinary, 'natural' characteristic of everyday life (Shields 1992). Some commentators argue that advertising and retailing now function as the religion of consumer culture (Jhally 1990: 200–3). The notions of the sacred and the profane which used to flow from organized religion now issue from the gates of the advertising industry. Individuals define their sense of community and difference around the symbolic universe of the world of goods (Baudrillard 1975). Advertising, fashion and commodity aesthetics in general are treated not as epiphenomena of material production but as the dreammachines of everyday life.

Several consequences for the organization of leisure identity, practice and association follow from this. Cohen and Taylor (1992) maintain that the dream-machines of consumer capitalism provide, as it were, the dream-stuff for exercises in *imagined otherness*. For these authors everyday life is characterized by sentiments of escape and possibility. People day-dream about consumption experience: dream holidays, purchasing luxury commodities, sexual fantasies and so on. These are the fantasy escape routes which make ordinary life possible. Whereas under Modernity 1 leisure is seen as a segmented part of life, here it is regarded as a constant supplier of symbols and images which we use to negotiate daily life.

Cohen and Taylor are notoriously equivocal on the questions of freedom and control. Their study fully recognizes the manipulative effects of consumer culture; but it also acknowledges the initiative and tenacity of people who ordinarily and habitually slip through paramount reality and the grip of the culture industry to find meaning and fulfilment in consumer culture. The authors therefore simultaneously claim that consumption is a world of regulation and a world of escape. This is not a contradiction which causes them embarrassment. Rather the point of their cartography of everyday life is to show that work and leisure, the public realm and the private realm, are riddled with contradictions. The attempt of political movements like Marxism or feminism to transcend these contradictions is, on this account, seen as naïve and doomed to frustration.

A rather different view of leisure and consumer culture emerges in the work of Debord (1967). Debord was a leading figure in the Situationist movement in France during the 1950s and 1960s. The situationists regarded modern society as dominated by organized spectacles which, so to speak, replace real life. In the society of spectacle individuals float about in a semi-submerged state of consciousness. They are impotent spectators of the procession of spectacles which delineate the world but which also seem to be beyond the control of any individual or group. The term 'spectacle' is used somewhat loosely by Debord and his associates. It refers to anything from a Christmas day city parade, a popular film or a sports fixture to a train crash, a terrorist outrage or an international war. Because life is presented in spectacular forms, daily activity is experienced as flat, motionless and alienating. Real life always seems to be occurring to someone else somewhere else. Our experience of leisure is always a pale version of what we think it *should* be. This is because the spectacle makes everyday escape experience anti-climactic by presenting images of freedom and self-determination which ordinary leisure experience cannot match. 'Tourism, human circulation considered as consumption', writes Debord (1967: 168) '. . . is fundamentally nothing more than the leisure of going to see what has become banal. The economic organization of visits to different places is already in itself the guarantee of their *equivalence*' (emphasis his).

For the situationists, the political requirement in spectacular society is to highlight and celebrate the fundamental disorder of things. More concretely it is to expose the productivist ethic which shapes everyday life and the illusory content of the spectacles which claim to render life coherent and meaningful. As Plant (1992: 86), in her outstanding study of situationist history and philosophy, elaborates:

For the situationists, the tactics and subversions of spectacular relations did not
need inventing, but only a name. The subjectivity which produces, consumes, and is
itself produced and consumed by the spectacle is already busy looting it as well. It
does not passively consume and obediently produce as the spectacle ostensibly
intends; it sabotages, steals, plays in the supermarkets and sleeps on the production
line. The spectacle feeds on this energy at the same time as it denies its dependence
on the imagination and creativity which sustain it, but as soon as the subject realises
that power 'creates nothing, it recuperates', the spectacle's own myth of its self-
sufficiency collapses.

Although violence was not excluded from revolutionary tactics, irony,
humour, poetry and lifestyle were presented as more practical responses to the
power of the spectacle. The revolutionary approach is perhaps best summed
up by the situationist attempt to develop and popularize the concept of
détournement. This term refers to both diversion and subversion. It uses the
found materials and symbols of spectacular society to challenge and reverse
spectacular order (Plant 1992: 86–7). *Détournement* involves heightening the
gap between what leisure and consumer culture promise and what we experience. Play and experiment were seen as the primary tools in reinventing life.
For the situationists revolution was not only about annihilation but also about
amusement (Marcus 1989: 163–72). Having fun was seen as one of the main
attractions of leisure. Might not this appeal to fun as an end in itself fuel
right-wing complaints that the situationist view of leisure is itself conservative?
For just like functionalist sociologists, what the situationists appear to associate with leisure is freedom, choice, self-determination and life-satisfaction.
But this is to infer that the situationists prioritize the pleasure content of
leisure over the political content. In fact, although the situationists insist on
the necessity of having fun in leisure and everyday life it is, as it were, 'serious
fun'. That is, the political content of activity is paramount. If fun is to be had
in leisure, argue the situationists, we must remember that it is in a context of
the alienation and monotony produced by spectacular society. The political
object is to transcend the spectacle and to rehumanize society.

Flânerie

Modernity 1 tended to conceive leisure as purposeful activity harnessed to a
rational goal. One visited the seaside to improve one's health and one read
novels to improve one's mind. Wasteful leisure activity tended to be associated
with the absence of application, energy and will-power. This condition was
defined as a state of idleness. And as Smiles (1894: 90) proclaims, idleness

is equally degrading to individuals as to nations. Sloth never made its mark in the
world, and never will. Sloth never climbed a hill, nor overcame a difficulty that it
could avoid. . . . [Idleness] always failed in life, and always will. It is in the nature of
things that it should not succeed at anything. It is a burden, an incumberance, and
a nuisance – always useless, complaining, melancholy, and miserable.

Yet, paradoxically, Modernity 1 vastly multiplied the number of occasions for idle watching, wandering, browsing, waiting and wishing. The mathematical complexity of relations in the city ensures that much free time is spent in a state of indolence or semi-indolence. One drinks an unnecessary cup of coffee in a sidewalk café and watches the world go by while waiting for an appointment. One sits in a traffic jam killing time by idly gazing at the other drivers and the surrounding milling world of the metropolis. Baudelaire (1964) argued that these conditions have created a new psychological character in the metropolis – the *flâneur*. The *flâneur* is defined as a constant seeker of impressions and stimuli. As a biologist takes specimens of nature from the natural world, so the *flâneur* snips scenes and characters from the social world. But he does so in a spirit of idle curiosity, without any object of learning anything or reaching understanding. Rather, the joy of *flânerie* lies in indolently opening oneself up to the sensations that modern life offers. The impersonal and episodic character of industrial civilization is itself a source of boundless fascination. The city provides endless imaginative possibilities for strolling, daydreaming, watching and being watched. As Baudelaire (1964: 9) puts it:

> For the perfect *flâneur*, for the passionate spectator, it is an immense joy to set up house in the heart of the multitude, amid the ebb and flow of movement, in the midst of the fugitive and the infinite. To be away from home and yet to feel oneself everywhere at home; to see the world, to be at the centre of the world, and yet to remain hidden from the world . . . we might liken him to a mirror as vast as the crowd itself; or to a kaleidoscope gifted with consciousness, responding to each one of its movements and reproducing the multiplicity of life and the flickering grace of all the elements of life. He is an 'I' with an insatiable appetite for the 'non-I', at every instant rendering and explaining it in pictures more living than life itself, which is always unstable and fugitive.

Benjamin (1970) regarded the *flâneur* as the quintessential man of leisure. 'His leisurely appearance as a personality', writes Benjamin (1970: 54), 'is his protest against the division of labour which makes people into specialists. It is also his protest against their industriousness.' The *flâneur*, then, cultivates polymorphousness and discontinuity in leisure. Rather than moving forward he enjoys standing still and observing. He makes a virtue out of idleness and values the senses above reason.

Wolff (1990) has criticized the account of *flânerie* provided by Baudelaire and Benjamin on the grounds that it ignores women's experience. She deplores the argument that Modernity 2 created new opportunities for idly gathering impressions and acquiring experience because this argument logically implies the emergence in the nineteenth century of the *flâneuse* – the female 'passionate spectator'. According to Wolff (1990: 47), 'such a character was rendered impossible by the sexual divisions of the nineteenth century.' But this view is at odds with the arguments of other feminist writers like Hayden (1981) and Wilson (1985). They argue that there was a clear curve of growth in the independence of women in the nineteenth century. In fashion, aesthetics, rational recreation, welfare and medicine women became steadily more *visible* and *mobile* in public life. Of course, women were not as pre-eminent as men in leisure or the public sphere. But they were successful in challenging and exposing the collusions and brutality of male power. On this account the action of Modernity 2 eroded patriarchy by undermining spheres of sexual exclusivity.

The Global and the Local

The nation-state was the primary unit of analysis for Modernity 1. This bias is reproduced in many studies of the political economy of leisure today (Wilson 1988; Glyptis 1989; Henry 1993). Yet many commentators argue that a pre-occupation with the nation-state is now difficult to sustain (Touraine 1974; Robertson 1992). These writers argue that 'globalization' has weakened national divisions. The term 'globalization' tends to mean different things to different people. However, at the heart of the matter is the proposition that the social, economic, political and cultural composition of individual industrial societies is now so interdependent that a global culture has been created.

Elements of the argument can be found in theories of social development produced in the 1960s and 1970s. For example, McLuhan (1967, 1973) argued that communications was moving from print culture to electronic culture. He predicted the rise of the 'global village' in which news, debate and entertainment would be instantaneous from Sydney to New York and from New York to London. For McLuhan, patterns of leisure consumption in individual industrial nations were already parallel. His work forecast increasing coalescence in leisure identities and practices. Another influential argument can be found in the works of Touraine (1974) and Bell (1974). They argued that the trajectory of development in the knowledge and service base of industrial economies would inevitably produce post-industrial society. These writers held that individual nation-states are gradually moving towards a common culture. By this they meant the lifestyles and leisure experience of individuals in different countries would increasingly interlace. Similarly, Kerr et al. (1973) argued that the industrial economies are converging in respect of their individual political systems, industrial relations arrangements, welfare schemes and cultural characteristics. They argued that 'the logic of industrialism' ensured that all industrial nations are fated to embrace the characteristics of 'pluralistic industrialism'. All of these writers shared the belief that the technological change was on the brink of shifting industrial society from a work-centred to a leisure-centred existence. With Riesman (1964: 162), they believed that modernity was on the brink of producing 'the sudden onrush of leisure' for everyone in society. A shorter working week, flexible time, longer vacations, higher real incomes and a comprehensive system of state welfare would combine to produce real freedom and real choice for the individual.

However, even at this time doubts were raised about the quality of leisure produced in industrial society and the lack of policies to deal with change. For example, Marcuse (1964), following Adorno and Horkheimer (1944), pointed to capital's organized manipulation of mass leisure. He equated global game shows, sports events, pop crazes, with mass conformity and gloomily concluded that society was already hopelessly 'one dimensional'. Riesman (1964) was more sanguine. However, he insisted that society was ill-prepared for the leisure boom and he was troubled that the multiplication of leisure time would be filled for the masses with empty and meaningless experience.

Many of these hopes and fears resurface in the current debate about globalization. Robertson (1992: 8), who defines globalization as 'the compression of the world and the intensification of consciousness of the world as a whole', points to four key features of globalization:

(1) *Legal conventions*. This refers to the growth of international agreements regarding standards of world trade, civil rights and regulation of the environment.
(2) *Communications*. This refers to the development of, first, mass global print culture markets and, second, through film, popular music and television, mass electronic culture markets. It also refers to the development of speedy and efficient transport networks which facilitate the mass movement and diffusion of populations throughout the world.
(3) *Knowledge*. This refers to the internationalization of knowledge. Theories of child-rearing, personality regulation, economic management, welfare regulation and cultural organization become, so to speak, common ground for policy formation in advanced nation-states.
(4) *Economic interdependence*. This refers to the internationalization of corporate interests and power. Industrial giants such as Ford, Sony and Toyota locate their production and distribution services throughout the world thus administering an international regulative effect upon business culture and economic activity.

Robertson (1992: 58–9) believes that the globalization process can be traced back to the 1870s. But he is careful to avoid the platitudes of McLuhan and the post-industrial society theorists. For Robertson, globalization must not be thought of in monolithic terms as leading to increasing universalism, harmony and 'the end of history'. On the contrary, the globalization process inevitably carries with it the seeds of conflict and resistance. For example, he characterizes the period beginning from the late 1960s to the present day as 'the uncertainty phase'. This is typified by, among other things, the accentuation of fears about global ecology, the rise of deglobalizing/reglobalizing movements such as Islam, the heightening of problems of multi-culturalism and poly-ethnicism, the intensification of debates about 'rights' and 'obligations'. Robertson's work suggests that it is wrong to regard local conditions as infinitely malleable. Like Giddens (1990: 22) he seems to endorse the idea of a dialectic between the local and the global.

This dialectic parallels the dialectic between the globalizing, ordering effect of Modernity 1 and the de-differentiating, disordering effect of Modernity 2. With regard to leisure relations, it is evident that the tendency to generate global culture has been obstructed, both by the unintended effects of processes of globalization and by organized resistance. For example, Hebdige (1979, 1987) argues that local cultures are not subordinated to global culture. Instead they cut out bits of global culture and combine them with elements in their own tradition and other sources. For Hebdige, then, fashions in leisure cultures, especially youth leisure cultures, operate by methods of 'cut and mix' rather than manipulation. Similarly, Craik (1993) argues that body and dress fashions are not a matter of designers in Paris, New York and London telling us how we should look, but of practices located at street level combining the local with the global in a dizzy, vertiginous attempt to express style and personality, often *against* the projected trends of designers.

The subject of globalization raises important questions about place and community. The sense of community generated by proponents of the globalization thesis is regularly criticized for being an 'imagined community' (Anderson 1983). The inference that we are all jet-setting around the world, engaging in instantaneous communication with one another and deciding the news and entertainment we get is an unfortunate product of the globalization debate. Featherstone (1991: 145–7) argues that instead of thinking of common culture in terms of universalization and standardization, it is more accurate and fruitful to think of it as a common *ethie*, that is, a common set of symbols, myths, memories, events, cult figures, landscapes and traditions which penetrate popular consciousness. People living in Tokyo or Toronto, Melbourne or Manchester may be perfectly *au fait* with this common *ethie* without necessarily reading it or using it in uniform ways.

Another important aspect of the globalization question is considered by Massey (1984). She maintains that the question of globalization should not be divorced from the questions of stratification and power. By implication she suggests that exactly the reverse has happened in the globalization debate. According to Massey, a strata of highly mobile people *may* have emerged in the advanced industrial societies. Perhaps they share a range of leisure and cultural interests which make a nonsense of national barriers. They may even be said to lead a decentred existence in that they do not recognize themselves as belonging to any place but regard themselves to be 'citizens of the world'. However, concludes Massey, this is an elite stratum for whom the 'global village' envisaged by McLuhan is more like a high-class hotel where they check in from room to room without really participating with the local at all. The experience of this stratum must be contrasted with that of the masses. The latter are divorced from any real decision-making power in the globalization process. For them, argues Massey (1984: 26), experiencing 'the global' may amount to little more than 'eating British working-class style fish and chips from a Chinese take-away, watching a US film on a Japanese television; and not daring to go out after dark'. Massey's insistence that stratification must be at the centre of any worthwhile account of global culture and global leisure raises the question of what *kind* of stratification is relevant.

Students of cultural studies maintain that our opportunities in leisure and in all aspects of life are dictated by our place in the class system; feminists argue that gender is the key determinant of life chances; Hebdige (1987) argues that the whole of our critical traditions in the study of culture and leisure should be recast to take account of the black immigrant presence. For someone coming to the field for the first time the situation is bound to appear confusing and paradoxical.

One useful way of combining the issues of globalization with stratification is suggested by the work of Wallerstein (1979, 1980, 1984). Wallerstein writes from a Marxist perspective, so the process of class domination and struggle is central to his approach. However, it is possible to use his model of 'the world system' analytically without placing class at the forefront. Wallerstein divides the globe into *core*, *peripheral* and *semi-peripheral* powers. The core powers are the dominant industrial, financial and cultural centres. The development gap between them and semi-periphery and periphery means that they are paramount in shaping the global economy and global culture. According to Wallerstein, the core powers historically, and practically today, maintain their wealth through the exploitation of labour and nature both in their own core boundaries and elsewhere in the world economy. The *periphery* consists of underdeveloped economies which are financially, industrially and culturally dominated by the core. The powers of the *semi-periphery* operate between core and periphery to oil the workings of the global system of exploitation and interdependence. Although subordinate to the core in terms of power and influence, they none the less have an effect in shaping the global economy and global culture by reinforcing the pattern of domination and dependency between core and periphery with their own direct mechanisms of exploitation.

Critics have been less than happy with Wallerstein's classification system. Among the regular complaints made is that Wallerstein exaggerates the coherence of core, periphery and semi-periphery; he underestimates the independence of local effects (such as national and regional policies) in disrupting the world system; and he exaggerates the importance of economic factors over cultural factors in the management of order (Skopcol 1979; Aronowitz 1981; Robertson 1992: 65–71). However, leaving these criticisms aside – and in doing so I in no way wish to imply their irrelevance – there are many ways in which Wallerstein's model helps us to better understand stratification in global culture and global leisure. Three points might usefully be made.

To begin with, there is a recognizable sense in which core powers influence global leisure patterns. As Ang (1985) showed convincingly, popular television programmes like *Dallas*, *Miami Vice* or *Cheers* may emanate from the USA but they penetrate households throughout Europe, Latin America, Asia and Australia, creating a global audience adept in the narrative and symbolic repertoire of the programme. Of course, the audience may interpret the programme in various ways, including ways which subvert the meanings intended by the producer of the programme. Even so, there is a real sense in which the global consumption process perpetuates common discursive frameworks and forms of behaviour.

Second, the model allows us to examine the multiple, continuous and contradictory forms of stratification which exist in global culture. For *within* core countries one can also differentiate a periphery and a semi-periphery. Their relation to the periphery and semi-periphery *outside* the core is complex. But by using Wallerstein's distinctions we can trace how periphery and semi-periphery within core powers link up with the periphery and semi-periphery outside the core to influence core leisure patterns. The diffusion of Afro-Caribbean music and culture to the capitalist core and the collusions and adaptations with the new host culture which this music and culture has made is one case in point. In Australia and New Zealand the 'rediscovery' of Aboriginal and Maori culture, its collusions with and criticisms of white culture and its imagined or real connections with other peripheral cultures in the world economy provides another example. Similarly, the development of 'world cuisine' in the core demonstrates how peripheral and semi-peripheral cultures penetrate with patterns of leisure in the core countries.

   Third, Wallerstein's model allows us to examine how divisions of class, gender and ethnicity coalesce and divide within and between the core, periphery and semi-periphery. By treating the model as a geo-political set of distinctions we gain more mobility and flexibility than treating stratification in the global culture in terms of either class, gender or ethnicity.

Leisure Space

Leisure space – free space, areas of choice, vistas of self-determination – these, and other clichés, seduced the leisure-seeker, the citizen of Modernity 1. If the word 'seduction' seems too extreme, let us remember what Modernity 1 promised to its leisure-seekers: release, self-knowledge, temporary uncluttered fun, liberation, maturity. After the 1840s these abstractions were pointedly translated into the material realm. The snooker rooms and general games rooms that began to be incorporated as standard design components of middle-class households represented controlled metres of freedom safely sequestered from the rude streets abounding in the real and imagined physical and social dangers of the exterior (Rojek 1993a). The sense of freedom that these rooms created was constructed upon a regime of control. That is, their effect depended upon the separation of the outside realm from the interior. The private sphere allowed the individual to support the illusions of escape manufactured by the culture industry of Modernity 1. Here a sense of personality, originality and continuity could be cultivated to contrast with the impersonal, anonymous, episodic commodity relations that dominated in the outside world. In the leisure space of the middle-class household, argued Benjamin (1970: 168–9), the individual aimed to create a place of refuge by 'stripping things of their commodity character by means of his possession of them . . . [here] he dreamed that he was in a world which was not only far-off in distance and in time, but which was also a better one.' But although Modernity 1 was, above all, a *private* society, it recognized public duties. After the 1840s these extended into relations of health and leisure. Public parks were designed to be the lungs of the city. Here nature could be conveniently accessed in the very heart of industrial civilization. Here too, hoped the rational recreationists, the physical and moral improvement of the masses could be promoted. As Robert Glendenning, an activist in the Manchester rational recreation movement, put it:

> All parks . . . are surely intended for other and more important objects than mere promenading, swinging and skittle playing. *To feed the mind and exercise the body*, are both compatible in a public park. (Glendenning quoted in Manchester City Art Galleries 1987: 33; emphasis mine)

The parks symbolized human control of nature. But as public expressions of the superiority of industrial civilization and as places of refuge from the teeming metropolis, they had to be carefully divided from the outside world of concrete and traffic. The building plans for Central Park in New York illustrate this very well. The designers, Frederick Law Olmsted and Calvin Vaux, associated nature with moral value. They envisaged the park as a moral retreat in the expanding asphalt jungle of Manhattan (Fazio 1979: 201). But its existence was also seen as an expression of the astonishing fertility of Modernity 1. The commercial and industrial titans of New York took with one hand and gave back with the other. They plundered nature to accumulate value, yet they preserved partitioned areas of the natural world to symbolize restraint, tamed nature and the power of industrial civilization to deliver free time and free space to the masses. The desire to preserve was translated into a fastidious self-effacing attitude with regard to the design and management of the parks. For example, while Olmsted and Vaux wanted to extend the industrial principles of convenience and accessibility into the exhibition of nature displayed in Central Park, they were also concerned to protect the integrity of their vision of nature. This vision would be obviously compromised by the presence of traffic routes into the park. The solution was to hide the roads. As Olmsted (1979: 214) put it, the roads were to be

> sunk so far below the surface. . . . The banks on each side will be walled up to the height of about seven feet . . . and a little judicious planting on the tops or slopes of the banks above these walls will, in most cases, entirely conceal both the roads and the vehicles moving in them, from the view of those walking or driving in the park.

The architects of leisure under Modernity 1 can therefore be said to treat leisure space as the antithesis of work and living space. If this was true of the public parks it was also true of the seaside resorts, amusement centres, hotels and boarding houses that emerged over the same period (Kasson 1978; Walton 1983). In all of them the aim was to demarcate leisure space from everyday life and to isolate it from the mundane, industrial world of routine and constraint.

Of course, from the standpoint of Modernity 2 this purist desire for 'counter-space', for zones of freedom, self-determination and choice, is an illusion. Lefebvre (1991a, b) is perhaps the fiercest critic of the concept of leisure as 'counter-space'. As he puts it:

> Leisure spaces are arranged at once functionally and hierarchically. They serve the reproduction of production relations. Space thus controlled and managed constrains in specific ways, imposing its own rituals and gestures (such as tanning), discursive forms (what should and should not be said), and even models and

> modulations in space (hotels, chalets, – the emphasis being on private life, on the genital order of the family). Hence this space too is made up of 'boxes for living in', of identical 'plans' piled one on top of another or jammed next to one another in rows. (Lefebvre 1991b: 384)

For Lefebvre, the notion of 'ludic space' is incompatible with a society based upon the personal accumulation of wealth. This is because the freedom and choice which ludic space promises for the many is always an object for individual capital investment. The effect of building roads, exercise areas, hotels, motels, souvenir shops, beer gardens, restaurants and amusement arcades as accessories of ludic space is to annihilate the sense of freedom, choice and self-determination which this space is supposed to radiate. To quote Lefebvre (1991b: 59) again:

> The truth is that all this seemingly non-productive expense is planned with the greatest care: centralized, organized, hierarchized, symbolized and programmed to the *n*th degree, it serves the interests of tour-operators, bankers and entrepreneurs . . . in the spatial practice of neocapitalism (complete with air transport), representations of space facilitate the manipulation of representational spaces (sun, sea, festival, waste, expense).

Lefebvre thus identifies leisure space with the level of signification and he reduces its meaning to ideology: the organization of an illusory sphere of freedom and choice which encourages a conformist and uncomplaining attitude in the masses. Lefebvre therefore associates leisure space with capitulation and control, the exact opposite, in fact, of the freedom and self-determination which the chancellors of Modernity 1 attribute to leisure in the modern order of things.

Lethal Leisure

Under Modernity 1 the individual was free to pursue pleasure within the limits of personal conscience and the dictates of the law. Even here there were serious conflicts because what was a social pleasure for one person was often seen as a social cost for others. However, the constant innovative and revolutionizing aspects of modernity clouded the meaning of many established pleasures. Several popular leisure pastimes such as smoking, eating fatty foods and drinking alcohol were revealed by medicine to have morbid effects upon health. Similarly, the private motor-car and the cosmetics industry, which for most of the twentieth century were promoted as signifying increased freedom and choice for the individual, were attacked by environmentalists for having destructive effects upon the ozone layer and the general level of pollution. What were once generally seen as 'innocent' pleasures are now widely castigated as forms of leisure which may have lethal consequences for body and society.

In recent years the moral panic over lethal leisure has concentrated upon AIDS. The virus has been widely described as 'the gay plague' or 'nature's revenge'. As many commentators have observed, AIDS is not simply a physi-

cal condition it is a cultural construction with political motives and consequences (Altman 1986; Watney 1987). For the New Right, the virus is the
inevitable effect of the liberalization of sexual politics that occurred in the so-
called 'permissive society' of the 1960s. The crassest formulations of this
argument submit that gay and lesbian emancipation directly led to the virus
and corroded the moral fabric of society to boot. In Britain the Conservative
government of Mrs Thatcher effectively enshrined this argument into the law
with the notorious 'Clause 28' of the 1988 Local Government Act which limited the 'promotion' of homosexuality by local authorities. But the censure of
homosexual lifestyles has also radicalized gays and lesbians. 'The young doctor who told me this morning I was a carrier of the AIDS virus was visibly
distressed,' wrote Derek Jarman (1987: 16), 'I smiled and told her not to
worry.' Elsewhere, in a journal entry written in September 1989, Jarman (1991:
149) elaborates:

> As I sweat it out in the early hours, a 'guilty victim' of the scourge, I want to bear
> witness how happy I am, and will be until the day I die, that I was part of the heated
> sexual revolution; and I don't regret a single step or encounter I made in that time.

This represents one – relatively privileged – person's response to the virus. If it
sounds like martyrdom, it is only fair to observe that Jarman (1991: 25) also
explicitly deplores 'the element of worship' that surrounded him after the
public announcement of his illness. The point of quoting him is to show that,
despite all of the public opprobrium and labelling, AIDS carriers are far from
being cowed and self-recriminating about the virus. With other homosexuals
they have participated in marches, publications, protests and other statements
which deplore the moralistic reaction against gay and lesbian lifestyles and
expose the puritanism of the New Right.

But the AIDS crisis, and the response to it, is a particularly clear example of
how leisure and lifestyle are encoded under modernity. In the 1960s and 1970s
homosexuality and bisexuality were publicly recognized as expressions of
emancipation. Recoding in the 1980s and 1990s has left the public picture
more ambiguous. Many powerful agents now unhesitantly denounce sexual
emancipation as having lethal consequences. The targets of the moral campaign against AIDS in fact extend much further than gays and lesbians. Media
attention on the apparently higher incidence of the illness in Haiti and certain
African countries has provoked some people to lay the 'blame' for causing
AIDS at the door of non-whites. The tourist industries of these countries have
certainly suffered through this unfortunate association. But stigmatization
has also had a more general effect in fixing these spaces and their populations
as 'unclean', 'risky' and 'dangerous'.

Deviant Leisure

The picture of leisure painted by Modernity 1 made allowance for deviant
leisure practice – but only to chastise and reject it. 'Normal' leisure had

nothing to do with consuming mind-expanding drugs, stealing, trespass, vandalism, sexual sadism or sexual masochism. But of course, the more these practices were outlawed from the dominant order of leisure the greater their attraction as a focus for the formation of alternative identities and subcultures. Benjamin (1979: 215–22), in his rather earnest description of the effects of hashish, focuses on the playful and oppositional consciousness associated with the drug. The pleasure he takes in unravelling a ball of string or ordering oysters in a restaurant when high is not merely a question of bio-chemical reaction: it is also a matter of transgression, stepping outside social conventions, playing with norms.

From Becker's (1963) study of marijuana users to Garber's (1992) work on cross-dressing and transsexuality there is a rich literature documenting how subterranean worlds of leisure support alternative lifestyles. Pearson's (1987) study of young heroin users vividly demonstrates the rituals of initiation, subterfuge, dealing, hustling and robbing that dominate the leisure experience of the heroin drug culture. What emerges most powerfully from his account is that users are attracted to heroin as a way of entering a realm of experience which they perceive as being richer and more colourful than the mundane order of ordinary life. It is as if the freedom, self-determination and choice offered by Modernity 1 are rejected in favour of the possibility of transcending experience. But even if this search for transcendence ends in addiction, the medical efforts to rehabilitate the addict can have unexpected consequences for leisure behaviour. Dorn and South (1989) argue that drug group therapy often creates leisure networks which can have important effects of social bonding and consciousness-raising between users and their families.

There is little evidence that the order of things laid down by Modernity 1 has ever been very successful in eliminating lifestyles and practices which it labels 'deviant'. For example, respectable society's attempt to banish 'hooligan' behaviour through the development of rational recreation and harsh sentences for offenders in the late nineteenth and early twentieth centuries was only a qualified success. Humphries (1981) argues that the authorities were wrong to see street gangs, social crime, larking about and civil disobedience as a problem of idleness. He submits that these activities in working-class youth culture 'helped to loosen the bonds of obedience and deference that many institutions were attempting to secure' (1981: 26). Humphries sees these leisure forms as processes of rebellion against a form of society which systematically oppressed the working class. Similarly, Berridge and Edwards (1987), in their careful history of opiate use in Britain, show that the 1920 Dangerous Drugs Act, which made illegal possession of opiates a criminal offence, failed in its attempt to eliminate drug use. Instead it gave a fillip to the development of subterranean drugs cultures organized around the recreational use of narcotics.

What emerges most unequivocally from the literature is that it is a mistake to see deviant leisure practice simply in terms of the mindless or spontaneous infraction of rules. In pursuing leisure activity which breaks the law, the deviant necessarily challenges the moral authority and practical wisdom of the law itself. This is perhaps most obvious in the case of the use of illegal drugs. Here many commentators argue that the law is pointlessly mechanical. Narcotics cannot be disinvented and outlawing them simply generates a black market for supply which is perhaps more dangerous to the user and to society than controlled legal prescription (Berridge and Edwards 1987; Dorn and South 1989).

Another example refers to trespass. There is a long history in Britain and the USA of demanding freedom of access to recreational land. Malcolmson (1973: 107–10) and Cunningham (1980: 57–75) cogently demonstrate the effect of the eighteenth-century enclosure movement in uprooting common land rights, destroying time-worn leisure pastimes and wrecking communities. The game laws of eighteenth-century Britain reinforced the tendency to limit access to the countryside by endorsing the traditional hunting rights of smallholders (Thompson 1975; Ford 1977). Donnelly (1986) describes the various and ongoing attempts made to regain access from the formation in the 1820s of a number of Ancient Footpaths Societies and Rights of Way Societies to acts of organized mass trespass such as the Kinder Scout trespass in 1982. He shows that deviant leisure behaviour is often deeply politicized. It resists and challenges legal views of the distribution of property, rights of access and the management of leisure space.

Conclusion

The 'paradoxical unity' to which Berman (1982) alludes in his description of modernity is perhaps now clearer. There are indeed contradictory forces in modernity which simultaneously pull in the direction of greater unity and greater disunity, more standardization and more diversity, further centralization and further de-centralization. The atomized existence of the individual in the market for leisure is akin to the atom of nuclear physics: it is being continuously split and recombined, released and controlled. In modern society leisure forms are both ascetic and hedonistic, integrating and disintegrating, active and passive. All of this leads to confusion, lack of certainty and violent disagreement among commentators. As I have argued elsewhere, leisure studies is an intensely antagonistic field of enquiry. It conforms to a 'gladiatorial paradigm' or a gladiatorial way of normally presenting research findings and theoretical arguments. By this I mean that contributors seem to evaluate the power of their own arguments with the absolute destruction of the arguments of others who represent competing traditions. Instead of recognizing unities, disunities are abruptly and bluntly stressed. In these belligerent conditions any project which seeks to find common ground between traditions tends to be confined to the periphery of research and debate (Rojek 1989).

However, from the discussion of Modernity 2 in this chapter, three things seem to be beyond doubt. In the first place, Modernity 1's attempt to arrange the rational differentiation of society generated irresistible de-differentiating tendencies. Modernity 2 should be understood basically in terms of a process

of de-differentiation. Lefebvre's (1991a, b) analysis of leisure space reveals
the dialectic between differentiation and de-differentiation with admirable
clarity. To quote him once again:

> The space of leisure bridges the gap between traditional spaces with their monu-
> mentality and their localizations based on work and its demands, and potential
> spaces of enjoyment and joy; in consequence the space is the very epitome of con-
> tradictory space. This is where the existing mode of production produces both its
> worst and its best – parasitic outgrowths on the one hand and exuberant new
> branches on the other – as prodigal of monstrosities as of promises (that it cannot
> keep). (Lefebvre 1991b: 385)

For Lefebvre, leisure space under capitalism is a 'prodigal monstrosity' precisely because it cannot insulate itself from the processes of commercialization
and commodification which characterize society. The ideas of 'free' zones and
areas of 'choice', continues Lefebvre, belong to the ideology of capitalism.
They are sharply contradicted by people's actual experience in using modern
leisure space. But this contradiction is generally evident in leisure. That is, it
extends to cover leisure identities, practices and forms of association. All have
a liminal character 'which suggests their arbitrary, cultural nature' (Shields
1992: 8). And this liminal character is an unavoidable feature of leisure under
modernity.

Second, analysing leisure solely in evolutionary terms is not satisfactory.
Leisure is a combination of continuous and discontinuous processes. This
recognition is missing from the functionalist sociology of leisure which blandly
sees leisure as the expression of social progress. It is therefore quite incapable
of explaining the various forms of leisure activity which oppose the dominant
values in society. But critical positions are also deficient in exaggerating the
evolutionary aspects of leisure. Thus, for example, cultural studies and feminism are wrong to treat 'freedom' in leisure as one link in a metonymic or
material chain leading back to class mystification or the rule of patriarchy.
They are wrong because in refusing to acknowledge de-differentiation they
remove the individual's experience of leisure from historical process. Instead
they posit the evolutionary lineage of oppression across all historical and cultural differences.

Third, differentiation and de-differentiation call upon us to place people's
experience at the centre of analysis. Experience tends to be an assumed category in most treatments of leisure under the gladiatorial paradigm. That is, it
is 'read off' from a person's sex, race, age, income level, regional location and
so forth. The dialectic between differentiation and de-differentiation suggests
that everyday experience is more contradictory and many-sided than these
analytical practices allow.

The next chapter attempts to describe the relevant categories of leisure experience in modern society. It is hardly an exhaustive cartography, more a rough
guide. Furthermore, it pays particular attention to the unresolved ambiguities
and de-differentiating effects of Modernity 2. This is because I believe these
tendencies to be marginalized in the literature on leisure studies. That literature
has been cast against what I call Modernity 1 – a formation which prioritizes

order over disorder, structure and agency over process, rationality over irrationality. By focusing on Modernity 2 I wish to emphasize that most people's experience of leisure is messy. The satisfaction which they get from a given leisure activity is often punctuated with anti-climax or a sense of meaninglessness and killing time. There are no guarantees that pleasure in leisure practice can be repeated. Leisure is regularly experienced as not being categorically different from work, or 'free', 'self-determining', 'flexible' and 'spontaneous'. It does not follow from this that we should see it as an arena of 'false consciousness', 'manipulation' and cynical control. What needs to be injected into the debate is a sense of the inherent ambiguity of leisure – a sense which is perhaps best captured in the concept 'liminality'. For liminality carries with it the idea of thresholds of freedom and control rather than the idea of absolutes. A more shifting, various and conditional picture of leisure emerges, one which I think fits better with people's experience of 'the transitory', 'the fugitive' and 'the conditional' in the modern life-world.

6

THE PHENOMENOLOGY OF LEISURE

Phenomenology is a daunting word. But what it refers to could not be more commonplace. Phenomenological sociologists study everyday experience and ordinary life. They are interested in how people construct meaning and negotiate social interaction. Meaning and negotiation are always treated as a practical matter for the individual. That is, in all social interaction we focus with one part of our minds on what we think is *really* going on.[1] Of course, our reading or interpretation of what is really going on may be faulty or utterly mistaken. But for phenomenologists these faults and mistakes are revealing because they tell us about the shared nature of social reality.

In terms of methodology, phenomenological sociology approaches the world from the standpoint of the naïve or native subject. That is, it endeavours to make sense of the world by using the categories which ordinary people apply in daily life. It is therefore often very critical of the categories of 'positivist' or 'critical' sociology. For example, phenomenological sociology posits that we cannot assume that all car-workers and waitresses will see the world in the same way. The background assumptions and taken-for-granted assumptions which make up our life-worlds are not uniform. With Heidegger (1949: 24) we may all recognize as a basic principle that 'Being-in-the-world is, from the outset, being-with and existing-with' (*das In-der-Welt-sein ist gleich ursprunglich das Mitsein und Mitdasein*). However, the ways in which this 'being-with' and 'existing-with' are produced and reproduced in everyday life are enormously varied.

On the face of it this sounds like a very 'open' and 'undisciplined' attitude to research. To be sure, phenomenological sociology is often criticized for being incapable of generating anything other than a descriptive or semi-journalistic view of the world. By extension this criticism leads to the proposition that phenomenological sociology is morally reprehensible since it carries no brief to change social conditions which are horrifying, dehumanizing or degrading. With Marx (in Marx and Engels 1968: 30) these critics complain that phenomenologists 'have only *interpreted* the world, in various ways; the point, however, is to *change* it' (emphasis his). Phenomenologists respond by insisting that positivist and critical sociology are incapable of understanding the world. Instead both are castigated for imposing order and meaning onto existence with the result that the strategies of management and change which they formulate tend to be inconsistent with, and inappropriate with regard to, ordinary experience.

Phenomenologists therefore reject the charge of methodological indiscipline.

They insist that their 'openness' is a strength because it enables them to interpret what is really going on accurately. It follows that they regard their
methodology to be highly disciplined because it requires the researcher to
assess how the meanings and negotiations of social reality made by individuals correspond with 'the real thing'. As Goffman (1974: 10) writes:

> I start with the fact that from an individual's point of view, while one thing may
> momentarily appear to be what is really going on, in fact what is actually happen-
> ing is a joke, or a dream, or an accident, or a mistake, or a misunderstanding, or a
> deception, or a theatrical performance, and so forth.

Everyday Life

What is 'the real thing' for phenomenological sociology? The question is relevant because reading 'deceptions' or 'mistakes' in social life only makes sense
if it occurs against a standard of 'reality' or 'normal understanding'. Goffman
(1959, 1974) used the term 'paramount reality' to refer to an overarching or
ultimate set of assumptions and beliefs which enable us to judge meaning and
truth. More commonly, phenomenologists use the term 'life-world'. According
to Berger et al. (1973: 62) the term 'life-world' refers to 'the overall structure
of meaning within which . . . particular patterns and symbols are located and
from which they derive their collectively shared significance.' The life-world
structures 'the business of living'. Central to the concept is the idea that social
life is composed of *typifications*. A typification refers to what persons will
ordinarily expect when they inhabit a given social setting. For example, we
know what to typically expect when a doctor examines us in a medical surgery,
or when a policeman interviews us after we have been stopped for speeding.
Similarly we know what typically happens in leisure events like visiting the cinema or attending a concert. Typifications provide, as it were, 'ongoing
maintenance' in the life-world.[2]

Although the concept of life-world is necessary for understanding what is
really going on in social interaction, it is not sufficient. The life-world forms,
as it were, the backdrop to our personal sense of everyday life. The concept of
everyday life, as Lefebvre (1991a) recognizes, is residual. He argues that everyday life is defined by '"what is left over" after all distinct, superior, specialized,
structured activities have been singled out' (1991a: 97). By 'distinct', 'superior',
'specialized', 'structured' activities Lefebvre means the technical functions
produced by Modernity 1 to maintain social order, for example the education
system, the health system, the police, the judiciary and the various branches of
the state machine. Both positivist and critical sociologies of modernity
acknowledge that these institutions shape human life. But, continues Lefebvre
(1991a), these approaches are wrong in assuming that human relations are a
mere reflection of these institutions. For Lefebvre (1991a: 97) 'the something
left over' is in fact 'the substance of everyday life – 'human raw material' in its
simplicity and richness'. This account regards everyday life as consisting of
friendship, love, humour, play, eating, drinking, walking, communicating and

browsing. There are, perhaps, similarities with the concept of *flânerie* discussed above (pp. 90–2), except that *flânerie* is generally accepted to be the expression of a conscious lifestyle choice whereas everyday life is, as it were, incidental to conscious lifestyle and is merely the unavoidable stuff of modern existence.

Modernity 2 emphasizes the messiness and untidiness of human relations. The concept of everyday life is a powerful metaphor of these things. It reminds us that in real life people have a chronic habit of thinking and acting in ways which are contrary to the theorems of positivist and critical sociology. Michel de Certeau's (1984) work on the culture of the contemporary city argues that everyday life has a critical edge. For de Certeau (1984: 48) society is composed of 'foreground practices and institutions' which provide ordinary human experience with gravity and stability. The everyday consists of 'innumerable other' 'relatively minor' 'organizing discourses' which exist in a state of tension with the foreground. According to de Certeau, these tensions stem from the fact that these minor organizing discourses utilize 'tactics', 'poaching techniques' and 'memories' which are not homologous with foreground categories and practices. Everyday life chronically refracts or subverts the foreground order, bringing new meanings and practices into play.

Fiske (1989a, b), draws on the work of de Certeau to highlight the 'knowledgeability' and 'creativity' of ordinary consumers in making consumer and leisure choices. He argues that consumption and leisure practice should be studied at the level of micro-politics instead of the level of macro-politics. That is, instead of exploring leisure in terms of freedom, class domination, patriarchy or the civilizing process it should be approached at the level of specific interactions between people. Although Fiske recognizes that the 'life-world' or 'paramount reality' which contextualizes specific interactions is 'white, male-dominated, commodity capitalism', he does not explore this context in any detailed way. Instead he concentrates on the various ways in which consumers resist and defy this context.

However, in the work of both Fiske and de Certeau the celebratory tone in which consumer practice is treated leads to problems. Three points must be made. In the first place it tends to automatically cast the consumer in an heroic role, endlessly unmasking the deceptions of the capitalist culture industry while remaining mobile, flexible and free. As McGuigan (1992: 72–3) observes, this picture comes perilously close to the stereotypical argument of capitalist entrepreneurs that the market delivers genuine freedom, choice and self-determination for consumers in their leisure and consumption activities. The second problem is that micro-politics does actually occur in the context of the macro. It might be fashionable to deplore the use of concepts like class, gender and race in understanding everyday life, but they are rather more than empty abstractions. Positivist and critical sociology undoubtedly exaggerate the explanatory power of these concepts even to the point of implying that micro-level behaviour is simply a reflection of the macro. One has sympathy with phenomenological sociologists when they throw up their hands in despair at this. However, it is surely indisputable that class, gender and race are vital categories of analysis in understanding what people actually do and experience in their leisure.

This brings me to my third point. In concentrating on the micro, de Certeau and Fiske are in danger of producing an ahistorical, asocial view of the social actor. Actions seem to occur outside of structures of motivation; effects seem confined to immediate interaction experience; actors are quite misleadingly reduced to a common plane of empowerment, producing a zero-sum model of life chances and leisure choices. All of this is objectionable at both the level of social theory and the level of ordinary observation.

A somewhat different, and unjustly neglected, view of everyday life is supplied by Cohen and Taylor (1992). They see everyday life as a mixture of 'chained activities' which render collective life predictable, and 'escape attempts' which aim to utilize these activities as a precondition of freedom. Everyday life, they argue, consists of 'multiple life-worlds'. Escape attempts in modern society reflect this variety of forms. But all share in common 'the individual's assertions that this is where he really lives, where he suspends self-consciousness because the activity in itself provides an adequate opportunity for self-expression' (Cohen and Taylor 1992: 97). Among the escape attempts documented in their study are hobbies, games, sex, sport, holidays, gambling, fantasies, drugs, therapy, anarchist politics, communes and criminal activity. Of course they acknowledge that assertions of authenticity may in fact turn out to be organized deceptions or manipulations. For example, this is clearly apparent in the typical escape messages of consumer culture. They entice the consumer with fantasies of leaving routine and monotony behind without supplying any of the means of empowerment to make the trip possible. Escape messages might therefore have the effect of tightening the chains of conformity and monotony instead of delivering genuine opportunities for self-expression. 'The fantasies of popular culture', write the authors (1992: 85), 'may support and enhance paramount reality. The advertisements for rum, cigars or perfume which are set on a white Jamaican beach might indeed provide the source material for fantasies but they hardly send people rushing to Jamaican beaches, for they provide no script for such a journey.'

Leisure features prominently in Cohen and Taylor's argument. It is in leisure that the chained activities of everyday life threaten to engulf consciousness with their denial of choice and freedom. Precisely because leisure promises to free us it can give us a demoralizing sense of anti-climax and even despair when, instead, it leaves us feeling trapped. But leisure is also the axis in society for the richest forms of fantasy-work and identity development. The authors (1992: 97) distinguish three basic leisure forms which are commonly used to launch escape attempts from the chained activities of modern society:

(1) *Activity enclaves*. This refers to behaviour which is designed to emphasize freedom, choice and self-determination. Examples include hobbies, sex, sport and games. Activity enclaves are compatible with the routine of everyday life but they none the less provide regular opportunities for puncturing monotony and restraint.

(2) *Landscaping*. This refers to transforming one's immediate or habitual environment in order to realize escape fantasies. Examples include holidays, interior design and adventures. Landscaping satisfies our craving for variety and difference. By turning our house into a customized environment which through the use of furnishings, decorations and architecture signifies the distant in space and in time, or by physically leaving home behind through travel, we can break the links of the chained reality that surrounds us.

(3) *Mindscaping*. This refers to transforming one's inner self or expanding one's state of consciousness. Examples include the use of drugs and various therapies. Mindscaping provides us with a way out by taking an inner voyage into the self. By unlocking our inner lives we satisfy our yearning for depth – a yearning which is often denied by the haste and hurry of routinized modern existence.

Cohen and Taylor argue that all of these leisure forms have the potential to deliver genuine escape experience. All the same, they are careful to acknowledge that the contingencies of modernity may neutralize or weaken all three forms. 'Activity enclaves, landscaping and mindscaping,' remark the authors (1992: 136), 'can be seen as well-established tunnels out of paramount reality. But their walls are precarious and they threaten every minute to cave-in.'

Cohen and Taylor provide an extremely rich analysis of everyday life and leisure forms. Their study is virtually a primer in demonstrating how everyday life and leisure are influenced by the sense of 'imagined otherness', that is, the sense of being free from one's partner, one's class, one's sex, one's race, one's country and even one's self. However, in the end their argument is rather equivocal. They conclude that everyday life and leisure provide genuine experiences of imagined otherness and authenticity while at the same time chronically undermining our escape attempts. This reinforces their proposition that everyday life consists of multiple life-worlds. However, in terms of theorizing leisure it is rather like having your cake and eating it. The difficulty is that the meaning of current leisure activity is rendered imponderable by this approach. One can only decide leisure meaning after leisure practice has occurred. So the leisure analyst is confined to a sort of smug retrospective wisdom while the meaning of contemporary everyday life and leisure remains frustratingly elusive.

Restlessness

All of the commentators on modernity refer to the depth and pace of change of modern life. Change is described variously as 'tumultuous', 'white-hot', 'thrilling' and 'immense'. While these remarks are generally addressed at the level of society, they also apply to the level of the human psyche. Simmel (1978: 484) refers to the 'secret restlessness' and 'helpless urgency' which dominates modern consciousness. We are consumed, he continues, by the search for ever-new stimulations, sensations and external activities. Thus it is that we become entangled in the instability and helplessness that manifests itself as the tumult of the metropolis, as the mania for travelling, as the wild pursuit of competition and as the typically modern disloyalty with regard to taste, style, opinions and personal relationships. (Simmel, 1978: 484)

Modern life seems to be fractured and subject to impersonal, implacable forces of change. Human relationships are experienced as episodic and incomplete. Nothing matches our fevered expectancies of happiness and satisfaction. Even the much-mooted consensus upon which society is based finally appears 'evasive, unwieldy, unpredictable' (Bauman 1987: 139). The young Marx (1964) also acknowledged these traits in modernity. He writes of the 'excess' and 'intemperance' of civil society (1964: 147). Individuals, he continues, fall 'into *contriving* and ever-*calculating* subservience, to inhuman, unnatural and *imaginary* appetites (emphasis his). 'Fantasy', 'caprice' and 'whim' dominate consumer culture giving it an expansive quality which is rudely frustrated by the paucity of escape opportunities.

The dialectic between Modernity 1 and Modernity 2 can be understood as producing a perpetual sense of corrosive restlessness in the human psyche. This is reflected in leisure behaviour in, for example, the endless pursuit of novelty. We crave the latest commodity or commodified experience but forget them almost as soon as we have consumed them. We are captivated by the style and boldness of the latest advertising campaign or fashion craze but we have trouble remembering anything about them six months later. Our leisure seems to be crunched up in the endless search for novelty and variety but leaves nothing memorable behind. Modern leisure experience, it might be said, is often marked by a disappointing sense of anti-climax – a feeling that despite all of the excitement that surrounds us there is nothing really exciting left to do any more.

Simmel's sociology distinguishes two basic mental responses to modern culture's bombardment of the senses: neurasthenia and the blasé attitude. As Frisby (1989) shows, both mental responses are relevant to understanding the tone of contemporary leisure practice. Neurasthenia refers to the tightening of the nerves. It is the response of our besieged senses to the constant assault of the ever-changing sensations integral to modern culture. Our emotions are accelerated and heightened. Leisure is passed in a state of tension and expectancy. We flit from activity to activity always in search of genuine escape and satisfaction. But we are divided by the 'inner barrier' between people which is 'indispensable' to the modern form of life.

The blasé attitude refers to an incapacity to react to new sensations. The ever-changing stimuli of modern culture flood our senses. Unable to commit ourselves to any of the ephemeral stimulations that we encounter, we are nonetheless incapable of living without them. Leisure is experienced as colourless, unvarying and incapable of providing genuine release. Our leisure activities simply become ways of killing time. Nevertheless, because our craving for escape has not been satisfied, we are driven on to helplessly search for excitement, escape and release.

The motor of this craving is the fundamental dynamic action of modernity. But it is expressed most nakedly in the showplace of consumer culture. For Simmel this is a hive of change and restlessness. As he puts it:

> The way in which the most heterogeneous industrial products are crowded together in close proximity paralyses the senses – a veritable hypnosis where only one message gets through to one's consciousness: the idea that one is here to amuse oneself. Through frequency of repetition this impression overwhelms countless no less worthy impressions, which because of their fragmentation fail to register. (Simmel 1991: 119)

Simmel's sociology presents modern culture as locked into a condition of chronic fragmentation, differentiation and de-differentiation. Leisure offers the dream of completeness and fulfilment but it is incapable of avoiding the flux and incompleteness which define modern experience. The point is not that leisure activity is incapable of delivering excitement or a sense of escape, but rather that these experiences are themselves momentary. 'This excitement and euphoria,' remarks Simmel (1991: 96), of the leisure experience of the retreat into nature, 'which drive the emotions to a level more intense than normal, subside remarkably quickly. The uplift which a view of the high Alps gives is followed very quickly by the return to the mood of the mundane.' Even music leaves us with a sense of anti-climax. 'All of the verve and heightening that music brings out in us,' writes Simmel (1991: 96), 'and which we claim as our own, fades away with the notes and leaves the state of one's soul exactly at the point where it was before.' Our leisure is a restless quest for choice, freedom and self-determination in the heart of modern culture which is objectively unable to deliver these experiences except as momentary diversions.

Homelessness

Just as the primary characteristic of traditional society is rootedness – rootedness of identity, place, practice and hierarchy – the primary characteristic of modern society is homelessness (Berger et al. 1973). Modern society is the first societal form in which the minority live, work and die with people they were born with. Instead the typical modern experience is uprootedness. As children we follow our parents as their work takes them from place to place; university is a significant *rite de passage* symbolizing a major break with the familiar order of home life; after university we may spend some time travelling the world before finding work; our working life may require us to migrate to several towns in more than one country; in retirement we may settle in a place that we only know from holiday visits; and most of us will die in hospitals cared for by strangers.

Sennett (1977) depicts this complex and many-sided societal transformation in terms of the *privatization* of society. He argues that modernity atomizes social existence by extending social mobility, social diffusion and the division of labour and accelerating the pace of economic change and the circulation of ideas, information, commodities and human bodies. Despite all of the panoply of universal citizenship rights ushered in under its auspices, submits Sennett, modernity actually denudes civility. It brings about the stark, unremitting fall of 'public man', the withering away of hospitality, trust and mutual help. Sennett (1977: 265) writes of 'the perversion of fraternity' in modern communal experience. As he explains:

> The narrower the scope of a community formed by a collective personality, the more destructive does the experience of fraternal feeling become. Outsiders, unknowns, unlikes become creatures to be shunned; the personality traits the community shares become every more exclusive; the very act of sharing becomes ever more centred upon decisions about who can belong and who cannot. . . . Fraternity has become empathy for a select group of people allied with rejection of those not within the local circle. This rejection creates demands for autonomy from the outside world, for being left alone by it rather than demanding that the outside world itself change. The more intimate, however, the less sociable. For this process of fraternity by exclusion of 'outsiders' never ends, since a collective image of 'us' never solidifies. Fragmentation and internal division is the very logic of this fraternity, as the units of people who really belong get smaller and smaller. It is a version of fraternity which leads to fratricide. (Sennett 1977: 285–6)

In passages like this Sennett seems to reduce modern culture to little more than a Hobbesian tribal war in which the rules of *politesse* conceal selfishness and brute force. Leisure, in this view of things, is essentially sectarian. It signifies distance and difference quite as much as closeness and belonging. And because this distance and difference can never be distilled into a finite nucleus, a 'collective image of "us"', it is doomed to be restless, unsatisfying and alienating.

Yet in a later work Sennett (1992) radically modifies this picture. He describes modern culture in terms of plastic, uneven, ambiguous 'narrative space'. Modern culture is uneven, serrated, jagged, split, endlessly shifting and mutating in unforeseen ways. This very untidiness endows it with a demotic quality because, in spite of the strictures of Modernity 1, it is impossible to precisely regulate this culture, as it were, 'from above'. There will always be bald spots in which centralized control has no remit and loose ends which resist the 'steering capacity' (Habermas 1973) of established society. Play and leisure forms here can be read as open links enabling connection and identification. The density and irrepressible character of modern culture force people to cross 'boundaries' and look over 'walls'. They spin the static order of Modernity 1 into a vortex where no division – fratricidal, sexual, ethnic – finally holds together.

Sennett, then, offers two contrasting views of homelessness. The first presents the individual as essentially privatized. As Sennett (1977: 282–3) puts it, people believe that they must 'withdraw from social interaction in order to know and feel more as a person'. Leisure becomes sectarian, a way of separating oneself from the 'outsiders' and 'strangers' who signify a threatening presence. The paradox of privatization is that in withdrawing from life individuals cease to feel at home in themselves. They become prey to the fantasy world of the domestic interior and consumer culture which is unable to offer integrative and sustaining meanings. They alienate themselves and their being atrophies.

The second view is more generous. Here Sennett presents homelessness in terms of mobility. Modern transport and communications systems are depicted as freeing consciousness from the bars of sectarianism. Through travel, play and leisure individuals extend their narrative space. In common with Berger et al. (1973), Sennett argues that modernity produces the inevitable pluralization of life-worlds. Homelessness is part of the fate of modern life and is not necessarily a reason for despair or anguish. A more subtle and complex view of modernity emerges here than the raw simplicities of the privatization thesis offered in *The Fall of Public Man*. It depicts modernity as a combination of privatization and the opening up of new public spaces, of amalgamating high and low culture and of mixing narratives instead of marginalizing them.

Narcissism and Hedonism

Narcissism may be formally defined as 'a disposition to see the world as a mirror, more particularly as a projection of one's own fears and desires' (Lasch 1979: 33). This state of self-absorption both reflects and reinforces conditions of restlessness and homelessness. Not having anything in society or any moral universe to adhere to, the individual becomes totally self-centred, and drifts from passing fancy to passing fancy. Authority figures have little credibility for the narcissist. Any attempt to impose social and moral control upon society is dismissed as shallow rhetoric. This fierce rejection stems from a profound lack of faith. For the narcissist, no authority figure can truly appreciate what goes on in his or her mind. By definition, narcissists stand alone. Because no one can really understand them, they have no genuine respect for others. And here the contrast with the ideology of Modernity 1 must be forcefully stressed. This ideology celebrated the rugged individual who utilizes the world as a resource to be shaped to his or her own design; it distinguishes between the private realm and the public realm; it depicts the individual ageing process as the gradual accumulation of wisdom; and it portrays death in triumphalist tones as the culmination of a life well lived. The narcissistic personality inverts these distinctions. Narcissistic personalities see the world as beyond control and fetishize personal survival above all other planetary considerations; they regard the public realm as the extension of their own private fancies and fantasies; their leisure is a defiant statement of their inner self; typically they want to stay permanently young and they view their own death as the end of everything.

Lasch (1979) associates narcissism with fundamental hopelessness, powerlessness and a sense of withdrawal from public life. 'Having no hope of improving their lives in any of the ways that matter,' he writes, 'people have convinced themselves that what matters is psychic self-improvement: getting in touch with their feelings, eating health food, taking lessons in ballet or belly-dancing, immersing themselves in the wisdom of the East, jogging, learning to "relate", overcoming the "fear of pleasure"' (1979: 4). Narcissism is therefore diagnosed as a way of avoiding challenge and development. By implication it

is infantile because it prevents the individual from maturing. Immediate gratification becomes an all-consuming lifestyle. Leisure is dominated by
unrealistic wants of total satisfaction, fulfilment and mastery.

Anxiety and depression are integral to narcissistic personalities. Their lives
are dominated by the search for a perfect reflection of themselves. Every relationship and experience is devalued because nothing is ever enough to
encompass who they are. There is always something less than ideal in others.

In a later work Lasch (1984) anticipates Beck (1992b) by arguing that
modernity is a high-risk society. That is, it is prone to sudden dislocation
caused, *inter alia*, by economic depression, ecological disaster, terrorism and
social protest. The result is that the withdrawal tendencies of narcissism have
mutated into a siege mentality which always expects the worst. Lethargy, indifference and numbness are the typical responses to the crises of life. Narcissistic
leisure is an empty experience because it cannot provide an escape from the
listlessness of daily life. Self-love consigns one into the vortex of permanent
dissatisfaction. Unable to fight off physical decay or to find the perfect partner or consumer lifestyle, the narcissist lapses into a semi-coma of indecision
and nostalgia.

Veblen's (1925) theory of the leisure class provided an early glimpse of the
relationship between narcissism and leisure. Modernity 1 taught that leisure
was given by providence to renew the body and mind for work; but the leisure
class cultivated leisure as an end in itself. The emphasis was not upon action
and productivity but upon the cultivation of feelings and traits of status.
Accomplishments which were practically useless, such as the mastery of
ancient dead languages, arcane sports and heraldic iconography, were enthusiastically embraced as marks of distinction and breeding.

The expansion of leisure time for the masses in the twentieth century has
changed the relationship between narcissism and leisure. The masses do not
lead lives of leisure. On the whole, they have not devoted themselves to the cultivation of arcane knowledge, language and practice. On the other hand, they
have enthusiastically embraced the opportunities for the cultivation of a narcissistic lifestyle offered by consumer culture. The body-beautiful culture
consecrates narcissism as a legitimate life-goal for the masses. Advertising
reinforces self-preservationist perceptions of the body (Featherstone 1982:
18). The camcorder enables everyone to be the star, script-writer and director
of his or her own life-story. Society offers the individual countless opportunities for immediate gratification in leisure activity. The result is that infantilism
is a big component of ordinary leisure experience.

Giddens (1990: 174–9) has criticized Lasch for exaggerating the passivity of
the narcissistic individual under modernity. The notion of the narcissistic personality, continues Giddens, suggests not only social introspection but also
social paralysis. This notion is sharply at odds with the vitality of ordinary life
and the ceaseless innovation that we all observe and participate in as a part of
normal existence. Lasch is accused of exaggerating the prominence of narcissism in the organization of ordinary experience. If narcissism was truly
dominant, contends Giddens, social life would be impossible since

introspection, withdrawal, self-love and indecision would cancel out the ordinary routine selfless activities which hold the life-world together.

This is doubtless a criticism that Lasch himself would accept. What Giddens misunderstands is that Lasch believes that a degree of narcissism is unavoidable in a society which places such relentless stress upon personal appearance and impression management. When Lasch refers to 'pathological narcissism' he is not drawing attention to the choices that individuals make, rather he is emphasizing that narcissism is a *fait accompli* in a society preoccupied with images, spectacles and surface appearances. Far from viewing narcissism as a relapse into infantilism, Lasch's argument presents the cultivation of narcissism as a perfectly mature and rational strategy to achieve personal success in consumer society. The stress is not so much upon the passivity of the individual as upon the demands that society imposes upon the management of the self in everyday life. *Contra* Giddens, it is precisely the poverty of choice offered to the individual, rather than the choices which they make, that Lasch describes as 'pathological'.

Narcissism is closely related to hedonism. Hedonism is the belief that the accumulation of pleasure is the prime goal in life. It is the richest expression of Dionysian culture which reverses Apollonian order by privileging instinctual drives over the standards of civilization. According to Campbell (1987: 85–91), consumer culture intertwines narcissism with hedonism. It prioritizes the wants of the individual above the wants of the community and it associates commodity consumption with life-satisfaction. Campbell links narcissism and hedonism to the inability to form deep, emotional relationships with others. Both psychological states involve obsessive fantasy work. The individual is fanatically enwrapped in daydreams of the perfect relationship and total consumer fulfilment. People and objects encountered in the external world are necessarily less than perfect. 'Longing and a permanent unfocussed dissatisfaction,' writes Campbell (1987: 87), 'are complementary features of that distinctive outlook generated by self-illusory hedonism.' The day-dreams of pleasure are never matched by the realities of experience.

Hedonism is often expressed in artistic form as a revolt against society. For example, the performance artist Carolee Schneemann argues that the centre of Modernity 1 is phallic culture, which supports a life-world of repression and taboo. The result is that people pass their lives in a kind of oblivion which retards human capacities. Her performances are calculated to shock the audience into a state of self-realization through the use of nudity and controlled outrage. A typical example is her 1964 performance work *Meat Joy*. This was first performed in Paris for Jean-Jacques Lebel's Festival of Free Expression. The performers were semi-nude and the performance consisted in a frenzy of smearing each other with dead fish, chicken parts and raw sausages. Schneemann (1979, 1991) has developed her critique of society through a variety of other performance works and writings. Common to all, she writes, is the desire to achieve 'a healing or a shock; an imposition; a slicing. The healing may be slower but sometimes there's a glimpse of feelings and conceptual connections that take off' (1991: 75).

Karen Finlay, whose performance work was banned in London during the late 1980s, also uses nudity and political satire to explore sexual inhibitions and social repression. 'I think we don't feel,' she comments,

> To me, what's important is a connection and a centering: really listening to things our selves, because we're always listening to things outside ourselves. . . . I think this is why people feel better after seeing my work; a lot of people are spending their lives trying to 'forgive and forget' things that happened to them in their childhood. Whereas in my work, it's more like: 'These people are bad, they're ass-holes.' (Finlay, 1991: 44)

Finlay's shows involve her smearing her body with chocolate, sticking candy hearts symbolizing 'love' all over her body, wrapping herself up in tinsel and at the end of her performance washing herself clean. The purpose of the show is to highlight how phallic culture coerces women to play the roles of sex object or housewife and, when they have reached a certain age, systematically rejects them.

Other performance artists, like Annie Sprinkle, Linda Montano and Diamanda Galas, work in broadly similar areas and use similar performance techniques. Performance work of this kind celebrates hedonism. But it does so against the backcloth of a social order which is defined as brutal and de-humanizing. In other words, it should ultimately be interpreted as a form of social critique.

However, these choreographed appeals to hedonism are part of a general resistance under modernity to puritan values (Cohen and Taylor 1992). This social reaction is a key element in Modernity 2. It has a long history including the work and life of Oscar Wilde, the Dadaists, the situationists and the punks (Marcus 1989). The dramatic expressions of Wilde, the situationists and the punks, fed off the culture of everyday life and stimulated it in complex ways. It should certainly not be assumed that simply because we know more about artists who preach hedonism that the ordinary blows against the culture of repression made by people in daily life, and which, for the most part, pass unrecorded, are of negligible importance. On the contrary, the tendency of Modernity 2 is precisely to pitch the individual against the walls erected by the order of things laid down under Modernity 1. Because these acts often involve displaying or exposing the body they often involve narcissistic elements in their motivation and results.

Critics of hedonism focus on its alleged triviality and parasitism. For example, Bell (1976: 70) fulminates against the 'world of hedonism' on the grounds that it is a 'world of make-believe', 'immediate gratification', 'sexual licence'. Hedonism, he continues, leaves society with no moral or transcendental ethic (1976: 71). In a striking parallel with Giddens' criticism of narcissism, Bell contends that hedonism always culminates in social paralysis. Although it appears to be quintessentially about escape it is actually locked in to the system of repression which it rejects. This is because all of its creative energy comes from attacking the paramount life-world rather than constructing or exploring alternative life-worlds. In addition, Bell argues that hedonism is a threat to society because it supports an acquisitive culture instead of a donatory culture. Self-interest overrides concern for the collective good. The hedonist gorges on immediate experience and has no interest in co-operating with others to address wider work or leisure needs. However, these strictures may themselves be criticized on the grounds that they equate hedonism with pathology. What this ignores is that hedonism is an unavoidable feature of highly controlled and regulated life-worlds. The hedonist is seeking ways of escaping from the confines of 'normality'.

The Infinity of Wanting

Market society seems to offer us an infinite universe of commodities and commodified experience. Marxist sociology has long argued that consumer culture operates to seduce the consumer with illusory wants and phantasmic projections of satisfaction and fulfilment (Haug 1983; Clarke and Critcher 1985; Clarke 1992). But recently, under the influence of semiotics and phenomenological philosophy, it has been argued that consumption experience has become focused upon wanting rather than having. Advertising, television and commodity aesthetics support a symbolic universe of objects and experiences. Instead of connecting primarily with the commodity, the consumer connects with the image or symbol of the commodity. Day-dreaming about commodities and commodified experience dominates the mental life of the consumer and is, in part, a substitute for owning. The consciousness of everyday life changes. 'What happens,' writes Campbell (1987: 85), 'is that the process of day-dreaming intervenes between the formulation of a desire and its consummation; hence the desiring and dreaming modes become interfused, with a dream element entering into desire itself.' Lasch (1984: 30) makes a similar point:

> Consumer production and consumerism alter perceptions not just of the self but of the world outside the self. They create a world of mirrors, insubstantial images, illusions increasingly indistinguishable from reality. The mirror effect makes the subject an object; at the same time, it makes the world of objects an extension or projection of the self. It is misleading to characterize the culture of consumption as a culture dominated by things. The consumer lives surrounded not so much by things as by fantasies. He lives in a world that has no objective or independent existence and seems to exist only to gratify or thwart his desires.

Lasch emphasizes the fantasy psychology of the consumer as the key factor in abolishing the distinction between reality and illusion. Others have developed this theme in novel ways. Earlier (pp. 107–8) I referred to the theme of imagined otherness that ripples through the consumerist dreamworlds of the present day. In shopping malls, department stores and media adverts we are bombarded with images of alternative identities which are presented as just being within our reach so long as we buy a particular commodity. I noted that possession of these commodities is often anti-climactic. The promised sense of total fulfilment does not materialize once you have installed your new CD player in the living-room or purchased the camera of your dreams. Something appears to be missing. In trying to answer what this something might be Ferguson (1992: 34–6) concentrates upon the dimensions of the 'dream psychology' that obtain in modern relations of consumption. He argues that the market produces a haunting sense of absence in consumers even though it seems to offer them everything. Consumer culture appears to be infinite in its range of goods and experiences. But it is impossible to conceive of owning examples of every item on display in the market, not least because the market is constantly redesigning and relaunching commodities. None the less the dreamworld of consumer culture presents wishing to own everything as a legitimate response. But wishing can never be translated into having. This leads to four typical sources of dissatisfaction in the psychology of the consumer:

(1) *Incompleteness*. The consumer is conscious that the endless variety of commodities on display can be nothing but an arbitrary sample from an ideal set of infinite possibilities. What he or she encounters in the local shopping mall is defined by what is absent – namely the remaining glittering world of consumer culture.

(2) *Arbitrariness*. Because consumption experience is unavoidably incomplete, dreams of wanting are necessarily marked by an arbitrary quality. Commodities are purchased, as it were, by circumstance rather than free choice. 'Objects,' writes Ferguson (1992: 35), 'are lightly taken up and cast off. None has lasting value, and none become the *telos* of an inner process of self-realization.'

(3) *Fragmentation*. The incompleteness of the market and the arbitrariness of consumer choice mean that the individual experiences the world in a fragmented fashion. The failure to have 'whole', 'personal' relationships with the commodity world translates into fragmented relationships in private life.

(4) *Indifference*. Mass-production is based upon standardization and equivalence. Commodities bear arbitrarily distributed inner values and are therefore experienced as identical. The consumer becomes indifferent to commodity choice. Each commodity appears to resonate with the same effect of ultimate dissatisfaction.

Leisure experience does not escape these processes of commodification. We dream of the perfect holiday or the totally satisfying weekend, and even when we think that we experience happiness we are vaguely aware of a sense of absence and incompleteness. The leisure world seems to offer so much varied experience that we become oppressively aware that it is impossible to experience everything or to determine whether our current experience is the best choice that we are capable of making. What fascinated us a year ago now seems remote and a matter of complete indifference. The uses we make of our leisure and our decision to spend it alone or with people seem arbitrary. We are always aware that things could be other than they are. The experience of leisure itself seems to be utterly contingent. We do not decide on the quality of our leisure experience while it is happening, rather it is only in a future stage of reflection that we judge if the ball game or the movie gave us 'real' pleasure. The freedom which our leisure time delivers never seems free enough. We always want more.

Nostalgia

In South London there are two Elvises. One performs at the Il Carretto restaurant, Streatham. He is a Scottish singer called Albert Laing. Five yards away at La Pergola, the other Elvis entertains the diners every night. He is Kim Bridges from Peckham. Mr Abraham Hulusi, the Turkish Cypriot owner of La Pergola, claims that 'We were the first to have Elvis.' Speaking of the promoter of the other Elvis, Mr Giovanni Monachello, who owns Il Carretto, Mr Hulusi alleges: 'The agency sent him a Pakistani Elvis, an Irish Elvis, a Scottish Elvis. Il Carretto knows we've got a professional cabaret Elvis, Kim Bridges. He looks like the King, he sings like the King, he acts like the King.' 'I don't think he can sing,' responds Mr Monachello. 'Our Elvis is 100,000 times better than the other one.' Wearing a spangled suit with flares and a high collar, Albert Laing explains that he has been doing his act since winning a 'Best Scottish Elvis' competition four years ago. At La Pergola, Kim Bridges says he's been doing Elvis for twelve years. 'I watched the films and thought, "That's how I want to be." I'm a fan before I'm a singer' ('The Elvis Wars', *London Evening Standard*, 20 July 1992).

The example is amusing. However, contrary to first impressions it is of more than mere trivial significance. What 'The Elvis Wars' illustrate is the depth of both hyperreality and nostalgia in contemporary life. I shall take up the question of hyperreality and examine it at length later in the book (see pp. 149–51). Here I want to address the question of nostalgia. Given that modernity is usually described in terms of change, restlessness, fragmentation, differentiation and de-differentiation, it is hardly surprising that a common psychological response to these conditions is the idealization of the past and the concomitant longing for stability and security. To be sure, the idealization of the past is not specific to modernity. O'Loughlin's (1978) scholarly work on the concept of leisure in the traditions of Homer, Virgil, Horace and Montaigne clearly establishes that from the time of ancient society the past has been celebrated as a golden age. Moreover, the leisure experience of this golden age is depicted as more fulfilling, more whole and more satisfying than anything that the present can muster.

Heller (1978) argues that the Renaissance fatefully changed the relationship between the individual and history. From that time, the past is not merely reproduced or mechanically celebrated. Rather, it starts to be expanded, treated and enhanced. Renaissance painting is one obvious way in which the past is given colour and life. But of course, to treat something is also to introduce an external influence into its make-up. By refusing to treat the past as simply something that is *given* and instead treating it as something that is *chosen*, the Renaissance made the past into a resource for imaginative transformation.

Lowenthal's (1985) superb study of post-Renaissance attitudes to the past develops Heller's argument. He explores art and architecture to reveal how the past has been designed by the values of the present. The nineteenth century, he argues, was stricken with a revulsion against aged things. The expansiveness of the era decreed that life was for living and that all interest must be focused upon the new. Ancient things were cleaned up, modified, aestheticized and in some cases simply destroyed. The past was required, so to speak, to look new. Lowenthal contrasts this with the present-day view which tends to venerate decay in ancient objects because it conveys a sense of their antiquity. Objects in museum collections, classical paintings, old buildings are all now restored in ways which do not violate their patina of charming decay.

Jameson (1991: 19–21), in a commentary on the grip that nostalgia holds on the modern mind, remarks on the power of contemporary film to reconstruct the past. He argues that commercial film-makers have deliberately raided the recent past to produce mesmeric 'glossy mirages' of reality. Movies like George Lucas' *American Graffiti*, Polanski's *Chinatown*, Coppola's *Rumble Fish*, Kasdan's *Body Heat*, contends Jameson, are set in an 'eternal thirties' or 'everlasting fifties'. The view of the past which they convey is distinctive in being, precisely, out of time. Pastiche and stereotypes are applied to present the simulacrum of historical reality. For Jameson the critical point is that these nostalgic representations have nothing to do with real history and should, instead, be read as 'symptoms of the waning of our historicity'.

The nostalgia industry refers to the embellishment or re-creation of the past by the use of artifice for commercial purposes. It is important to distinguish this from the heritage industry. As several commentators have noted, heritage sites are one of the leading attractions in the modern leisure industry (Hewison 1987; Urry 1990a). For example, in 1989 the stately homes and other properties owned by the National Trust in the UK attracted over 4 million visitors per annum. Although the commercialization of stately homes frequently involves the construction of on-site tourist facilities such as restaurants, gift shops and adventure playgrounds, the dominant managerial policy is preservationism. The National Trust guide for Plas Newyd, home of the Marquess of Anglesey, is typical. It stresses the Trust's role in maintaining the authentic period appearance of the building, which dates back to 1470. The visitor is offered a piece of preserved history as opposed to the interactive spectacles and staged attractions more common in centres of nostalgia. The heritage industry sees itself as saving the past from the juggernaut of modernity. Thus, at Linley Sambourne House, Kensington, owned by the Victorian Society, the visitor is presented with a 'magnificent "artistic" interior' which has 'survived largely unchanged'. Similarly, the tourist leaflet for Keats' House in Hampstead, now owned by the London Borough of Camden, emphasizes that 'the exterior of the house remains very much as it was' and that 'the poet's sitting room is practically unchanged; it retains the original windows with their folding shutters and the shelves on which Keats kept his books.' One could proceed with more examples. However, perhaps enough has been said to establish the general point that the heritage industry is concerned with

maintaining the 'reality' of the past rather than using artifice or dramaturgi-
cal techniques to 'enhance' history.

Nostalgia sites and artefacts use techniques of embellishment and artifice
liberally and, in the view of some critics, chronically to re-create the past. In
studying them it is helpful to make a distinction between *performance* attractions and *tableaux*. Performance attractions use actors, stages and directors to
re-enact the past. Examples include cinema and television costume dramas
which use pastiche and charade to self-consciously 'periodize' or 'costumize'
the past (Bromley 1988: 146–7); and commercial heritage centres such as the
Way We Were centre at Wigan Pier, the Beamish Open Air Museum in County
Durham, the programme of historical displays such as medieval combats, cru-
sader pageants, Napoleonic and Civil War battles choreographed by English
Heritage (which follows the slogan of 'Bringing History Alive'), the Plymouth
plantation in New England, and the Sleepy Hollow restorations in New York's
Westchester County, all of which employ actors dressed in period costume to
produce an interactive presentation of the past. *Tableaux* refer to the use of
audio-animatronics, holographs, models and soundtracks to re-create the past.
Examples include the Hall of Presidents centre in Disneyland, the Tales of
Robin Hood centre in Warwick, the Royalty and Empire exhibition in
Windsor, the Pilgrim's Way centre in Canterbury and the London Experience
in Piccadilly, where 'the latest in sound and light technology' enables you to
'share the horrors of the Plague and the Great Fire, join the hunt for Jack the
Ripper and experience the devastation of war-ravaged London.'

The nostalgia industry panders to the longing for stability and security.
This, rather than any fidelity to historical accuracy, is its prime motivating
force and organizing principle. Typically it presents the past in terms of a dra-
matized plot which ends in a formal moral climax such as the triumph of
good over evil, or right over might. All the same, one should be wary of 'dominant ideology' models of nostalgia which fasten upon the role played by
entrepreneurial manipulators and class controllers to the exclusion of everything else. As Urry (1993) correctly maintains, much of the impetus behind the
nostalgia industry comes from the masses. The motive for conserving derelict
coal-mines, steel-mills, steam traction engines and canals has sprung from the
popular desire to save 'our history'. By the same token, the concessions made
to the entertainment values of the nostalgia industry in saving these sites have
been popularly rationalized as part of the unavoidable price to pay for
conservation.

Wood (1974) distinguishes between two layers in the nostalgia industry.
The first centres on the long-vanished past beyond the reach of living collective memory. The second is rooted in the recent past, a time within the reach
of living collective memory, such as the nostalgia for the rock and roll years of
the 1950s, the swinging 1960s or the bell-bottomed 1970s. The distinction is
important because it suggests that nostalgia is a permanent feature of modernity. No sooner has one fashion trend died away than it begins to return in
nostalgic form. The trend symbolizes vanished youth, or simpler times.
Sociologically speaking, nostalgia is essentially blank space. It provides a

repertoire of genre images which distract us. However, ultimately, it is a lifeless entity which is incapable of supporting any viable motivation for the future. Nostalgia, as it were, immobilizes development because it is only concerned with providing an attractive and unchallenging view of the past.

Nostalgia has also featured as a resource in the twentieth-century aestheticization of everyday life. Featherstone (1991) argues that there are three dimensions to this process:

(1) *Surrealism and the avant-garde.* The intense questioning of reality and the rediscovery of the imagination and the repressed associated with Dadaism and the surrealist movement in the 1920s disturbed the distinction between art and everyday life. The aesthetic values of the surrealists and avant-garde began to spill over into architectural design, fashion, forms of entertainment and so on.

(2) *Dandyism.* This refers to the quest for originality and status superiority through the use of an uncompromising style of dress and personal appearance. It was associated with the ideas of Beau Brummel in England in the early nineteenth century. It became an important theme in the construction of artistic counter-cultures in the mid- to late-nineteenth century. Today the idea of 'the look', personal dress and mannerisms as the gauge of lifestyle and individual worth, is a prominent feature of consumer culture.

(3) *Sign-economy.* This refers to the rapid flow of signs and images from advertising, film, television and other branches of the mass media which saturate everyday life. These prefigure in the dreamworlds of consumer consumption and, according to critical theorists like Adorno and Horkheimer, they are the nucleus of commodity fetishism.

Although nostalgic elements can be detected in each of the three dimensions, it is in the area of the sign-economy that it is most evident. Here nostalgia supplies a rich fund of images which can be reworked to launch new desires in the consumer. Zukin's study of 'loft living' in New York provides a clear example. Zukin shows that the fashion of converting disused factories into residential accommodation caught on in New York in the 1970s. Before that time the idea of living in an industrial neighbourhood would have offended middle-class sensibilities of refinement and power. A variety of influences combined to change this. The cost of real estate in Manhattan made entering new purpose-built housing prohibitive for the middle class. At the same time, the conversion of derelict factory space into studio space by artists like Robert Rauschenberg and James Rosenquist in the 1950s and 1960s endowed lofts with a bohemian cachet. Similarly, the desire to retain privacy but maximize convenient access to the attractions of the city made loft conversion attractive. Because of the structure of many smaller factory lots, most lofts are entered directly from the elevator thus dissolving the distinction between the public and the private which is at the heart of Modernity 1's division of social space. Finally, in the midst of ever-changing residential styles and values the loft represented solidity and authenticity. Zukin (1988: 67–8) goes so far as to claim that 'loft living is a part of a large modern quest for authenticity . . . living in a loft is an attempt to replace modernism's mass production of the individual with an individualization of mass production.'

In a choice aside, Zukin (1988: 59) points to the ballast of nostalgia that underpins the fashion for loft living. The romantic attachment of living in converted factory space, she argues, only exists for people who have never known 'steam and sweat'. Similarly, the wrought-iron ornamentation that decorates the exterior of many lofts is valued by the inhabitants as a relic of the good old days of craftsmanship and individuality. Ironically, as Zukin points out, the façades of many loft buildings that were constructed between 1820 and 1880 were cast in standardized iron parts that could be ordered from a catalogue and taken apart at will. The weight of nostalgia in modern life makes 'the mass production of an earlier industrial era look to our eyes like individuality' (Zukin 1988: 59).

Zukin's observation appears to deny the force of the nostalgia industry in shaping popular culture by demonstrating that historical research can finally separate illusion from reality. It also implies – although this is not an implication that Zukin herself would necessarily accept – that scientific method can establish the truth of things. However, while this argument is technically correct it is wrong to push it too far. It should be remembered that Zukin's scholarly argument is a *privileged* practice. In the so-called 'three-minute culture' of today most people do not have the time to engage in systematic research to discover the real facts of a particular case. Moreover, a negligible number read the work of scholars who can do some of this demystifying work for them. Rather, popular culture is dominated by the mass media, which pump out nostalgia messages and images more or less continuously. Our automatic idea of the Wild West relies on simulacra provided by John Ford movies and successful television series like *Bonanza* and *The Little House on the Prairie* rather than active historical research. Similarly our notion of Edwardian London has been fatally coloured by films like *Mary Poppins* and television shows like *Upstairs, Downstairs*. If this is correct it follows that the immediate standard against which nostalgia sites are judged in popular culture is itself of dubious authenticity.

The Poetics of Leisure

The question of poetics has been conspicuously ignored by students of leisure. Yet surely part of what draws people to sport, the cinema, theatre, literature, dancing, sexual adventure and other types of leisure activity is the scent of poetry which is neutralized by the mechanical density of work and bureaucratic routine. In singling out modernity as a spectacularly poetic age, Baudelaire (1964, 1970, 1983) demonstrated both irony and penetrating originality. In what sense can the era of iron and steel be described as 'poetic'? For Baudelaire the answer is that both iron and steel are born through fire. Industrial society generates constant upheaval, excitement and energy. In the arcades, the crowds and the characters of the city, Baudelaire discovered end-less ambiguity and poetry. Of course it would be wrong to imagine that modernity is uniquely poetic. Medieval and Renaissance society were known for their distinctive poetics of expression, dress and carriage. But only in indus-trial society is poetry for the common man and woman born out of dichotomy and contradiction. For Baudelaire it is precisely the knowledge that things do not hold together, that nothing really fits, that inspires and entrances. The use-lessness of much social activity, including leisure activity, has poetic value, especially in an age still influenced by utilitarian philosophy.

However, it is perhaps to Gaston Bachelard (1968, 1969, 1971) and not Baudelaire that we must look for the profoundest discussion of poetics and modernity. For Bachelard, modernity is a universe of corners, private spaces, exterior spaces, nests, miniatures and shells. The boundaries of modern life are ambivalent and constantly invite transgression. In Bachelard's view the effect of transgression is to enhance the appreciation of the elements – earth, fire and water. 'These images blot out the world', writes Bachelard (1969: 233), 'and they have no past. They do not stem from earlier experience. We can be quite sure that they are metapsychological.' Bachelard, then, is making a direct connection between the barrage of stimuli in modernity and the poetic return to the elemental. In the swirling, exploding turbulence of the metropolis we are drawn to basic and in Bachelard's view pre-social images of poetry.

The work of Kasson (1978) and Rearick (1985) on *fin de siècle* popular entertainment in America and France reinforces the connection between mod-ern leisure forms and poetics. Electric light was commonly used to give a sensation of the marvellous. Luna Park on Coney Island was installed with a quarter of a million electric lights; and in an attempt to eclipse this nocturnal display leisure entrepreneurs running the adjacent park of Dreamland installed a million electric lights, 100,000 for one tower alone (Kasson 1978: 66, 85). Velocity also figured prominently in amusement park attractions. Coney Island offered a variety of speed rides on mechanical railways, shoot-the-chutes and roller-coasters; while in Paris looping the loop in an automobile and 'circles of death' tracks enjoyed immense popularity (Rearick 1985: 204).

In partaking of the *flânerie* of the Parisian streets, Baudelaire and Bachelard may both be criticized for assuming that the alchemy of modernity works a universal spell. They appear to conclude that at all times and everywhere modernity produces a yearning for the poetic crystallization of the eternal and the elemental from the flux of passing stimuli and impressions. Even if we qualify this argument by insisting that Baudelaire and Bachelard meant it to apply only to persons of a certain receptive sensibility, there is much about it that is unconvincing. For one thing it implies that modernity produces the con-ditions for pure, unmediated reflection in human consciousness. Yet this is to ignore one of the most obvious effects of modernity which is that it fractures and dislocates consciousness. Baudelaire and Bachelard seem to grant a uni-versal quality to poetics which they withhold from all other aspects of modernity. Beyond this, both authors appear to forget that our ideas of the eternal and the elemental are themselves social constructs. As the managers of the great *fin de siècle* amusement parks discovered to their cost, popular perceptions of the marvellous and the poetic are not set in stone. New specular technologies have a dissolving effect upon the specular regimes of old, rendering them uncommercial and redundant. Thus, for example, as the relative costs of long-distance travel declined and with the emergence of radio entertainment, the gramophone, the cinema and television as mass leisure forms, Coney Island and the amusements of turn-of-the-century Paris ceased to be honeypot attractions and fell into decline.

Are these arguments sufficient to refute the association between poetics and leisure? The question cannot be answered in the affirmative. What leisure offers is the charm of fulfilment which the density of everyday life negates. That this charm is actually symbolically connotated rather than directly experienced in leisure activity matters not one jot. We all know that leisure signally fails to deliver total fulfilment or real escape. Rather it is part of the dreamworld of escape and fulfilment with which modernity illuminates daily life. This dreamworld has a tangible poetic quality. For the modern imperative is defined by the inexorable process of de-differentiation which has the net effect of increasing the gap between dream and reality and ultimately making all of our experience dream-like.

Regions and Staged Authenticity

Goffman's (1959: 108–40) sociology identifies front and back regions in social organizations. Front regions refer to the 'face' of the organization, that is, the area in which staff and public meet. Examples include reception rooms, dining areas, foyers and booking stalls. Back regions are areas where members of the organization relax or work. Examples include kitchens, boiler rooms, computer control areas, prison cells and observation points and power stations. MacCannell (1976: 91–107) argues that modernity has transformed many back regions into tourist attractions. The disruption of the divisions between the spheres associated with de-differentiation and the immense circulation of bodies, information, commodities and signs has produced a fascination for the 'real life' of others. Our leisure becomes coloured by the desire to get behind appearances and discover solidity and authenticity. The fleeting images and signs generated by consumer culture heighten our awareness of the artificiality and superficiality of life. In reaction to this we hanker for reality and truth.

The leisure industry caters to this desire by creating what MacCannell evocatively calls 'staged authenticity'. This refers to the calculated construction of 'reality' or 'naturalness' in leisure settings. As examples, MacCannell (1976: 101) mentions themed drinking and eating areas where plastic or foam decorations are used to simulate a 'real' environment (the pirate's retreat or the Harvester restaurant), and simulated moon-walks for television audiences and live sex shows in Berlin where the customer can pay to watch interracial couples having sex according to his own specifications.

Since MacCannell's book was published the range of settings using staged authenticity in the leisure industry has multiplied. For example, Shields (1990) comments that historically remote and geographically distant decorative settings are regularly used in the design of shopping malls. Chaney's (1990) revealing analysis of the Metrocentre in Gateshead lists the use of themed sectors such as the Antique Village, the Roman Forum and the Mediterranean Village as essential parts of the shopping experience. In the USA entire 'European' villages have been constructed complete with full-time staff dressed in the appropriate regional costume and shops full of authentic 'local' goods. For example, the Alpine Village, which advertises itself as a chunk of Old Bavaria, is situated in Torrance, California; and many miles further to the south-east in Georgia lies the town of Helen which boasts a full-scale reconstruction of a Swiss mountain village, again complete with costumed staff and 'Swiss' merchandise. In Japan, similarly, an artificial village called British Hills, complete with church, pub and school, has been constructed north of Tokyo where Japanese students can go to learn about British culture as well as the English language.

Staged authenticity is also, of course, a common feature of nostalgia performance sites and *tableaux*. I have already mentioned the use of actors dressed in period costume at the Way We Were centre at Wigan Pier and the Beamish Open Air Museum in County Durham (p. 120). Here a distinction is made between the directors and actors, who stage authenticity, and the audience. But that distinction does not obtain in many nostalgia leisure organizations, where staged authenticity is embraced as an indispensable part of leisure lifestyle. For example, consider the California-based Society for Creative Anachronism (SCA). It stages regular medieval and Renaissance fairs and tournaments. 'Welcome to the current Middle Ages,' reads an SCA leaflet.

> Picture a meadow ringed by bright pavilions, penants flying overhead. Lords and ladies stroll about . . . or turn to watch the centre of the meadow where knights in armour strive with sword and shield. Minstrels play lutes and harps . . . their songs blend naturally with the clangour from the field. In the shadow of a tent, a King and Queen confer with a richly dressed circle of advisers . . . a green-cloaked herald strides into the field and announces a Royal Court. The people in their finery begin to gather around the thrones.

The SCA aims to recreate the best qualities of bygone times. It divides America into a series of ancient and secret kingdoms each with its own king and queen, baronies, provinces, shires and canons. The 'known world' – that is, the part of the globe recognized by the SCA – consists of two dozen kingdoms and principalities, stretching from Atlanta in the east to Caid in the west, and from the Kingdom of Trimaris (named after its surrounding seas) to the Kingdom of An Tir, consisting of the Sherwood-like forests of the Pacific north-west. Interestingly, the SCA emphasizes the educational value of these fantasy experiences. Society members, it explains, learn the real skills of combat, needlework, woodwork and cookery used in bygone days. 'You really don't have to know anything about the Renaissance to become a member,' explains Hilary Powers (a.k.a. Mistress Hilary of Serendip), the SCA president in 1991.

> Anyone can join, although most people come with at least a basic knowledge of the era and a desire to learn more. The one thing that we require is that members participate and make their attempt at producing pre-17th Century clothing, wares or equipment. And older members are always willing to teach and help. (quoted in Cody 1991)

The SCA is hardly unique. Many other leisure clubs and organizations in North America and Europe actively require members to adopt artefacts of nostalgia as essential parts of leisure lifestyle. In the UK English Heritage is perhaps the organization with the biggest number of full-time members. However, there are many other local and specialized leisure organizations from Dickens Festival members to Civil War societies which require members to embrace nostalgic dress and mannerisms as an essential part of the leisure lifestyle.

Many of the developments in staged authenticity in the 1980s have focused upon history. However, it would be wrong to regard staged authenticity simply as a matter relating to reconstructing times past. Staged authenticity also presents us with the simulacrum of spatial flexibility. Reconstructions of places which are geographically distant have been a common attraction in theme parks since the days of the great international expositions of the late nineteenth century. For example, the Paris Exposition Universelle in 1889 offered visitors a compressed world tour featuring reconstructions of a Swedish chalet, an Indian palace and a Japanese garden. 'Wandering amid blue cupolas, golden domes and minarets, pagodas and towers of every style,' observes Rearick (1985: 120,) 'cartoonist and writer Frederic Bac felt himself "reborn to a new world," one filled with the "magic of the new times" by "ingenious sorcerers"'. Today, Chessington World of Adventures boasts reconstructions of a Wild West Calamity Canyon and The Mystic East; the American Adventure on the edge of the Derbyshire Peak District offers a 'totally themed' park revolving around reconstructions of American life; while in the USA Busch Gardens in Williamsburg offers reconstructions of 'typical' English, French, Italian and German villages.

The enumerated examples of staged authenticity reinforce Heller's (1978) thesis that one of the distinctive features separating modern and pre-modern society is that today history can be chosen. We select how to relate to the past and remote places and what parts we want to isolate and work upon. History and geography do not weigh on our shoulders with ineluctable gravity. In addition, TV and video mean that we can elect to drop in to the past or remote places without leaving home. Of course, the sense of flexibility and dropping out is artificial and contrived. But that has hardly diminished their attraction in the leisure industry. Indeed the sense of interacting with a spectacular form of staged authenticity which openly presents itself as artificial and contrived may enhance its crowd-pulling power.

Satisfaction

Leisure as mass deception, leisure as myth, leisure as empty time-filling activity, leisure as control – these are some of the most prominent themes in the critical sociology of leisure. And yet as Rybcznyski (1991) reminds us, the weekend and vacation time continue to be immensely popular attractions in modern time budgets. For many, real life only occurs *outside* the workplace. It is here where their emotions and interests are genuinely engaged. And here where they experience real satisfaction. These people live for leisure.

Are we to grandly attribute false consciousness to them? Must we insist that they are poor drabs who confuse the vulgar pleasures of patriarchal capitalism with real freedom? These are pertinent questions. There is in fact no doubt that the critical sociology of leisure has opposed the complacency of conservative accounts with exaggerated claims of repression, alienation and woe in our leisure experience. None the less, the sources of dissatisfaction in modern life are indisputable. It is important to draw attention to four of the most important ones.

(1) *Mortality*. We are, in Heidegger's famous phrase, 'born dying'. The consciousness that personal time is running out is usually only dully felt. However, there are stages in the *rites de passage* of modern life where it is sharply stressed: marriage, parenthood, the first unequivocal signs of bodily decay, grandparenthood and retirement. Leisure, it might be argued, concentrates our awareness of time passing. In moments free from the cares of work and the responsibilities of family life, who among us does not think of where he or she is going in life and how long they have left to live? Encroaching mortality is the velvety backcloth against which all of our passing joys and hopes are finally weighed and judged.

(2) *Inequality*. Weber's (1968) sociology recognized three lines of stratification: class, status and party. He associated class with the market position of the individual; status with particular lifestyles; and party with membership of voluntary organizations with direct influence over political processes. Common to all three is the idea of power. Class, status and party influence the *life chances* of the individual, that is, the opportunities for achieving success in work, marriage and play. Weber's schema has been criticized for ignoring gender and race. Neither can be reduced to his tripartite model. Each suggests powerful objective restrictions on the life chances of the individual. The fact of inequality obviously breeds a variety of dissatisfactions in everyday life. It is the essential context for studying choice and self-determination in leisure practice.

(3) *Change*. As I have had occasion to note at several junctures in this study, endless change is one of the fundamental characteristics of modernity. We are oppressively aware that nothing lasts. Fads and fashions captivate us for a moment and then disappear from sight. Production and consumption relations are based upon constant change. One generation's certainties are another generation's doubts. The dialectic between Modernity 1 and Modernity 2 generates dislocation and disruption. In such circumstances, convictions seem to be things made of plaster-board, things which cannot last.

(4) *Myth*. Barthes (1973) argued that modernity is a kaleidoscope of myths. The beliefs by which sexuality, nationality, democracy, business and pleasure are organized can be deconstructed and shown to be nothing but calculated delusions. A figure like the tycoon Robert Maxwell is so formidably larger than life that we are seduced by his rhetoric and forget to notice the swindles he perpetrates until it is too late to do anything about them. Similarly, the familiar ideas in leisure studies that self-discipline is tantamount to freedom or that choice is equivalent to the options offered by consumer society are also mythologies of daily life. Exposing them reveals the fictional basis of everyday reality. It calls into question the validity of our own conceptions of identity and truth.

There are good reasons, then, for arguing that satisfaction in modern society has a delusional quality. Modern life is so multi-dimensional and multi-layered that it is unreasonable to suppose that satisfaction in one area can be matched in all of the other dimensions or layers. And this dissonance is the direct reflection of the circulation of commodities, information and bodies in market society. Simmel (1991: 119–20) writes

> One's curiosity is constantly aroused by each new display, and the enjoyment derived from each particular display is made to seem greater and more significant. The majority of things which must be passed creates the impression that many surprises and amusements are in store. . . . Every fine and delicate feeling, however, is violated and seems deranged by the mass effect of the merchandise offered.

PART 3
POSTMODERNISM AND LEISURE

7
POSTMODERNITY AND POSTMODERNISM

Despite the tendency in common parlance to treat them as equivalent, post-modernity and postmodernism do not mean the same thing. Postmodernity refers to a generalized change in social conditions. The criteria of change are multi-dimensional. Among other things they include the collapse of the division between high (elite) and low (mass) culture; the replacement of a teleological view of history with a view that stresses discontinuity and 'open', 'unfinished' qualities; the attachment to a conventionalist model of knowledge (which emphasizes myth, symbol and the play of shared assumptions) over a scientific model (which adheres to concepts of reality, truth and the grand ambition of discovering the laws of natural and social motion); the superimposition of local, community and national distinctions with a global, ever-changing sign-economy; and the practice of a politics of impression instead of a politics of problem-solving. At this point in the discussion I will simply list these criteria. Later in the chapter, when specific theoretical contributions to the debate on postmodernity are considered, I will expand upon the points at issue.

In contrast with postmodernity, postmodernism refers to a change in social consciousness. The most distinctive features of this change are: (a) a sense of disquiet with the categories of thought and action associated with modernity; and (b) a disposition to anticipate that the thrust of change is in the direction of the abstract form of postmodernity. One might say that the self-image of postmodernism is of a sensibility born between the gradual collapse of one era and the slow, uneven crystallization of another. Of course, postmodernism was not dramatically conjured out of thin air. Rather it was the product of a medley of specific events and developments which fuelled speculation in academic and popular culture that the era of modernity was beginning to crumble. Among the most important of these events and developments were the following:

(1) The rise of feminism, which challenged many of the conventional

authority structures installed under the male order of modernity. Feminism exposed many of the modernist categories of closure as strategies of male power. It contributed to the postmodernist sense of the place of illusion, difference and diversity in everyday life.

(2) The expansion of the international tourist industry and mass communications, which vastly increased the global circulation of bodies, information and symbols – the net result of this was to undermine the modernist distinction between the local and the global.

(3) The transfer of cheap labour to the core industrial economies and the development of distinct ethnic quarters in core metropolitan centres which directly signify difference, contrast and cosmopolitanism.

(4) The politicization of gays and lesbians, which exposed the collusions and restrictions of the heterosexual power order of modernity.

(5) The collapse of communism in Eastern Europe, which weakened the teleological view of history underpinning Modernity 1 and 2. The collapse also damaged the modernist belief that social change could be rationally planned and managed.

(6) The development of ecological consciousness, which pointedly insisted that the unrestricted economic and industrial growth demanded under the expansionist dynamic of modernity imperilled the ecological necessity of human survival.

(7) The weakened steering capacity of the core economic powers to manage the global economy and combine high employment rates with low inflation and sustained economic growth.

(8) The explosion of information technology, which increased the mobility and flexibility of data retrieval systems, improved the speed and accuracy of communications through networking and e-mail systems and multiplied the use of simulated models in business management, research, the household, the education system and leisure activity.

These events and developments have combined to produce a general feeling of scepticism about the capacity of traditional political parties to solve anything. Under modernity the key rallying points for political action were parties based upon class, gender and ethnicity. They based their appeal and political programmes upon the putative universal needs of elites or masses. But since the late 1960s these organizations have been increasingly challenged by identity politics which criticizes them for being remote, abstract and ineffective. Identity politics focuses upon particularistic issues, recognizes the inevitability of difference and heterogeneity and distrusts political vocabularies which revolve around the images of the universal and the mass. They analyse present-day society as being in a chronic state of de-differentiation. And they make virtues out of flexibility, mobility and anomaly in political action.

Postmodernism, then, has emerged in the context of profound economic, political and cultural destabilization. With Modernity 2 it shares a heightened sensitivity to the velocity and relativity of change in industrial society and an ironical awareness that all intended actions have unintended consequences.

What separates it from both types of modernity is the conviction that the categories of modernist thought and action are incapable of producing a
realignment in the system or replacing the defective system with a planned
alternative. The standard modernist rebuke to this position is, of course, that
destabilization is merely cyclical and that postmodernism offers no solid proof
to support the proposition that society is moving into a condition of
postmodernity.

Decentring

Decentring is a term derived from the phenomenological philosophy of de
Man and Derrida. These writers maintain that meaning and reality are structured by language. What we take to be truthful and objective is merely an
effect of language. In the works of de Man and Derrida decentring is used to
undermine the categories of order and authority that constitute the corner-
stones of modernity. There is no need to go fully into the details of their
argument here. Two examples from the field of leisure will be enough to suggest its radical implications.

First, let us consider leisure as an expression of language. This proposition
means that the freedom, choice and self-determination and flexibility conventionally associated with leisure are not real but the reflection of linguistic
conventions. If this is allowed it follows that the attribution of *presence* to these
qualities must also be marked by the trace of their *absence*. To put it less
abstractly, what freedom means linguistically only makes sense if we also have
a conception of restraint and unfreedom. The attribution of freedom in leisure
therefore carries with it some trace of unfreedom or restraint. Hence perhaps
the feeling of restriction or confinement that often accompanies our 'free'
time experience. Leisure is not like an open clearing that we reach once the
density of industrial life has been left behind. Rather it is part of the representational and symbolic machinery that we use in order to negotiate daily life.

The second example refers to leisure policy. One of the dreams of liberal
society is to create leisure for all. This underwrites much of the public funding
in recreation and the arts and it is seen as part of 'the good life' which market
democracy alone is said to deliver. But state expenditure in leisure is frequently
criticized. It is not only a question of inadequate budgets to meet people's
needs and demands; it is also a question of competing interests. Political economy perspectives on leisure and sport have done more than enough to
establish the general point that public funding involves a complex bartering
system between the state and the competing pressure groups in which needs
and demands are concentrated and managed rather than simply being satisfied
(Henry 1993). But most contributions to political economy assume that real
needs can be identified and that effective policies can be formulated to address
them. Decentring violates these assumptions. It treats needs and policies as
links in a metonymic chain in which meaning is permanently unstable. What
meaning represents and symbolizes is therefore open and mobile as opposed

to being closed and fixed. The presence of need and policy are, in de Certeau's (1984: 212) phrase, effects of 'scriptural operation'. Assessing leisure policy is therefore projected from the arena of so-called *Realpolitik* to the plane of communication. It is in the representational and symbolic universe of language that we must search for meanings and responses to leisure instead of the myth-ical world of 'real' interests and 'effective' policies.

Contrary to the view of most critics it does not necessarily follow from this that postmodernism is apolitical. The subject of the politics of postmodernism is not well understood. Too often postmodernism has been wrongly equated with mere nihilism. For this reason I wish to consider the issue separately and at length in a later section of the book (see pp. 169–74). At this point in the discussion it is enough to note that decentring is much more than an analyti-cal accessory. It amounts to a radical critique of dominant and critical traditions in Western social science which foreground an integrated subject – whether it be conceived of as 'the individual', 'class', 'elite', 'gender', 'race' or 'leisure'. In the light of this critique leisure studies is reduced to the mere play of signs and symbols. The goal of understanding the real world of leisure, either by creating a pure science of leisure or constructing valid critical theory, is dismissed as empty pretence.

Conditions of Postmodernity

Before moving on in the next chapter to consider some of the concepts in post-modernism which are relevant to the study of leisure it might be helpful to examine some of the leading theories of postmodernity that have emerged in the 1980s. Although these theories have all been inspired by the notion of seismic change in the condition of society there are significant differences in their analyses. I propose to consider these differences under five headings: knowledge, authority, culture, communication and the economy. It will be clear in what follows that the work of particular postmodernist theorists does not fall neatly into these divisions. For postmodernism draws attention to connectivity in social change and discounts prime-mover theories of history. None the less, commentators on postmodernism do give more significance to some key changes than others. It is for this reason that the divisions are pre-sented here.

Knowledge

The proposition that the crux of postmodernism is a crisis in knowledge is most closely associated with the writings of Lyotard (1984, 1992). He argues that modernity is essentially a clash between grand narratives which aim to underpin life. Thus, Modernity 1 sought to impose order on the basis of the philosophy of liberal individualism and the market system. Modernity 2 strug-gled to uproot this regime through scientific, quasi-scientific and inspirational blueprints and treatments of morality and society. For Lyotard the condition

of postmodernity amounts to the delegitimation of the grand narratives produced under Modernity 1 and Modernity 2 concerning the purpose of life and
the means by which it should be lived. Individuals employed in the knowledge
sector of society have shifted their interests from a concern with the ultimate
ends of human life to pragmatic concerns relating to the optimal performance
of means. There has been a move from social engineering to performativity.

One can see this in the fields of cultural policy and leisure studies. In the
1960s and 1970s debate was fixated upon 'the leisure society'. Kerr et al.
(1973) viewed the leisure society to be the inevitable consequence of 'the logic
of industrialization'. This deterministic thesis held that modern productive
forces require standard social, political and cultural support systems. Hence
the commitment to industrialization was held to lead to the convergence of
social forms. Regardless of their current religious, historical, ethnic, cultural
and political background, argued Kerr et al., each industrial society is destined
to move towards market organization, democratic liberalism and a strong
centrally funded leisure sector. Similarly, Haworth (1977) expatiated on the
leisure society as a festival of free choice and self-determination. 'In the leisure
society,' he writes, 'people will confront an environment so open that their days
and nights are taken up with activities that reflect uncoerced choices of their
own' (Haworth 1977: 48). The rationale for the leisure society was a semi-
mystical belief in the irrepressible power of productive forces. What was
missing was an adequate historical and comparative dimension to social analysis. Hence the political options facing industrial elites were simplistically
stated. Pontificating on 'the leisure society' or championing a supremacist
belief in the power of productive forces to determine our leisure would, today,
be seen as eccentric.

The cutting edge of debate has shifted to investigating the different ways in
which leisure is structured and the diversity of leisure experience. The radical
interest in social transformation and extending leisure provision remains.
However, it is expressed in the context of general scepticism about universal
concepts such as 'the leisure society', 'progress' and even 'individual experience'. Lyotard attributes the shift in interest from a discourse of ultimate ends
to a discourse of performativity to changes in the acquisition, classification
and exchange of knowledge. The key metaphor here is the computer. Lyotard
maintains that computer technology has transformed scientific and communicative practice. It has created irresistible demands for flexible and accessible
systems of knowledge. Within the academy research has become more fragmented and compartmentalized. The old divisions between the disciplines
have been over-run. The postmodern condition is one in which it is recognized
that there no single theory or meta-narrative is capable of embracing everything. It regards theories which aim at law-like certainties and ultimate truths
as objects of nostalgic interest.

While it raises many important questions, there is little which is original in
Lyotard's work. Wittgenstein's philosophy questioned the validity of truth
and regarded knowledge to be the effect of 'language games', that is, agreed
discursive conventions between actors. Moreover, in the 1960s Foucault (1973,

1974) developed a position which thunderously attacked the notions of universal history and grand meta-narratives. Similarly, Kuhn (1970) used the term 'scientific revolution' to refer to the collapse of governing systems of scientific knowledge and their replacement with antithetical systems. However, Lyotard's (1984) study coincided with the computerization of society. The computer is indeed the indispensable metaphor in his discussion of the transformation of knowledge and also the key to understanding why his work on postmodernity made such a big impact. At the level of popular consciousness, the computer symbolizes the openness, elasticity and pragmatics of knowledge which Lyotard claimed for the level of knowledge organization. Two points must be made. In the first place, networking provides immediate communication access to users. Instead of waiting for information to be published in the form of articles, reports or books, the user has the opportunity of reaching data when it is still in a mobile, fluid state. The second point is that computer hacking and viruses enable the user to enter protected and private terrains of knowledge. Traditional notions of secrecy and privacy are thus violated. Lyotard's study also coincided with the erosion of the boundaries between academic disciplines. For example, with the rise of cultural studies, sociology became more open to ideas drawn from literary criticism, philology and aesthetics. This reinforced the proposition that the entire ground of society and culture was shifting.

Interestingly, despite his general hostility to meta-narrative, Lyotard insists that postmodern society is still capitalist in form and content. Indeed, his writing about the fate of the intellectual under capitalism (1992) parallels the pessimistic thoughts of the Frankfurt School. 'Capitalism isolates them,' he writes, 'speculates on them, and delivers them muzzled to the culture industry' (Lyotard 1992: 72). Elsewhere in this work Lyotard (1992: 79–80) argues against seeing postmodernism as a radical break with modernism. Instead he asks us to regard it as the latest episode in the evolution of the avant-garde. Postmodernism, he contends, operates to expose 'the West's "modern neurosis" – its schizophrenia, paranoia and so on, the source of the misfortunes we have known for two centuries' (1992: 80). This is tantamount to backsliding on what Lyotard is generally understood to have said – which is that postmodernism represents a complete rupture with modernism. Yet, as Tester (1993: 158–9) has shown so astutely, there is a palpable sense in which Lyotard's early work *never* claims more than that postmodernism is a ground-clearing exercise. It creates a space from the bounded categories of modernist thought and practice. In this space counter-factual discussion about the possibilities of identity, association and organization occurs.[1]

Lyotard, then, depicts an ambiguous picture of the postmodern condition. He argues that postmodernity is characterized by a crisis in knowledge caused by a generalized scepticism about truth claims; yet at the same time he insists that postmodernists represent the leading front of the avant-garde and can be relied upon to give accurate knowledge about the direction in which society is moving. None the less, his work powerfully expresses the sense of chronic crisis in the categories of modernist culture. Modernist institutions like the law, religion, education, the police, medicine and social work are widely seen as suffering from delegitimation. It is not so much that we no longer believe their analyses and prognoses but rather that we are acutely aware that knowledge is contingent and not self-contained. What is written in tablets of stone in one period is trashed as misleading dogma in another. This is translated into the field of popular culture not as a general decline in enthusiasm but as a decline in constancy. We subject ourselves to a new diet and keep-fit regime in January only to forget all about it by June. Our leisure becomes a matter of faddism and hopping from one activity to another. We are not directed by an overall aim or purpose. Instead our leisure becomes mere consumption activity and changes in its pattern and variety reflect the machinations of the market.

Authority

Authority is closely related to power. Sennett (1980: 126) maintains that authority is 'a matter of defining and interpreting differences in strength'. Weber's sociology distinguishes between three types of authority: traditional, charismatic and legal. Traditional authority refers to strength which derives from custom or convention. The archetypal example is the respect given to village elders in tribal societies. Other examples include the respect which is given to the monarch and the aristocracy. Charismatic authority derives, writes Weber (1968, I: 241), from 'a certain quality of an individual personality by virtue of which he is considered extraordinary and treated as endowed with supernatural, superhuman, or at least specifically exceptional powers or qualities'. Examples include national leaders, film stars, pop stars, sports celebrities and 'heroic' business leaders. Legal authority is associated with bureaucratic organization. Here an individual's strength flows from the official position which he or she occupies and the impersonal rules of behaviour which support this position.

Weber is often understood to argue that authority in modern society moves on an evolutionary basis from charismatic and traditional forms to the legal form. In fact his position is more complicated and radical. Like Durkheim (1902), Weber submits that many forms of conflict in industrial society are associated with the persistence of traditional forms of authority. Time-worn ways of doing things inhibit both the charismatic leader and the bureaucratic personality. Furthermore, rational-legal authority which is unchecked by ethics can produce unrivalled technical efficiency but a morally repugnant doctrine of ultimate ends.

Bauman's (1989) extraordinary study of the logic of Nazi rationality in supervising the Holocaust is a case in point. Rational-legal authority is founded upon expertise which is impersonally exercised over demarcated boundaries of jurisdiction. For example, the medical doctor exercises expertise over the human body, the car mechanic over the automobile, the lawyer over the ordinances of the law and so on. Yet the intersection of expertise is far from being neat and tidy. Rather it generates competing knowledge and authority claims which are then pursued through ever more baroque courts of

enquiry, investigation procedures and dispute settlements. The result is grid-
lock. 'There is hardly any way left,' remarks Bauman (1987: 123), 'from this
self-propelling, self-perpetuating, self-divisive, autonomous and self-sufficient
mechanism of expert knowledge.' With this realization comes the encroaching
sense of scepticism against all forms of authority which, for Bauman, characterizes the postmodern condition.

Under modernity, authority is based upon paradigmatic closure and rigid
categorial thinking. As we have seen (pp. 36–78), the differentiation of spheres
of competence is the principle *par excellence* of Modernity 1. Modernity 2 is
a de-differentiating process which challenges the authority of the dominant
order through alternative inspirations and ideologies. Social movements like
Marxism and feminism aim to construct a better order of things. Under postmodernity, images replace ideologies and the authority of any foundationalist
philosophy, social movement or functional institution is inherently problematic (Lash and Urry 1994). In leisure this is evident in the decline of traditional
modernist centres of pleasure and excitement such as the sea-side resort. As
more and more leisure facilities become compatible with privatized settings the
public leisure space of the resort loses its appeal. A common entrepreneurial
strategy followed by leisure entrepreneurs faced with this situation is to extend
the range of indoor games and activities available to the public. Hence the
growth of computer game technology in English sea-side resorts like Weston-
super-Mare and Brighton.

Of course, postmodernists argue that the crisis in authority goes much further than the restructuring of resort attractions. Under postmodernity, it is
submitted, the steering capacity of the state to manage socio-economic problems and the capacity of parties and political leaders to achieve consent is
diminished. Under modernity variety, contingency and ambivalence tend to be
regarded as threatening. Authority is attached to the notion of the rugged integrated personality, that is, a moral, rational being capable of making difficult
choices. The foundation of this notion is an evolutionary definition of agency.
From childhood, individual progress is seen in terms of a learning curve. The
individual learns from his or her mistakes and, through this, attains maturity
(Rojek 1993a: 105–7). But this definition rests upon a notion of constancy
which is denied by postmodernism. Instead social life is presented as irre-
trievably varied, contingent and ambivalent. The integrated personality, who
constantly strives to impose his or her personality upon social life, is, according to this view, guilty of self-delusion. Instead postmodernism tends to
present social relations in terms of disintegrative personalities. It makes greater
allowance for the dimly felt, the unconscious, the symbolic, the ambiguous and
the transparent in human relations. It highlights the sense of not knowing what
we really feel about our leisure.

Culture

In the view of many commentators the key to the condition of postmodernity
is cultural change. For example, Huyssen (1986) argues that postmodernism is

the result of the collapse in the division between high (elite) and low (mass) culture. Similarly, Jameson (1991) contends that postmodernity is the consequence of the destruction of the autonomy of the cultural sphere. Both writers see postmodernity in terms of the decomposition of modernist categories and the decentring of cultures. The processes of decomposition and decentring are explicitly linked to a legitimation crisis in society. 'Within decentred cultures,' writes Collins (1989: 141), 'no *Zeitgeist* can emerge as a dominant; nor can any one institution – whether the university or prime-time television – be considered the sole "official" culture responsible for establishing aesthetic ideological standards for entire societies.' Jameson (1991) places great analytic weight upon the postmodern 'effacement' of history. He argues that under modernity historical evidence was deployed to separate illusion and fantasy from the rest of life. However, under the retro-cultures of postmodernity the past is always being recycled, treated and revised so that the detachment and authority which it used to convey has disappeared. Postmodernism, contends Jameson (1991: 18), involves 'the random cannibalization of all the styles of the past . . . [so that] the past as "referent" finds itself gradually bracketed, and then effaced altogether, leaving us with nothing but texts.' Postmodernism opposes the pivotal image of transcendental reality, which literally held life together under modernity, with the image of agency and structure as games of representational strategy. The modernist belief that cultural practice can get behind the veneer and distil the reality or the purity of things is dismissed as mere wishful thinking.

Architecture is often cited as clearly embodying the spirit of postmodernism (Venturi et al. 1972; Jencks 1984; Harvey 1989: 66–98). The Postmodern Visions exhibition organized by the Deutsches Architekturmuseum, Frankfurt and the Williams College Museum of Art and displayed at the IBM Gallery of Science and Art, New York, in the autumn of 1987 presented a notable portrait of postmodernism in architecture. The exhibition flyer noted that the slogan of modernist style was 'form follows function'; under postmodernist architecture, which is periodized as starting in 1960, the slogan has been radically adapted to 'form follows not just function, but fiction.' Modernist style was absolutist. It venerated homogeneity, clarity and purity as the highest design values. It was intolerant of historical or local reference, narrative, fantasy, embellishment, emotionalism or irrationality in architecture. This was the constraining backdrop against which postmodernist architects like Charles Moore, Robert Venturi, Michael Graves, Aldo Rossi and Arata Isozaki developed their designs in the 1960s and 1970s. Postmodernism celebrates theatricality, frivolity, symbolism, eclecticism, the circumstantial and the ordinary. Purity of form is rejected for structures which playfully mix forms and historical styles. Harvey (1989) and Jameson (1991) trace similar processes of mixture and exchange in contemporary fiction, film, music, art and dance. They point to a culture of mixed elements in which circulation and discontinuity prevail over evolutionary categories.

The cultural form which expresses these changes most dramatically is the spectacle. Echoing the situationists and especially the work of Debord (1967), postmodernists argue that we live in the society of the spectacle. Popular culture and leisure are hypnotized by the mass spectacle such as 'global pop concerts' (Live Aid and Mandela Day) and international sporting events. The spectacle emphasizes instantaneousness, drama and the staged dislocation of daily life. It presents complex arguments in simple and direct messages. It provides a temporary focus for collective consciousness. But it is also stodgily self-referring. Unable to posit an outside or a beyond, except by using unlikely, exaggerated images, it becomes captivated by itself (Rojek 1993b). This is the side of postmodern culture which attracts most critical attention: the self-fascination, the preening, the apparent political indifference to others or to a future that might be better than our present. It is as if postmodern culture supplies mere distraction from the big and difficult questions in life and instead dreamily luxuriates in imprecision, vagueness and play (Callinicos 1989; Norris 1990; Gellner 1992).

But where critics see only self-indulgence and a sort of cultivated, pleasurable ennui in the postmodernist *mentalité*, adherents find the promise of emancipation. Vattimo (1992: 8–9) equates postmodernism with

> the liberation of differences, of local elements, of what could generally be called dialect. With the demise of the idea of a central rationality of history, the world of generalized communication explodes like a multiplicity of 'local' rationalities – ethnic, sexual, religious, cultural or aesthetic minorities – that finally speak up for themselves. They are no longer repressed or cowed into silence by the idea of a single true form of humanity that must be realized irrespective of particularity and individual finitude, transience and contingency.

Bauman's (1992) interpretation of postmodern culture is broadly similar. Like Vattimo he argues that the disintegration of universal 'meliorative' strategies, the acknowledgement of contingency, have the potential to translate into new standards of emancipation, tolerance and empowerment. From this standpoint it is precisely those unbending forms of modernist thought that posit objective universality, historical inevitability and moral absolutism which bring obfuscation and authoritarianism in their wake. Similarly Lash and Urry (1994) equate postmodernity with the invigoration of local and community consciousness. They argue that the depthlessness of global hyperspace, with its endless procession of superficial spectacles and images, promotes the mobilization of localized collectivities anxious to preserve their particularity and traditional way of life. On this reading, leisure can become the focus for new oppositional strategies based upon local, particularistic interests. Examples might include preserving the local disused coal-mine, farm, mill or factory as a leisure resource.

There is, then, discernible controversy about the value and effect of postmodern culture. Its slowly emerging contours are seen by some as the ascent to genuine freedom in social relations, while others see only another obstacle to group-particularistic mobilization and the rational transformation of society. One view points to a depthless culture of anomaly, play and drift; the other points to the emergence of critical pluralism in the body politic in which identity politics acts as the sap of political life.

Communication

Many metaphors compete as the master-key to postmodernity: speed, seduction, the orgy, cloning, fatality, transsexuality, artificiality. But it is perhaps the communication circuit – the network of information exchange – which, above all, holds and horrifies. Modernity was indeed horrified by the idea of turning a human into a robot. From Marx to Marcuse the image of a mechanical body and a mechanical mind in humans is presented as a living death. Reification – endowing processes with a 'thing-like' quality – is reviled as the worst sin of modernist philosophy and politics. However, there is a paradoxical element in this reaction. Robotic existence denies choice and is therefore abhorrent to one of the main elements in Modernity 2's view of the good society; but it also represents the predictable, regular regime of relations that Modernity 1 identifies with order and peace. Under postmodernism it is as if the tension between these positions collapses. Pure mechanical action is now identified as the arena of our sociability and humanity. The fears which even exponents of Modernity 1 entertained about the mechanization of the world and the concomitant loss of humanity have vanished.

In comparing the postmodern individual to a 'monitoring screen' or a 'terminal of multiple networks' Baudrillard (1987: 12, 16) is usually understood to be engaging in overstatement. However, to appreciate his comments properly they should be placed in the context of his (1983a, b, 1990) argument that the social has imploded and that the private sphere has disappeared. Baudrillard maintains that the dissolving effect of continuous change, demythologization and remythologization precisely leaves no solidity, truth or authority behind. The circuitry of communication becomes a transmission belt for a media elite who have nothing to say and a mass audience which has lost the sense of collective being. Kroker and Cook (1986: 270) develop the point by arguing, *contra* the Frankfurt School, that far from the communications industry manipulating the masses it has become a focal point for abstracted attention. The media, they continue, revolve around spectacle and entertainment and elevate electronic images as the sole means of communication.

How can commentators like Baudrillard, Bauman and Vattimo find in this sort of analysis signs of imminent liberation? Surely the image of empty media feeding a non-existent public serves only to heighten our awareness of the absurdity of existence. Common sense tells us that nothing comes from nothing. Postmodernism seems to present the world as strewn with the debris of failed programmes of emancipation. The idea that the debris can be reassembled is rejected as a fantasy. The communication industry is regarded as functioning to distract consciousness. Postmodernism seems to indicate that our attempts to escape the constraints of everyday life and to improve social conditions lead nowhere.

Of course, postmodernists see things differently. They argue that the modernist belief that perfect freedom derives from having perfect knowledge of the necessary structure of reality and conforming to it is no longer tenable. Communication is associated with exposing the impossibility of this modernist view.

> In the media society, the ideal of emancipation modelled on lucid self-consciousness, on the perfect knowledge of one who knows how things stand (compare Hegel's Absolute Spirit or Marx's conception of man freed from ideology), is replaced by an ideal of emancipation based on oscillation, plurality and, ultimately, on the erosion of the very 'principle of reality'. (Vattimo 1992: 7)

It is for this reason that Baudrillard (1987) uses the metaphor of ecstasy to describe communication processes. The media dissolve our sense of finality and reality. Instead what they stimulate is our sense of the world as a tissue of appearance, variety and infinite possibility. For Baudrillard the refusal to recognize the superficial, depthless, changeable character of contemporary life and instead to insist on a solid, unitary, stable and 'authoritative' reality is inherently neurotic. It is an insistence that must end in disappointment and bitterness.

Postmodernism indeed sets up a psychological distinction which has perhaps not received the attention which it deserves. It associates modernity with the heaviness of being, that is, a psychology dominated by responsibility, morality and guilt. The political rulers of Modernity 1, who attempted to govern social order on the basis of male, white domination, possessive individualism and free competition, demonstrate this clearly. But so do the political agents of Modernity 2, from Robespierre to Malcolm X, with their passionate denunciations of 'the system' in favour of 'the people' or 'the oppressed' and their intense visions of rational reconstruction and utopia. In contrast, postmodernism claims that postmodernity is associated with the lightness of being. It recognizes play, change and anomaly as the province of humankind. It urges us to live without guilt. This last sentiment should not be confused with a call to be without compassion. *Contra* the conventional wisdom, postmodernism does not wash its hands of the poor or morality.[2] Rather, in emphasizing the predominance of the sign and communication as the oil in postmodern culture, it concludes that those without open access to communication and the sign-economy are politically marginalized. As Bauman (1992) avows, the whole thrust of postmodernism is to include more and more people within the polity of communication so that more and more voices can be heard and more and more desires achieved.

Naturally, some will object that the distinction is too coarse. After all, the history of modernity includes a gallery of figures from Baudelaire to Rimbaud, from Matisse to Picasso, who radiate the lightness of being. This argument is undeniable. However, what it ignores and what finally makes it miscarry are the distributive changes that have occurred in the organization of society. These changes are related to important changes in the structure of economic activity. It is this question which occupies the next section of the chapter.

The Economy

The economic reconstruction in the core economies that engendered the long postwar boom which lasted until the first oil crisis of the mid-1970s was led by

Fordism. Henry Ford's mass-production process of manufacturing has often been described as revolutionary. In fact, as we saw earlier (p. 13), it was the logical extension of the principles of scientific management laid down by F.W. Taylor and the reformism of the rational recreation movement.

Fordism consists of a hierarchical production system. Control of production is centralized in a managerial elite who apply the principle that work design and control must be separated from execution and skill. As with the scientific management system, Fordism breaks down the production process into a rudimentary division of labour. Workers are employed to fulfil standardized, repetitive work tasks on an assembly-line system of production. There is a strong attempt to demarcate work time and leisure time. Scientific management promoted productivity through incentive schemes which were typically structured around a piece-work system. The effect of this was to drive down the general level of wages as only successful piece-workers would gain higher reward. Their reward was, of course, directly tied to their productivity as opposed to the general work-rate of the labour-force. Fordism is apparently more generous in its system of reward. In fact, as is well known, Henry Ford attracted his workers by offering to pay them the unprecedented sum of five dollars for an eight-hour working day.

For apologists of the dehumanization and alienation created by Fordism, the rise in material prosperity enjoyed by the workers was sufficient compensation. Workers may not have been happy in assembly-line work but at least they had the benefit of earning high wages which they could spend on themselves and their families. On the other hand, critics of Fordism point out that the mass-production system is predicated on a mass-consumption society. The relatively high wages of the Fordist system are calculated to create the effective demand which mass-production needs to advance. Fordism is therefore criticized for being a total system of domination. For the commodities which the workers produce on the assembly-line are the same products which they consume and which dominate their leisure time. Demand is dictated by the supplier who therefore sets the economic and moral standards for all types of consumption activity, including leisure behaviour. The real needs of the workers are therefore secondary to the functional requirements of the system for a docile labour-force and consumer compliance (Braverman 1974; Aglietta 1979; Lipietz 1987).

The smooth operation and growth of Fordism depended upon the maintenance of relative equilibrium between supply and demand. By the mid-1960s a number of factors converged to imperil this state of affairs. Five points must be made. In the first place, economic restructuring in Japan and Western Europe produced a saturation of their internal markets. Labour shortages compelled industry to seek investment elsewhere. The lower costs of factors of production in South-East Asia and Latin America attracted investment resources from the core economies. The result was the growth of unemployment in the core regions and, as a corollary, a serious over-supply of commodities in the global market. Secondly, and by extension, disequilibrium fuelled inflationary pressures in the world economy. Disinflationary policies aggravated the unemployment problem and triggered a crash in property markets. The difficulties for the business and finance sectors in the core were exacerbated by the effects of OPEC's decision to raise oil prices. Third, the role of the USA as the broker of the global economy was compromised by the strains on the US economy of maintaining its military supremacy. The US trade deficit weakened internal demand in the US economy. The trend was reinforced by the abandonment of the gold standard in the early 1970s. The resultant devaluation of the dollar further weakened the US economy and, given the importance of this economy for international trade, the growth prospects for the global economy contracted. Fourth, the attempt of governments to ride through the storm of disequilibrium by printing more money stoked the fires of inflation. The core economies found themselves on a triple spiral of rising inflation, increasing unemployment and decreasing margins. Finally, the failure of the core economies to join together in effective remedial action intensified the triple spiral of world-wide economic recession.

Harvey (1989: 142–72) argues that the rigidities of Fordism, which strengthened the world economic system so long as economic equilibrium prevailed, became a serious handicap as soon as equilibrium could no longer be guaranteed. Investment programmes which had been geared up to mass-production were slow to adapt to the new conditions. Similarly, collective bargaining processes which had been developed around principles of full employment and guaranteed growth responded to the new conditions as if the structural changes in the world economy were simply temporary. This merely had the effect of increasing the attraction of the less restrictive labour markets of South-East Asia and Latin America for core investment programmes.

The crisis in Fordism destabilized the postwar economic and social order. However, it also created a series of new experiments in industrial organization and social and political life. Harvey (1989: 147) uses the term *flexible accumulation* to refer to the economic dimension of these experiments. By this term is meant a disposition to flexibility in labour processes, labour markets, products and patterns of consumption. This disposition translates into the multiplication of numbers employed in the service sector, that is, the knowledge, information and communication industries. The smart investment money in flexible accumulation is channelled to alternative ways of supplying financial services, new markets, new forms of marketing and developing innovative cost-effective technologies. Henry (1993: 181–7) cites the increasing investment in leisure as a means of economic regeneration, competitive tendering in local government leisure services and decentralization of service decision-making and delivery as examples of 'post-Fordist'/flexible accumulation strategies in the leisure sector. Also of note is the restructuring of defunct work-space (textile mills, coal-mines, machine rooms, farms and power stations) as leisure space (see Rojek 1993a: 146–53).

At the same time as generalized disequilibrium weakened Fordism, the nature of the production process was undergoing a dramatic change. As I have tried to indicate above, Fordism was predicated on the principle of a low-skilled, high-wage labour-force. This principle was shattered by the progressive mechanization of labour that became a key feature of the postwar period. Castells (1989) cites the introduction of the integrated circuit in 1957 as the start of this process. It was followed by the microprocessor in 1971, gene-splicing techniques in 1973 and the microcomputer in 1975. Marx, of course, recognized that the mechanization of labour was integral to capitalist organization. However, what is different about today's information technology is not simply that mechanical processes perform the tasks formerly conducted by labour more cost-effectively and efficiently, but also that production *and consumption* are increasingly knowledge-intensive.

Lash and Urry (1994) use the term 'reflexive accumulation' to refer to contemporary socio-economic processes. By this term they mean an orientation which recognizes that knowledge and information are central to contemporary economic organization. Knowledge here refers not only to the technical capacity to operate information technology but also to the ability to experiment and innovate. Further, Lash and Urry emphasize that there is an important aesthetic dimension to reflexive accumulation. It is an orientation which assumes adeptness in symbol-processing capacities. That is, it takes it for granted that consumers are capable of playing with the coded messages of advertising, commodity design and marketing; while at the same time workers are taken to be responsive to the communication systems which oil the reflexive economy. Finally, Lash and Urry argue that reflexive accumulation correlates with high labour mobility and flexibility. Fordist traditions of production and collective bargaining no longer structure work or consumption decisions for individuals. New strategies of accumulation destroy the permanence of employment and the integration of community with workplace enshrined under Fordism. So work, lifestyle, leisure and consumer choices are unblocked and individuals are impelled to become more independent, more risk-taking and more enterprising.

Marx believed that the mechanization of labour produced deskilling and the immiseration of the proletariat. The steady erosion of skills and replacement of men and women with machines was bound, he reasoned, to lead to working-class revolution. Against this, the work on flexible and reflexive accumulation posits, at least for a numerically large section of the population, the *reskilling* of labour in both production and consumption relations. While career patterns have lost the stability of Fordist days, there is much greater capacity in the system for retraining and reallocating labour. Crucially much larger numbers are now employed in the service sector.

A huge literature on the significance of the people employed in this sector has grown up (Bourdieu 1984; Lash and Urry 1987; Savage et al. 1992). Do they constitute a new class? Are they 'value parasites' (Harvey 1989: 347) who display mere fashion in the range and intensity of their attachments? Do they indicate a fundamental weakening in the power of the working class? These are some of the fundamental recurring questions in the debate. However, what seems to be widely accepted is that there has been an appreciable increase in the number of specialists engaged in the manufacture, circulation and transmission of intellectual, cultural and symbolic goods. Further, that this stratum has functioned to weaken some of the old barriers and symbolic hierarchies of modernity; and that it has expanded the audience for intellectual and artistic goods and experience. The growth of the service class, then, is often seen as increasing both the supply and the demand for symbolic capital. As a result the popular receptivity to some of the sensibilities and aspects of postmodernism has been augmented (Featherstone 1991: 125). However, the reskilling of large numbers of the population and the expansion of the service class does not extend throughout society. The structural changes associated with flexible accumulation and the roll-back of the state has also resulted in the multiplication of the underclass. The tendency for postmodernism to pass in silence over this stratum is taken by many critics to be evidence of its essential amoralism and social and political myopia.

The point of concentrating on economic change is not to propose that postmodernism and postmodern leisure forms are economically determined. However, changes in the economic and political structure clearly translate into the personality structures of individuals. Thus, people become more conscious of change and the need to be adaptable and flexible. Predictability in employment and consumption relations ceases to be associated with security. Instead it is associated with incapacity and rigidity. Symbolism and informality assume a greater profile in the organization of everyday existence. Individuals become more concerned with personal appearance and relating to others as opposed to dressing, speaking, thinking and acting to correspond with old social collective categories. Individuation, which refers to the demarcation of the individual as a specific person who is recognized as separate and distinct from others, becomes a more prominent feature of culture. Leisure activities becomes less continuous and more discontinuous, less rigid and more flexible. Leisure time is valued not simply as a relaxation time but as a resource in reskilling. Hence the increased emphasis since 1970 in the leisure industry upon entertainment as education. As Urry (1990a: 52–6) observes, the increasing popularity of museums, heritage centres, the arts, back-regions such as the nuclear reprocessing plant at Sellafield which attracts 150,000 visitors per year, and educational breaks where consumers study art and antiques, bridge, archery, watercolour painting, pottery, fly-fishing and so on all point to the closer interweaving of leisure with learning.

Flexible accumulation, greater geographical and occupational career mobility for those in paid employment, correspond with variable patterns of leisure. In the 1950s and 1960s sociologists used to cite stable leisure pursuits such as pigeon-racing or bingo as evidence of the immemorial character of social life in working-class industrial communities (Friedmann 1950; Tunstall 1962). Technological and cultural changes in leisure forms are, of course, recognized. The impact of television, cheap automobiles, domestic labour-saving devices, changed some aspects of leisure behaviour. Still the general impression conveyed by these studies is of sons and daughters following the leisure patterns of their parents. The growth of flexibility in labour markets has weakened this argument. Traditional leisure patterns obviously still persist. But they are superimposed upon flexible forms which emphasize the discontinuity of experience. The refusal to holiday in the same seaside resort, the relative decline in the cost of long-distance air travel, the development of multiple forms of leisure practice in one's leisure career as opposed to rigid, monolithic commitment to a single form, point to the enlargement of flexibility in leisure culture.

Willis (1990: 15–17) notes the trend away from homogeneous, collectivist forms of leisure practice in traditional industrial communities and the move towards variable, discontinuous patterns. However, rather confusingly, he chooses to interpret this as a 'victory for the working class'. Greater flexibility in leisure behaviour, he reasons, is evidence of the success of the working class in acquiring greater access to cultural capital. Old collective social categories, he insists, have not disintegrated under the impact of more individualism, variability and flexibility. Traditional classes and class antagonisms have not ended. However, as with all arguments that try to have it both ways, Willis's position is very unsatisfactory. To interpret greater flexibility and variability as evidence of the persistence of class solidarity is, to say the least, eccentric. Moreover, to argue, as Willis (1990: 17) does, that more individualism reinforces traditional collective social categories 'in surprising ways' is itself surprising! It is surely more plausible to interpret the enlargement of flexible leisure forms in traditional working-class communities as evidence of the decline in salience of the class nexus. If this is correct, flexible accumulation is directly related to the expansion of individuation, discontinuity and variation in leisure forms – just as the postmodernists claim.

8

POSTMODERN LEISURE

For reasons that should now be apparent, the term 'postmodern leisure' is an oxymoron. For one thing it implies that the condition of postmodernity has already arrived. As we have seen (pp. 6–8), this is a proposition which sharply divides postmodern writers. Some confidently believe that we live in a postmodern age, while others, just as confidently, maintain that we can see no more than intimations, glimpses or hints of postmodernity. Besides, the term 'postmodern leisure' is inherently contradictory. Postmodernity means boundlessness and protean flexibility; leisure is a modernist concept and refers to a bounded category of practice and experience. None the less, if we are to consider what postmodernism means for the study of leisure it is necessary to pursue the combination even if in doing so we are troubled by the nagging absurdity of what we are doing. For if there really is something different about postmodernism one must follow through the full implications as they apply to leisure studies. This is the chief objective of this chapter. A lesser objective is to present more concrete details about the meaning of postmodernity. In a series of subsections facets of the postmodern will be portrayed. The aim is not to produce a complete picture, since this is logically impossible given the protean, emerging nature of postmodernity. But the reader will be left with a collection of impressions which might help to capture the substance of this most mobile, perplexing and – for many authors – beguiling of concepts. Through this one hopes that the reader will see why students of leisure ought to take the term seriously. We are far from all being postmodernists now. On the other hand, we ignore the insights which postmodernity brings to questions of social order, lifestyle, responsibility, commitment and truth at our peril. For the postmodern debate has shifted the ground of discussion in sociology and the study of leisure.

Disembedding and Cyberspace

Zukin (1991: 27), in her thoughtful account of the dialectics of symbolic space, accurately identifies the main paradox of postmodern culture. That is, in making postmodern space more mobile and flexible it weakens our sense of living in situated geographical locales and increases our sense of being in universal cultural space. The growth of postmodern shopping malls, leisure centres and supermarkets provides the same aesthetic and spatial references wherever one is in the world. So these distinct geographical spaces become, to borrow Zukin's

(1991: 27) term, 'non-places'. Whether one is physically in the Yonge/Bloor shopping mall in Toronto or the Brent Cross Shopping Centre in London, one could be, in experiential terms, in the same globally nondescript space. The same illuminated, polished surfaces reflect our images; the same adverts for Budweiser, Calvin Klein, Hitachi and Ford bombard us. Giddens (1990) has used the term 'disembeddedness' to refer to the consciousness of universal cultural space. Our sense of identity and immediacy is permeated by geographically distant stimuli. Meaning and action are constituted by references which stretch over vast expanses of geographical space.

Zukin and Giddens both write about the 'phantasmagoric' elements of decontextualized space and disembedded action and meaning. They argue that models of social behaviour which prioritize the local as the arbiter of our sense of paramount reality fail to grasp how contemporary consciousness is structured by the global economy of signs. Their arguments are compelling, but hardly new. Foucault (1982: 25) referred to 'heterotopic space', by which he meant the 'juxtaposing in a single real place [of] several spaces, several sites that are in themselves incompatible'. However, many writers today believe that 'heterotopic space' and 'disembeddedness' do not adequately convey the unique features of postmodern space. This is because postmodernity involves the dissolution of the link between signifier and sign, referent and reality. As such there is no longer any basis for determining the local from the global or real space from fictional or fantasy space. For this reason the term 'cyberspace' is now often used to fix postmodern space more precisely. By this term is meant the encompassing world of computer technology which supports an admixture of codes of observing, commentating, imagining and fictionalizing to construct and support the immediate space in which human relations occur. Computer networking and hacking illustrate the disembedded nature of cyberspace. They refer to both contact and contagion between invisible nomads who only have representational purchase as signs. Since they demonstrate very clearly how information is accessed and distorted they highlight the contingency of information and meaning. Moreover, they emphasize that the information world heightens interdependence and multiplies encoding and decoding processes. But the examples of networking and hacking are in some respects misleading because they confine cyberspace to the interior. It is important to be clear that cyberspace is also a feature of the exterior. For example, it can be entered in shopping malls, leisure centres, amusement arcades and airport terminals. In all of these spaces fantasy, fictional and real references are combined to construct disembedded space in which meaningful human relations occur.

Venturi et al.'s (1972) study of Las Vegas is a precursor of the subject of cyberspace and disembedding. In some circles this statement might appear to be rather eccentric since the authors do not use the terms 'cyberspace' or 'disembedding' in their book. However, the tendencies and trends which they describe anticipate most of the key features that now feature in discussions on the subjects. They argue that the Las Vegas Strip is indicative of a new type of space in postwar culture. 'The Strip,' they remark, 'is virtually all signs'

(1972: 9). It could be anywhere. Figurative and abstract graphic symbols in the form of billboards, hotel logos and electronic direction markers abound. The Strip is typically approached from the highway where these signs dominate the horizon. 'They make verbal and symbolic connections through space,' write Venturi et al. (1972: 13), 'communicating a complexity of meanings through hundreds of associations in few seconds from far away. Symbol dominates space.' The use of electronic light is essential in supporting cyberspace. Artificial light is not used to define boundaries but to abolish them. In the exterior space Strip-lighting bathes what Venturi et al. (1972: 49) term 'the autoscape' with neon brightness so that the division between night and day is eliminated. Within the interior – in the leisure centres, the gambling halls, the roulette rooms and the restaurants – the maze of electronic lighting creates ambient illumination which is independent of external light and space. It is the same for both day and night. The general psychological effect is one of comfortable disorientation. 'One loses track of where one is and when it is,' write Venturi et al. (1972: 49). For these authors the Strip is a zone of artificially constructed multiple meanings. Being on the Strip intensifies one's consciousness of the dramatic, imaginative, theatrical qualities of everyday life. The Strip is an elaborately staged performance and information zone. It resonates with the brittle, synthetic qualities of the postmodern landscape.

From a Marxist standpoint, the contention that cyberspace is an admixture of codes in which no single code is dominant is fallible. Marxists take it as axiomatic that capital has a tendency to reduce everything to its abstract form, that is, the form of monetary value. Instead of pointing to the neutrality and transparency of cyberspace, they stress that entrepreneurial culture is the connecting link which encourages consumers to appropriate the commodities and commodified experiences on display. Yet to emphasize this point above all others is surely to miss the somnambulant quality of cyberspace. Entering it is not quite the same as entering a dream since one is conscious of one's surroundings. Nevertheless, these 'non-places' offer a comforting, dream-like admixture of codes in which buying and selling is not necessarily paramount. Brand-names like Sony, Toshiba, St Laurent, support the sense of conducting behaviour in non-threatening, encompassing non-space. For Shields (1991, 1992) and Chaney (1993, 1994) they are external representations of the lack of cultural stability in structures of highly unstable identity, status and social placement. They nourish feelings of safety and continuity in conditions of high contingency and discontinuity. The simultaneity and anomaly of cyberspace and disembedding disrupt stability. The old (modernist) categories are no longer viable frames for organizing social practice. For example, in our free time we are acutely aware of a sense of confinement and a lack of choice; while in our work we feel that we soar and can do anything. In our homes we are able to observe distant events more closely and accurately through television than by 'being there'. Following Shields and Chaney, it is perhaps not too fanciful to speak of the self today in terms of multiple identities and plural statuses. And if this kind of phraseology seems reminiscent of symbolic interactionism and Goffman, one should remember that what differentiates postmodernism is the insistence that there is no paramount determination of these identities and statuses. That is, there is no 'outside' or 'beyond' the flux of parody/pastiche, allegory, analog, symbol and image of hyperspace. Cyberspace is, as it were, the 'empty meeting ground' of multiple identities and plural statuses (MacCannell 1992).

If this is correct it poses insoluble problems for leisure as it has been traditionally understood. For leisure is conventionally associated with the presence of freedom, choice, self-determination, escape and life-satisfaction. These are all, so to speak, determining codes of leisure experience. The concepts of cyberspace and disembedding negates the possibility of determining codes. Hence, the association of freedom, choice, self-determination, escape and life-satisfaction with leisure becomes insupportable.

Hyperreality

By hyperreality Eco (1986) means the abolition of the distinction between the real thing and the imitation, the signifier and the sign. Whereas Foucault's 'heterotopia' is notionally a residual category to 'reality' since it is composed of discordant determinate codes, hyperreality proclaims the collapse of the distinction between code and reality and the replacement of reality with sign-culture. Popular culture is pre-eminently iconic and ceases to have anything to do with 'community' or 'work' experience or a search for authenticity or reality. Artefact and symbol are equivalent in the loose matrix of postmodern signs. Eco claims that hyperreality imbues everyday experience with hallucinatory and ironic qualities. The consumer becomes a connoisseur of a kitsch culture composed of infinite reproductions and simulations. He or she retains a sense of the artificiality of life but does not translate this into a quest for the underlying order of things. Instead, hyperreality is savoured as an end in itself; and enjoyment derives from the fusion of nominally incommensurate signs and symbols.

However, although artefact and symbol are equivalent, there are still disputes over the quality of simulation. Thus, in the battle between 'the two Elvises' described above (p. 118), what matters is the quality of the competing imitations and not the correspondence of the imitation to the 'original' 'reality'. One also sees this in the recreation of the Wild West in the fake cowboy town of Old Tucson in Arizona; the assemblage of Bavaria in the German village in Torrance, California; and the simulation of America in the American Adventure leisure centre in Derbyshire. All of them revolve around discordant iconic symbols of the reality which they claim to reproduce. Thus the actors in Old Tucson sign autograph pads with modern ball-point pens and the authentic German citizens of Bavaria speak with American accents. The iconography of these sites is assembled from popular culture: film, television, fables and fictions. In effect the verisimilitude of these leisure sites is gauged by their correspondence or deviation from iconic codes of representation and not an appeal to historical 'reality'. But their combined effect is to weave a non-space which is no more or less real than local space.

The effect of hyperreality extends much further than the technologies of simulation employed in vacation sites. Baudrillard (1983a, b, 1993) argues that hyperreality has transformed politics. Struggle continues to be waged in the name of modernist categories of 'progress', 'value', 'liberty', 'freedom' and 'equality'. But there is a palpable dream-like quality to the process. One is no longer convinced that the concepts refer to anything tangible or realizable. They have become caught up in the fictionalized non-space which envelops everyday life. Political activity, contends Baudrillard, is now openly organized around the grid of gesture, fantasy display and ritual. The gestural repertoire and the surface manoeuvrings which extend from it disguise the basic emptiness of political activity. Politicians posture and preen but they are powerless to change anything fundamental. This is not to say that posturing has no purpose. Rather it contributes to maintaining a sense of order and normality. It makes the dream of justice more seductive. It is wrong, then, to dismiss hyperreality and postmodernity as having transcended politics. Rather, as Baudrillard (1993: 7–9) comments:

> Of the political sphere one can say that the idea of politics has disappeared but that the game of politics continues. . . . We are now in the transpolitical sphere; in other words, we have reached the zero point of politics, a stage which also implies the reproduction of politics, its endless simulation.

Vattimo (1992: 62–75) identifies the same characteristic in contemporary political life. However, following Foucault, he styles it in terms of a transition from utopia to heterotopia. The idea of utopia in the sense of a universal qualitative improvement in the organization of society and the concomitant unification of experience has disappeared except in the minds of political pundits and ideologues. It has been replaced by a heterogeneity of purpose. Factions, interest groups, associations, unions, pursue their narrow sectional interest without displaying any interest in, or responsibility to, the social whole.

Baudrillard's talk of 'the transpolitical era' and Vattimo and Foucault's discussion of heterotopia are diametrically opposed to the political strategies of the Left. Within leisure studies critical politics has always been organized around an orientation to total social transformation of the existing order of things. Thus, cultural studies authors still appeal to 'collectivist mobilization' and 'the end of capitalism'; while foundationalist feminists made the transcendence of patriarchy the aim of women's liberation. Postmodernist authors scorn as utopian these policies and the objectives which they support. It is therefore not surprising that the scepticism which Baudrillard, Vattimo and other postmodernist writers show to organized politics should be rejected by the Left as evidence of the bankruptcy of postmodernism (see Clarke 1992; Scraton 1993). But this indignation springs from a fundamental misunderstanding of the postmodernist argument. For, as should be clear from the arguments described above, postmodernists do not maintain that politics – or the things which make it necessary, such as injustice and prejudice – has vanished. Rather they contend that politics has become ever more gestural and performance-oriented. It is not what you say but how you say it; it is not what you do but the impression that you make – or the sign that you give – that counts. What appears to the Left as the immorality of postmodernism is actually a richly sarcastic reading of the potential of modernist political thought and action to change anything. For who, in the face of the fragmenting, disembedded self and the spawning divisions between people, can believe in the integrated individual or the collectivist whole? Modernist thought, which used to oscillate comfortably between the individual/society, real/utopia polarities, is unable to contend with the challenge of the fatal strategy, the unchained sign and hyperreality except by denying their validity *tout court*.

Aside from the question of politics, hyperreality challenges the stock idea that leisure and culture are segmented from the rest of life. When the rational recreationists of the nineteenth century spoke of 'civilizing the roughs' through organized leisure activity, they were echoing Matthew Arnold's meliorist notion that culture is a gift of the rich and educated to the poor and ignorant. What is abhorrent about this mould of thought is its lack of reflexivity, its failure to understand its own limitations and its patronizing attitude to subordinate cultures.[1] Arnoldian overtures are untenable under hyperreality, for the distinctions between high and low culture, reality and fiction, are said to have dissolved. And here another facet of the politicized character of hyperreality and postmodernism is revealed: if postmodernity erases utopia it also abolishes social closures in everyday life. It is not too fanciful, then, to claim that postmodernism legitimates a new openness and tolerance to the voices and narratives marginalized under modernity.

Neo-Tribalism

Maffesoli (1990, 1991) recognizes the tension in postmodern thought between the proclaimed disappearance of the social and the obvious popularity of social events. He tries to resolve it with the concept of neo-tribalism. One may wonder about the appropriateness of this term. For contrary to first appearances, Maffesoli is not saying that postmodernism produces the recrudescence of primitivism. Rather, he takes neo-tribalism to refer to the intense, episodic social attachments which take place in the midst of the generalized neutrality and transparency which characterizes postmodern society. 'Tribal groupings,' writes Maffesoli (1991: 12), 'cohere on the basis of their own minor values, and . . . attract and collide with each other in an endless dance, forming themselves into a constellation whose vague boundaries are perfectly fluid.' The momentary coherence of people in 'emotional communities' such as arts festivals, soccer stands, theatre auditoriums and so on are examples of what Maffesoli has in mind. But so too is the symbolic gathering situated around brand-names such as Nike, Apple Macintosh, Nintendo,

Calvin Klein and so on, where consumers recognize tribal status but retain an essentially nomadic existence.

Maffesoli's insistence on the presence of intense collective affectivity in the context of postmodern society might suggest to the reader that he is pointing to the emergence of new bases and standards of solidarity. But this is not the case. Maffesoli goes to some lengths to argue that, under postmodernity, processes of scattering outflank processes of gathering. For example, he insists that the gathering of tribes which is typically predicated on the spectacle, the game, the brand-name or the cult activity, is only meaningful because it is part of the massification processes of postmodernity which transform everyone into a cipher, a mere spectator of life (1988: 148).[2] It is because we take this process to be an ordinary, unexceptional feature of daily life that the concentrated spectacles revolving around acting and spectating draw us in with such intensity. Neo-tribalism is only attractive because it claims to support nothing but temporary emotional communities. Their ephemerality is an indispensable part of their attraction. In the condition of postmodernity a life permanently lived in intense emotional solidarity would at best be self-deceiving and at worst totally suffocating. For postmodernism treats solidarity merely as a mythological sign in the sign-economy. It refuses to treat it as anything solid or continuous.

There is, of course, an echo of Durkheim in Maffesoli's work on neo-tribalism. In the closing pages of *The Elementary Forms of Religious Life* (1915), Durkheim speculates that part of the business of the state in the era of fully developed organic solidarity will be to organize secular festivals, days of remembrance and processions which will concentrate collective consciousness. He recognized that industrial life perpetuates episodic meetings and anonymity. Leisure, he reasoned, might function as a point of gathering and moral remaking in the midst of generalized anomic disturbance (Rojek 1985: 51–5). However, while Durkheim attributed a binding effect to this function, Maffesoli insists that it is, at best, superficial and temporary. For Maffesoli the leisure spectacle is, so to speak, self-fulfilling. The integration which it temporarily delivers evaporates in the diffuseness of postmodern life. The individual returns to the condition of mobility and neutrality. Neo-tribalism in leisure and other settings is always ephemeral and discontinuous. At most it summons the momentary illusion of collectivity. This illusion provides the necessary reassuring balance to the fractious, episodic, anonymous conditions of postmodernity. But it cannot lead to a real 'leisure society'.

Risk

From global warming to the threat of biological warfare postmodern life seems to be besieged by risk. Doubtless it is an easy matter to show that risk is an historical constant. However, according to Beck (1992a, b), certain peculiarities differentiate risk today from all other times. He argues that risk is now uncontainable, unlimited and uncompensatable. Life has become more dependent upon contingencies which no one can control. The reason for this is twofold. In the first place the chains of interdependence between nations have lengthened and multiplied. For example, economic slowdown in one of the core capitalist economies affects the level of economic activity everywhere else. The second reason is that the current balance between culture, technology and nature is such that the pursuit of high-risk development strategies in one society has implications for all societies. For example, the depletion of the Brazilian rain forests or the excessive use of petrol in Europe and the USA increases the risk of environmental catastrophe for the whole world. The best example of the diffusion of risk in recent times was the nuclear failure at the Chernobyl power plant in the former Soviet Union which threatened large areas of North-Western Europe with radiation. But Saddam's decision to burn Kuwaiti oil wells during the Gulf War also risked the balance of the global eco-sphere.

Risk-escalation, continues Beck (1991), has led to a crisis in the Western insurance sector. A 'consensus of progress' prevailed in modernity. Under it nation-states accepted that technology and the extractive industries were permitted to prosper in order to maximize wealth creation. A global network of insurance developed to service these sectors by guaranteeing cover and protection. Today, continues Beck, this network can no longer service the aggregate level of risk throughout the world. Leading insurance companies like Lloyd's of London have suffered a series of claims for compensation which have threatened their very existence and forced them to change their business practices. We are moving to the condition of 'the uninsured society' in which certain forms of activity can no longer be covered. A parallel development is evident in the case of domestic insurance. In some quarters of the metropolis the domestic insurance premium to cover the risk of theft is now so great that people have stopped insuring their property.

Beck (1992b) is sanguine about our ability to adapt to risk-escalation. Indeed he presents the whole modernization process as one of increasing 'reflexivity'. By this he means that humans have a capacity to learn from their mistakes and from the threats posed to the survival of the species through the destabilization of the natural environment. As evidence he cites the greater awareness of environmental issues in the West and the spread of multi-lateral agreements regulating high-risk activities. Political pressures within nation-states, he believes, increase the propensity of governments to reach rational solutions to risk problems. Beck (1991) speaks of the need to establish international regulatory bodies to manage risk by laying down 'boundaries of scientific proof' and creating 'centres of discursive checking'. This faith in rationality has been strongly criticized for being over-optimistic. Lash and Urry (1994) argue that Beck belongs to the Enlightenment tradition which privileges rationality, order and progress. According to them, his work fails to give a convincing account of the place of irrationality in modernization and exaggerates the extent to which parties will recognize common rational interests as opposed to separate expressive interests.

A noteworthy and unfairly neglected counterpoint to Beck's work on risk is

supplied by Lasch (1984) in his commentary on present-day 'survival strategies'. Like Beck, Lasch argues that there is a contradiction between the
rhetoric and substance of modernization. The rhetoric ventilates on the progressive empowerment of the subject in history. Functionalist theory in leisure
studies takes this to a logical extreme by presenting leisure as the acme of freedom and choice. Also like Beck, Lasch attacks the foundation of this tradition
of thought. In his view it falsely privileges the psychology of self-assurance
and triumphalism over the psychology of insecurity and fear. Most people
today, he maintains, do not regard themselves as free subjects (1984: 96).
Rather they see themselves as victims of huge, uncontrollable forces. But
unlike Beck, Lasch takes a dim view of our capacity to manage risk. He
believes that the mass neuroses of our 'troubled times' stem from our sense of
powerlessness and our perception of encroaching and unavoidable personal
and global risks. The psychological response to this is complex. Lasch's use of
phrases like 'the minimal self' and 'the survival mentality' themselves run
the risk of over-simplifying the issue. However, in his detailed analysis (1984:
57–99, 251–9) he distinguishes between a variety of types. The most important
are as follows.

(1) *Emotional disengagement.* This is based on a sort of 'principled nega-
tivism' which sees the worst in all situations and deals with hopelessness by a
retreat into self-defensive strategies. Faced with a world which is defined as
unmanageable, the individual turns away from public questions and becomes
absorbed in protecting his or her private space and lifestyle. For it is only here
that individual actions seem to have some discernible impact on the course of
events. Private life is thus radically separated from public life. What happens in
the interior, in the domestic sphere and in personal relations with others is real;
the exterior and the political sphere are dismissed as imaginary realms.

(2) *Fantasy voyaging.* In this case the individual responds to the enormous
risks and implacable forces in daily life by denying social reality. Life becomes
a fantasy in which shared experience of the world is ridiculed. Personal existence ceases to refer to anything outside itself. We stoically accept that our
views and interests are unlikely to be shared by others. Because we find no one
like ourselves in our work or our leisure our lifestyle becomes fantasy-ridden.
Our leisure is dominated by fantasy situations in which we imagine ourselves
to be omnipotent or where our perceived lack of control is starkly emphasized.
For example, in the cyberspace of telematic technology we can either rig things
to achieve total mastery or experience the humiliation of being trounced by a
machine. The fantasy voyager is also prone to sadistic or masochistic episodes
in sexual behaviour. The control or subjection experienced here seems more
real than anything that happens in everyday life.

(3) *Fatalism.* Here the complexities of everyday life are managed by flatly
denying that we make our own history. Instead fatalists believe that everything
that happens is the will of superhuman forces. We survive by volunteering
our lives to these forces. The individual who adopts this outlook is likely to be
susceptible to traditional religious belief, mysticism and spiritualism. If this-
worldly existence is directed by extra-terrestrial powers, survival lies in

accepting our own powerlessness. Typically this form of thought presents our earthly life as a passage to a better form of existence after death.

(4) *Trivialization of risk*. Making light of risk, turning it into an object of humour or irony, is a widely practised survival strategy. Here the individual works with the belief that the worst will always fall short of our expectations. He or she dismisses warnings of ecological catastrophe, nuclear disaster or economic and political chaos. Those who dwell on catastrophe are rejected as doom-mongers, misanthropes and kill-joys. Instead a feel-good, boosterish attitude is celebrated.

Lasch is interested in risk psychology. It is easy to read postmodernism as a branch of this psychology. That is, the antipathy that postmodernism demonstrates to collectivism, utopianism, shared reality and privileged narratives is interpreted as a way of coping with the real risks of the present day. However, while this interpretation is certainly tempting it is also misleading. There is little in postmodernism to suggest that we live on the brink of catastrophe. On the contrary, it is precisely the secure, monotonous, repetitive character of simulation, spectacle, contingency, gestural politics and uncertainty that is stressed. It is the mundane orderliness of established systems of communication that enables the individual to experience what Baudrillard calls 'ecstatic' experience.

Still, Lasch's discussion does have relevance for understanding postmodernism and leisure. By emphasizing the prominence of our perception of risk in daily life he highlights the strategies of preservation which have taken root in leisure during the last thirty years. The obsession with preserving the body, beating the aging process, saving 'our' heritage, all point to a widespread feeling that we are surrounded by risk. From the country air we breathe, which might be laden with life-endangering pesticides, to local transport planning which threatens places of outstanding beauty, we seem to be enmeshed in a minatory, changing world of uncertainty. Our leisure practice reflects this with its increased sensitivity to the biological effects of the food we eat, the sun-rays we bathe in and the polluted air we breathe. It is no longer enough – and perhaps it never was – simply to have fun and pleasure in our 'free' time. Now we must ensure that our leisure minimizes risk to ourselves and the eco-system. In the nineteenth century much organized leisure was dominated by the desire for self-improvement. Now it is dominated by a twin responsibility to our bodies, others and the environment.

'Unhealthy' leisure practices such as drinking, smoking or lazing around are condemned for the risks they 'inevitably' bring in their wake. Those who indulge in such practices are lectured on the scientific links between the unrestrained use of stimulants or the lack of exercise and heart disease, cancer and the deterioration of respiratory functions. The message is that if you have this kind of fun you will die. But of course, the response from the heavy smoker or drinker is that we will all die anyway. By depriving ourselves of the simple pleasures of life we weaken the strength and depth of our experience. We diminish what we could be. Besides, everyday life abounds with counter-factual evidence which conflicts with the fatalistic arguments of the risk-preachers. Not only do many heavy drinkers and smokers seem to live for a normal life-span, they also attest to enjoying life. In a bar, talking with a man in his eighties who is drinking his fifth shot of Scotch and smoking his thirtieth cigarette of the day, it is hard to side with the doom-mongers of risk. This is not to say that the analysis of medical science is wrong. Bodily abuse kills. In a world in which everything is perceived as running down at an exponential rate our leisure assumes a last-chance quality. If we take that last calculated risk we may momentarily cheat the sense of general decay. But we may also die.

Contingency

Bauman (1992: 193) defines contingency as the belief of social actors that 'they have no overwhelming reasons for being what they are, and [that] they could be different if any of the participating agencies behaved differently.' Like Rorty (1989) and Tester (1993), Bauman maintains that contingency is one of the defining characteristics of postmodernity. All of these writers contrast the condition of contingency with that of determinacy. In traditional society destiny is determined by birth. One's family of origin structures one's life chances. Social order is reinforced by powerful religious beliefs which operate to legitimize inequality in this world by promising paradise in the after-life. As we have already seen, modernity uproots this order. It enlarges the social consciousness of conditioning processes which are external to the individual and the family but defined in secular rather than religious or mystical terms. The life course is no longer presented as a matter of destiny. Rather it is portrayed as a matter of contingent power relations. Thus, for example, the smaller life chances available to the lower strata in the social order are interpreted as the effect of the unequal and unjust power structure of society. Moreover, this structure is no longer understood as unchangeable but as something which is itself dependent upon contingent power relations.

Contingency connects up with the concepts of both neo-tribalism and risk. Maffesoli's concept of neo-tribalism rules out notions of fixed identities and historical destinies. It replaces both with a view of the masses as 'perpetually seething', polymorphous and super-mobile (Maffesoli 1988: 141). In Marxism the masses possess a coherent identity, almost a collective personality; in postmodernism social life has a molecular structure. Of course, people are conscious of the features of similarity between them but they possess no active class consciousness. Instead their consciousness is fatalistic. It focuses on the monotonous character of everyday life. We are aware that everything that is could be radically different. We see our lives changing through accident rather than design. Yet postmodernism also perpetuates a keen awareness that order is intrinsically precarious. This is why risk relates so closely to contingency. People understand that safety, under postmodernity, is never more than contingent. This applies to the level of the individual, the locale, the society and the planet. Thus, the individual is conscious that personal security might be extinguished by nothing more than the ignition of a faulty wiring circuit in the domestic lighting system of his or her domicile; the security of society might be put at risk by economic disaster or plague; and the planet itself might be at risk if the eco-balance is randomly disturbed. On the other hand, the fatalistic character of contingency-consciousness suggests that if disaster is going to strike there is little that can be done about it. If we become victims of catastrophe it is because we are very unlucky.

Acceptance that our lives will be dominated by forces which are too big to influence is the dominant mental state. Bauman (1992: 132–3) presents a generous picture of postmodern contingency-consciousness. He argues that it is profoundly distinct from modernist contingency-consciousness because it is based on the recognition of its own limits. Postmodern contingency-consciousness, he maintains, recognizes the inherent plurality of perspectives. It does not seek to exclude different perspectives or suppress them. Above all, it does not posit itself as transcending plurality by creating a new unifying order of things. Postmodern contingency-consciousness, he proposes, is *emancipation from false consciousness* (1992: 188). Through it one can no longer assert superior wisdom or total authority. For example, one can no longer claim – as the rational recreationists of the nineteenth century claimed – to lay down fixed principles geared to producing a universal programme of self-improvement. Instead postmodernism increases our sensitivity to the partial, value-laden character of all perspectives. For Bauman this results in an enlarged propensity for tolerance in daily relations. But he also recognizes that this is simply one expression of the postmodern condition.

A mental sensitivity to contingency can also lead to a permanent state of ambivalence and indecision in which no action seems worthwhile. Truth itself is acknowledged to have a history, that is, to be contingent. Without the conviction of truth the individual is unable to make the emotional leap of faith that inspires committed action. Instead he or she recognizes constant emotional mobility as the only meaningful life-option. The individual is therefore unable to settle down. He or she moves from emotional relationship to emotional relationship, from one free time activity to another, without ever feeling properly settled in a satisfying social position. If one were to use a single term to describe this mental condition it would be *restlessness* (Rojek 1993c).[3] The defining feature of this mental state is not that nothing seems worthwhile but rather that everything seems worthwhile. Hence making one life or leisure choice as opposed to another seems to be completely arbitrary. Since all leisure choices are defined as matters of circumstance, the individual who becomes totally absorbed in a single leisure pursuit is dismissed as a fanatic. Leisure becomes a hectic move from activity to activity. It is dominated by a consciousness which emphasizes the discontinuity of experience.[4]

Speed

A basic premise of postmodernism is that the pace of life accelerates exponentially. Everything speeds up so that our traditional perceptions of time and space are disrupted. In less than fifty years the transport revolution of the nineteenth century replaced the horse and cart with the railway locomotive. In the first half of the twentieth century the motor-car and jet engine continued the process of accelerating the speed of travel and communication. Now computer networking and telecommunications offer the prospect of immediate audio and visual communication. Electronic light seems to be on the brink of annihilating space and time.

The speeding up of life has a variety of effects. Most obviously, our consciousness of simultaneity is enlarged. By simultaneity I mean the awareness of spatially remote processes which co-exist with our immediate environment. Television and radio provide a continuous information stream into our private space. Computer networking systems extend this by giving us direct control over data accumulation. The development of fibre-optic communication systems promises to make visual phone links viable for the ordinary consumer. Simultaneity is generally seen as a progressive force (Smart 1992; Bauman 1992, 1993). Enlarging our information stream enriches our knowledge and understanding of the world. We become better citizens by knowing more. But this interpretation is perhaps too sanguine.

Virilio (1986, 1991) argues that popular consciousness of the increased acceleration of life increases psychological stress and tension. As we are bombarded with more information about what we might do and who we might be, our awareness of opportunity-loss increases. By the term opportunity-loss, I mean the consciousness of the multiple opportunities cancelled by choosing one opportunity option. For example, by choosing to watch a televised sports fixture at home we lose the opportunity of exercising in the gym or visiting the cinema. Every choice we make in our leisure and travel becomes, to borrow Virilio's (1991: 65) phrase, 'a little death'. We never know if the choices that we have eliminated would have been more fulfilling and rewarding. Since the quality and range of choices seems to be constantly expanding we have the distressing feeling of permanently missing out in our leisure, of not making the most of our time. For no sooner have we made one leisure choice than it is rendered obsolete by other leisure options.

At the level of the individual psyche the effect is to contribute to the tendencies of discontinuity, fragmentation and division. This reinforces our sense of hyperreality. The speed of life, one might say, tears individuals from a stable spatio-temporal context and floats them out through waves of ever-changing images and sound-bites. Since nothing is fixed or stable, nothing is tenable or real. Like Baudrillard, Virilio believes that the trend is towards the total mechanization of leisure and culture and the disappearance of the self. He predicts that in the near future the individual will be no more than 'an electronic terminal where we'd leave it up to the instruments to organize our most intimate vital rhythms, without ever changing position ourselves, the authority of electronic automatism reducing our will to zero . . . the vision of light moving on a screen would have replaced all personal movement' (Virilio 1991: 104).

Speed and simultaneity contribute to the general remoteness from public life that the individual feels in postmodern culture. From this it would seem that the programmes of moral regulation have come to an end. In postmodern culture the individual is free-floating and disconnected. The ephemerality of identity appears to reduce the capacity of the state to centre power on the individual.[5] However, there are surely dangers in pushing this postmodernist argument too far. Instant information might mean that the individual expands consciousness through a magnified view of the richness and diversity of the world. However, it also means direct policing since the state has the means to influence the subject without any intermediary confusing the issue. Electronic light carries with it the Orwellian nightmare of complete state control. Virilio's argument, then, regards acceleration as inherently contradictory. For the individual psyche, speed is divisive; but for society, it is potentially cohesive. The contradiction plays on the dual qualities of electronic light: it both gives focus and refracts. This is evident in leisure relations. The instantaneous character of communications makes it possible to speak of global events such as Live Aid, the Olympics and the World Cup, in which collective consciousness is genuinely concentrated.[6] On the other hand, it also creates networking between institutions and countries which undermines the sense of institutional or national collectivity.

Speed is, of course, a creation of culture. Through technology and telecommunications we are aware of the shrinking world and the dissolution of time. It is therefore perhaps in the realm of nature that the corrosive effects of speed are most starkly evident. For we are used to thinking of nature in terms of permanent natural rhythms and unchangeable patterns. The day's journey into night, the passing of the seasons and the life order of the ageing process have traditionally been presented in terms of an immemorial order. Speed changes this. Instantaneous communication throughout the globe eradicates the division between day and night. Jet travel creates a sense of amnesia which has the effect of extending the length of daylight and postponing the night. 'Where are we when we travel?', asks Virilio (1991: 61). And he finds the answer in the swift, engulfing consciousness of disjointed time and space. In a 747 there is no sense of space or distance. We receive up-to-date news bulletins and we have personal phone facilities just as we would at home. Similarly, in the privacy of the domestic interior we are awash with instant information about life in the exterior. From bulletins of the weather, traffic delays, trade agreements, terrorist threats, we are often better informed than the people on the spot. The effect is to heighten our awareness of the arbitrariness of traditional divisions of time and space and also to increase our sense of distance and remoteness from the external world. The individual takes a detour into a fantasy world of impressions, images and unchained signs.

Existence seems uncontained by restrictions of the body and time and space. Indeed, it is perhaps in the subject of the body that the effect of speed on nature is most palpably observed. Biotechnology is becoming increasingly adept at masking the degenerative effects of ageing. The natural speed of the ageing process is apparently reversed. Biotechnology disrupts the life order. Face-lifts, hair transplants, the suction of subcutaneous fats, cosmetic nipping and tucking, all contribute to the appearance of a more youthful body. This development is, of course, a response to the culture of hedonism which dominates consumer culture. To possess an ageing body is to lose relevance in the market. But a 60-year-old with jet black hair and no wrinkles punctures our sense of natural limits. Speed, as the cliché has it, kills. Yet through the effect of biotechnology it can also rejuvenate and invigorate. For example, Ronald Reagan's refusal to grow old may have just been a medically orchestrated illusion but it was an important power-prop during his time in office. The old boy seemed to defy the laws of nature and hence possessed the air of invulnerability. Even if in interviews and policy statements he often seemed slow-witted and forgetful, Reagan's surgically composed face and dyed hair signified the confidence of early middle age.

Necro-fever

Celebrity and the star system assume a prominent role in postmodernity. In conditions where daily relationships are widely seen as unreal, screen relationships attain a magnetic hold on consciousness. They seem backlit by glamour, vivacity, adventure and style. By comparison, our everyday lives at home and work seem undernourished and underdeveloped. It is the screen stars who really live. They say the right things; they wear the right clothes; they go to the right places; they find the right people to fall in love with; for them boredom and dissatisfaction are just temporary states of mind. We bathe in their radiance, but we cannot help noticing how limited our lives seem to be by comparison.

It is because celebrities are placed beyond ordinary experience that they mesmerize us. Death indeed holds no dominion over the social presence of the star. For example, images of dead stars such as James Dean, Humphrey Bogart, Elvis Presley, Jayne Mansfield, Clark Gable, John F. Kennedy, John Lennon, Sid Vicious, Jim Morrison, Kurt Cobain, abound. As McCann (1988: 199–200) writes:

> [Marilyn] Monroe is now everywhere, yet nowhere; her image on walls, in movies, in books – all after-images, images obscuring the fact of her permanent absence. For the movie industry, to place the consumer of its products in a constant position of desire is to bring him or her back to the cinema time and again, to crave an unattainable, flickering fantasy life.

McCann's discussion of Monroe is interesting. It amounts to the first in-depth sociological treatment of movie celebrity. But his suggestion that Monroe's death is in tension with her continued presence in daily life is open to objection. By attributing this presence to the machinations of the culture industry McCann ignores the point that experience of celebrity is typically mediated through a repertoire of images instead of physical presence. Stars may die, but their images permanently circulate through cyberspace. Physical termination is therefore relatively insignificant. The file of images remains in store and it can be perpetually formatted to comply with new contingencies. Three general categories of formatting have emerged to perpetuate the image files of dead celebrities.

(1) *Denial.* Images of the celebrity are recycled and developed, endowing the star with a timeless quality. The consumer grows old, but the dead star remains permanently young. Half-forgotten photo-sets are published as discoveries, discarded recordings are repackaged and rereleased, or original vinyl recordings are digitally remastered and sold in the 'cleaner', more 'authentic' CD format. The dead star is subject to a continuous process of disclosure and elaboration. Cloning is an important part of the denial process. Cloning refers to the surgical duplication of the star's physical appearance. For example, plastic surgeons advertise the 'Elvis look' and the 'Marilyn look' to would-be clones. Many leading entertainers self-consciously develop the physical assets of a dead idol. Riese and Hitchens (1988: 293–4) stop short of claiming that Madonna had plastic surgery to resemble Marilyn Monroe. All the same they insist that her persona is a calculated model of the Monroe image. Another branch of cloning refers to the mixing of classical film footage or original recordings with contemporary footage and recordings. So Woody Allen manages to interact with leading political figures and celebrities of the inter-war years in the film *Zelig*; and so, too, Natalie Cole scores a major hit in the 1990s with a vocal duet with her dead father who 'performs' in digitally remastered form; the film *Forrest Gump* uses similar juxtapositions. In cyberspace, where presence is a matter of image-repertoire, these fantastic occurrences are simply a question of clever editing. Marketing and design departments assist necrophiliac repackaging, reprinting and renewing. The dead star is a sort of open image which can be decked out in the latest fashions and inserted into the most up-to-date image streams. Recycling ensures everlasting vitality and flexibility. From hair gel to dental floss, from new cars to designer clothes, images of dead celebrities are used to sell products. The images deny mortality, but since they are part of the same image stream which typically supplies us with experience of the insubstantial, floating world of celebrity we do not notice their inherent implausibility.

(2) *Scandalization.* This refers to the ritual transformation of the death into an unnatural event. Sometimes it is as if the much-mourned idol has merely retreated into a denser zone of hyperreality. For example, Jim Morrison, Elvis Presley and B. Tavern – the thriller writer – are widely rumoured to have faked death so as to escape the glare of the media.[7] Elvis Presley is regularly sighted in the USA despite the official announcement of his death in 1977; and tape-recordings which purport to be conducted with the reluctant idol are sold in American book-stores (Rojek 1993a: 143–4).

Another form of scandalization technique is conspiracy theories. For example, the deaths of John F. Kennedy, Robert F. Kennedy, Robert Maxwell, Brian Jones, Andy Warhol and John Lennon are perpetually debated. Who really killed JFK? Can we really believe that Mark David Chapman acted alone to assassinate John Lennon? Do the muddled circumstances of Jim

Morrison's autopsy indicate an official cover-up? Did Robert Maxwell fall off his yacht or did he jump? Conspiracy theories on the death of Marilyn Monroe alone are enough to fill several bookshelves. Titles like *Goddess: The Secret Lives of Marilyn Monroe, The Strange Death of Marilyn Monroe, The Life and Curious Death of Marilyn Monroe, The Marilyn Conspiracy, Marilyn: An Untold Story, Marilyn Lives!* and *Marilyn Monroe Confidential* are typical. Scandalization techniques make the death – like the life of the idol – larger than ordinary life. They are a form of denial because they imply that only intrigue and crime can rob us of our beloved idols. But they also involve making new thematic connections and casting fresh light on reported events. Interestingly, conspiracy theories often develop around the theme of covert, criminal action by organizations which are usually presented as existing for the public benefit. For example, CIA agents are widely rumoured to have been involved in the deaths of John F. Kennedy, Marilyn Monroe and John Lennon, and the police and judiciary are colaterally rumoured to have been involved in cover-up operations. Perhaps these connections should not surprise us. History in hyperreality is never more than shared mythology. In the indiscriminate light of cyberspace, organizations like the CIA or MI5 are no more real (or false) than screen heroes or villains. Since hyperreality is essentially interactive, the consumer becomes a casting director, and history a game which can be reversed and elaborated at will.

Using the consumer as an active participant in extending or developing leisure experience is also evident in the growth of tours into the supernormal and supernatural. These are the ultimate escape breaks in necro-fever because they ostensibly allow you to re-enter history and solve a mystery. For example, the crime section of bookstores contain a variety of books which describe famous murders. We are invited to consider the clues, visit the sites of the killings and determine for ourselves what really happened.[8] The consumer becomes a private detective sifting through the evidence and challenging official accounts of reality. Similarly, popular interest in the paranormal is catered for by a variety of 'ghostly tours' and 'ghostly breaks'. Shropshire Tourism publishes an itinerary of hauntings in the county. For example, on platform 3 of Shrewsbury railway station the ghost of a Victorian passenger accidentally killed in 1887 is said to be seen pacing up and down waiting for his train;[9] in Ludlow at a building called Castle Lodge the ghost of a young girl wearing red gloves is regularly seen;[10] in Wenlock Edge a robber's rock is the scene of haunting; and the ghost-ridden Prince Rupert Hotel, Shrewsbury, offers ghostly weekend breaks to ghost hunters.[11]

What emerges most unequivocally from all of this is the immense interest in mysteries and the uncanny. Perhaps this is a universal feature of human existence. However, what is interesting in the context of necro-fever is the emergence of organized tours into the uncanny and the mysterious. Legends and rumours have been taken over by leisure entrepreneurs and we are offered the chance to become tourists into the realm of the inexplicable. In a culture in which nothing is seen as necessarily true or real, every item can be tested and questioned.

(3) *De-sacralization*

Ginger was reluctant to violate his privacy. Finally she opened the door and peeped inside. What she saw was Elvis doubled up face down on the floor with his buttocks elevated, in the fetal position. Clearly, he had been sitting in the black leather and chrome chair reading and had toppled forward onto the floor. The book was still lying on the chair. In falling, his head had struck a hair dryer that someone had left on the floor. If it had been anyone else Ginger had found in this condition, she might have been alarmed. With Elvis, this kind of thing was normal. . . . Walking over to him, Ginger called 'Elvis!' Then, suddenly she began to feel alarmed. . . . She reached down and touched him. He was as cold as ice. Again, this was typical. Sleeping for hours without stirring in a room whose temperature had been forced down twenty degrees by a powerful air conditioner, Elvis often felt icy to the touch. Finally, Ginger knelt down and turned Elvis's head around so she could see his face. Now, for the first time, she was gripped by terror. Elvis's face had become a grotesque mask, purple with engorged blood, his teeth set in his lolling tongue. Trembling, she raised one of his closed eyelids. The eye was blood red and motionless. (Goldman 1981: 686)

This is the climax of Albert Goldman's massive biography of Elvis Presley. It is a typical example of de-sacralization. This term refers to the systematic moral and physical denigration of the dead celebrity. The glittering reputation is ritually mired and the celebrity is reduced to an object of pity. Goldman's Elvis is a junk-food addict, a sexual degenerate and a massive drug abuser. He is an inveterate hypocrite who toadies with Presidents to stop drug abuse while privately glorying in his own narcotic intake. Goldman lists the drugs found in Presley's body after his death with gloating relish: codeine, morphine, methaqualone, diazepam, ethinamate, ethchlorvynol, amorbarbital, phenobarbital, meperidine, amitriptyline, nortriptyline, phenyltoloxamine (Goldman 1981: 685). Elvis is also portrayed as the lazy dupe of his manager, Colonel Tom Parker, who cheats him of his fortune and totally controls his career.

Goldman's (1989) biography of John Lennon is also an exercise in desacralization. Like Presley, Lennon is presented as a sexual degenerate who was helplessly dependent on drugs and, in his few moments of ordinary consciousness, consumed with bitterness against his former partners. Unlike Presley, Lennon was alleged to mix with terrorists and to payroll malcontents. In Ascot and Greenwich Village, Lennon is depicted as an agent of subversion.

Goldman, a former Professor of English and Comparative Literature at Columbia University, is one of the most successful exponents of de-sacralization. But his work is hardly unique. Another notable gourmet of celebrity tackiness and decadence is Kenneth Anger. His *Hollywood Babylon* series (1975, 1984) chronicles the sordid stories behind the images of the Hollywood dream factory. The addictions, sexual peccadilloes, murders and suicides of minor and major stars are savoured in Anger's knowing, matter of fact prose. Anger is captivated with the task of exposing the gap between the screen image and private reality. His shameless and captivating list of decadents, perverts, hypocrites, neurotics and paranoids is undoubtedly at odds with the dream factory's images of child stars, innocent waifs, male hunks and beauty queens. However, as with the Goldman books, the reader senses that he or she is being given a massively one-sided story – an account deliberately structured to show that the idol has feet of clay. And let there be no mistake – Goldman and Anger represent the top end of the de-sacralization market. Beneath them are the TV exposés, the tabloid revelations, the pulp portraits and the intimate teleplays. In the refracting space of hyperreality the celebrity is built up only to be knocked down. Allegations of degeneracy and inadequacy amount to nothing more than a twist of the image-repertoire. The open sign of stardom is so empty of content that anything is possible. And what reality can be deciphered from this?

Eco (1986), in his account of hyperreality, singles out the wax museum as an intense form of postmodern necro-fever. Here one can see models of movie celebrities, fairy-stories, historical figures and adventure stories. In the Movieland Wax Museum at Buena Park, California, Eco is struck by the meticulous attention to detail. A wax model of Jean Harlow, he notes, is surrounded with copies of period magazines. In the room inhabited by the model of Charlie Chaplin the walls are decorated with turn-of-the-century posters. The area where the *Dr Zhivago* exhibit is situated is artificially kept at a temperature of below zero centigrade in order to enhance the reality effect. 'Here', comments Eco (1986: 13–14) '"reality" is a movie, but another characteristic of the wax museum is that the notion of historical reality is absolutely democratized: Marie Antoinette's boudoir is recreated with fastidious attention to detail, but Alice's encounter with the Mad Hatter is done just as carefully.'

Postmodernism keeps everything at the same level – the 'original' object and the treatment, the clone and the 'real' thing, the dead and the alive. Another term for this function is the normalization of equivalence. Necro-fever achieves this by keeping the dead celebrity permanently alive in the image-stream of cyberspace. It is in this general sense of highlighting the unreality of telecommunication processes that it exercises its most important effect on leisure practice. However, at the same time, one should not ignore the intense feelings of affect that are generated around certain celebrity images. Some consumers systematically organize their leisure around celebrity image-streams. Elvis fans, Madonna fans, Barry Manilow fans, and countless other cult worshippers find their relationship with their celebrity image-stream to be more meaningful than other relationships in daily life. It is not uncommon for the death of a celebrity to be accompanied by a wave of suicides and attempted suicides as distraught fans decide they can no longer continue. For example, after Rudolph Valentino's death in August 1926, Anger (1975: 166–7) reports that 'two women attempted suicide in front of Polyclinic Hospital; in London a girl took poison before Rudy's inscribed photograph; an elevator boy of the Ritz in Paris was found dead on a bed covered with Valentino's photos.' Similar recorded incidents of suicide and attempted suicide by fans have followed the deaths of Jean Harlow, James Dean, Buddy Holly, Marilyn Monroe, John F. Kennedy, Elvis Presley and John Lennon.

Aesthetics/Ethics

Aesthetics refers to the philosophic investigation of beauty and the perception of beauty, especially in the arts. Postmodernity is associated with the aestheticization of everyday life. This is a corollary of the argument that the divisions between high and low art, elite and popular culture, have collapsed. It is not so much that life has become more beautiful but rather that, in comparison with modernity, questions of beauty and appearance exercise greater influence in our ordinary decisions about appearance, style and movement. For Jameson (1991), aestheticization reflects the enlargement of culture which postmodernity encourages. Under modernity, argues Jameson, social life is segmented into realms of culture, ethics, politics and economics. Because real life is associated with questions of how we should live, what systems we should abide by and where wealth can be generated, culture tends to take the back-seat to ethics, politics and economics. Culture is regarded as a realm of symbol and ambiguity. The realms of ethics, politics and economics are seen as realms of facts.

All of this changes with postmodernity. The sign-world infuses ethics, politics and economics, giving the behaviour conducted therein an ambiguous quality. Economic facts become converted into economic points of view and ethical truths into ethical values. Politics becomes increasingly concerned with style, presentation and gesture. Everything becomes perceived and explained in terms of culture. Class wars and gender wars are replaced with style wars. In conditions where appearance is said to have replaced substance as the focus of association, practice and identity, there is an obvious sense in which the quality of appearance comes to preoccupy social consciousness. Hence the pre-eminence of aesthetic questions in discussions of postmodernism (see Jencks 1984; Foster 1985; Kroker and Cook 1986; Jameson 1991; Featherstone 1991: 65–82).

Of course this focus on aesthetics is open to an obvious objection. *Prima facie*, aesthetics seems to ignore ethical concerns. More specifically, the questions of how we should live our lives, and what we should do to improve ourselves and our surrounding social conditions, seem to be obscured in favour of a complacent, self-sufficient philosophy of cultural appreciation. For those interested in matters of poverty and injustice, the subject of aesthetics therefore seems to be an irrelevance. Yet this criticism is itself vulnerable to two important objections. First, it implies that questions of aesthetics have no bearing on questions of poverty and injustice, and wider ethical questions. Second, it tacitly supports the proposition that a distinction can still be drawn between the realms of culture, ethics, politics and economics. The second point has already been addressed in the discussion of de-differentiation (pp. 79–85). But to come to the first objection, one might begin by addressing the burgeoning literature which has grown up around the people art of the New York artist Krzysztof Wodiczko (Smith 1992; Wright 1992; Hebdige 1993).

Wodiczko's work operates on the axis between aesthetics and ethics. In particular his design of the Homeless Vehicle and the Poliscar is, in part, a direct attempt to aestheticize poverty while at the same time offering a practical solution to the problems of homelessness. The Homeless Vehicle was first exhibited in New York in 1988. It is a mobile home for the homeless. The lower compartment consists of a supermarket trolley which is designed for storage – bags, clothes, blankets, food, water and empty cans. The upper compartment consists of an extendable sleeping area with a partially translucent metal roof with a conical nose. The nose is detachable and is used as a washbasin. But it also contributes to the viewer's impression that the vehicle is a projectile. As Smith (1992) and Hebdige (1993) comment, the projectile shape of the upper level enhances the appearance of the Homeless Vehicle as a counter to consumerist mores and values. 'The Homeless Vehicle', Smith (1992: 58) remarks, 'is an impertinent invention that empowers the evicted to erase their own erasure.'

Wodiczko developed the idea with his Poliscar which he introduced in 1991. The Poliscar is a triangular construction based on a frame with wheels to permit movement. It enables the homeless person to be securely inside and thus sheltered. The detachable conical washbasin is situated at the peak of the triangle. Inside the Poliscar there is enough room for more than one person to be comfortably seated and a window slot to permit navigation. But the most interesting features of the Poliscar have to do with the communications system installed inside. It includes a CB radio, external camera, TV monitor and a portable Microwave Link for transmitting visual images to other vehicles and receivers. Communication, argues Wodiczko, is an essential characteristic of civil society. By restoring communication facilities to the homeless the Poliscar contributes to their empowerment. In Wodiczko's words (quoted in Smith 1992: 59) it aims to overcome the contradiction 'that while they are physically confined to public spaces they are politically excluded from public space constituted as a space for communication.' But this political concern is not superior to the question of aesthetics. Wodiczko has designed the vehicle to have a startling, provocative presence. In Wright's (1992: 13) view the design has 'allusions to Kafka, Goya, Aldo-Rossi, Tatlin's famous tower . . . the visionary machines designed by Leonardo . . . fantastical robots . . . Dr Who's daleks . . . the first tanks that went into action on the western front in 1916.'

Wodiczko's vehicles are both art objects and practical solutions to the challenges of homelessness. One can appreciate them in the gallery or use them on the street. However, they are obviously designed to be noticed. The aesthetic quality is palpable. The 42nd Street Art Project in Manhattan is a similar enterprise. Here the hoardings of disused cinemas and massage parlours are used to display messages which are calculated to jar with the routine consumerism of the streets (see photographs opposite). Social criticism about the ugliness of urban-industrial life is targeted at mass consumption experience when alienation from others and commodification seem precisely to be most 'normal'. As you buy a soda on your way to Macy's you read that 'YOU ARE TRAPPED ON THE EARTH SO YOU WILL EXPLODE'; or 'MEN DON'T PROTECT YOU ANYMORE'. This is shopping with attitude, *flânerie* with politically correct style.

Arts Project, New York City, 1993

These projects can, of course, be criticized for producing a designer image of the homeless and injustice. Just as we have designer jeans, designer watches, we have designer poor and designer oppressed. However, this criticism is short-sighted. What it ignores is the determination of these artists not to treat the homeless or the oppressed in a stereotypical way. Wodiczko's vehicles are designed with the assistance of homeless people. They tell him what their requirements are, what will and will not work and what looks good. This stress on participation and pleasure contrasts sharply with how 'the leisure poor' are usually represented in leisure studies. For example, the cultural studies tradition tends to treat aesthetics as a compartment of resistance. Questions of fashion, music, art and attitude are read in terms of strategies of struggle. The density and mobility of urban life are examined – almost exclusively – in political terms. Insufficient seriousness is placed on the pleasures of seeing and being seen, mixing and wanting to stand apart. The Frankfurt School reading of aesthetics and leisure is, likewise, highly politicized. It tends to present the subjects of beauty and attraction in mass culture as effects of the culture industry. Underpinning this reading is a schema of high and low art which, although rarely stated with candour, colours judgements about all aesthetic questions. Hence, Adorno's notorious hatred of jazz: its delight in improvisation, participation and its general sense of *élan* simply conflicted with his sense of the serious purpose of real art.[12]

Against these positions, many writers on postmodernism hold that aesthetics necessarily carries an ethical dimension. In social conditions where 'reality' is assessed in terms of symbol and image, personal or institutional appearance is the most immediate point of social communication. Bauman (1992: 202–3) characterizes postmodernism as a general move from 'heteronomous control to self-determination'. By this he means a shift from behaviour governed by established social rituals and mores (stemming from class, race, status and gender) to self-governing behaviour. Judgements about 'normal' and 'bizarre' lifestyles and appearances cease to be matters of conformity and become matters of contestation. The celebration or denigration of forms of leisure is no longer automatic but becomes a question of dialogue, bargaining and negotiation. Bauman associates this with the aestheticization of everyday life because self-government involves 'self-monitoring, self-reflection and self-evaluation'. In effect his analysis yokes postmodernity with the enlargement of ethical consciousness. As he puts it:

> In the postmodern context agents are constantly faced with moral issues and obliged to choose between equally well founded (or equally unfounded) ethical precepts. The choice always means the assumption of responsibility, and for this reason bears the character of a moral act. Under the postmodern condition, the agent is perforce not just an actor and decision-maker, but a *moral subject*. The performance of life-functions demands also that the agent be a morally *competent* subject. (Bauman, 1992: 203; emphasis his)

Bauman's analysis can be faulted on two counts. First, he assumes that postmodernity universalizes access to ethical education and relevant information streams. By avoiding the problem of material inequality he implies that actors operate at the same ethical level. Yet since his discussion of post-modernity makes no provision for equalizing economic and cultural capital, this implication is implausible. Second, he envisages integrated moral actors as the norm under postmodernity. This runs counter to the argument made by Baudrillard (1983a, b, 1990), Kroker and Cook (1986) and Jameson (1991) that postmodernity proliferates super-mobility, unpredictable 'multiphrenic intensities' and profoundly *dis*integrated actors. Nevertheless, Bauman is surely right to emphasize that in a sign-dominated society ethics is integral to aesthetics. Ordinarily, social judgements on ethical behaviour do not derive from hours spent in the debating chamber or huddled over the appropriate philosophical works in the library. Rather they derive from the appearance of things, the chain of images that circulate in private and public spaces of met-ropolitan society. Moreover, the propensity of actors to believe that something is right and good is intimately connected with judgements of beauty. This is obviously objectionable to moralists since it suggests that postmodernity reduces ethical questions to matters of marketing, packaging and appearance. Yet this is precisely the case that Baudrillard, Kroker and Cook and Jameson make when they insist on the transparency and depthlessness of postmoder-nity. It is not so much that nothing is right or wrong any more but rather that everything – from shopping in a supermarket to reading a book – has an eth-ical dimension.

By stretching the ethical realm to cover everything in life postmodernity violates its depth and density. Unable to embrace the absolutism of mod-ernist thought or to believe in the transcendence of current conditions, the postmodernist falls back on the liberal ironism espoused by Rorty (1989) and others. Liberal ironism is a type of ethical conduct which recognizes itself to be contingent upon the circumstances of time, place and vocabulary. It is not inconsistent with caring about others or believing in self-improvement. Rorty makes it clear that a concern to alleviate suffering and enhance the condi-tions of life are perfectly valid responses of liberal ironism. However, what distinguishes it from other forms of ethical conduct is the insistence that one's own view of what suffering entails is not necessarily identical with the view of those who suffer. Most of us – certainly in the economically devel-oped societies – do not know what it is to be leisure rich or leisure poor. If we identify the leisure poor as enduring a state of suffering or the leisure rich as basking in a state of satisfaction it is because we choose to do so. The prac-tical part of Rorty's philosophy is that we should open ourselves up imaginatively to those that we instinctively think of as 'them' – whether 'they' be rich or poor.

Conclusion: Profiles of Postmodernism

It is always tricky to reach conclusions about a social transformation which is, so to speak, in mid-flight. Postmodernism really only took off as a subject of debate in social thought in the 1980s.[13] In the field of leisure the subject is only just starting to be explored. Small wonder then that modernist critics castigate postmodernist arguments for being unsubstantiated and overblown (Callinicos 1989; Norris 1990; Allison 1994). We are in the realm of speculation and possibility – a realm which modernism has always mistrusted because it lacks the clear, unambiguous lines of managerialist theory. However, it is important not to permit modernist indignation to stifle the realization that postmodernism sprang from the vivid failure of modernist thought to manage order or implement change by the lights of its own ambitions. As Bauman (1993: 3) points out, modernist thought routinely set itself targets which it could not reach. With regard to leisure it determined free time as the arena *par excellence* of authenticity. In the ideal of erotic love it expressed both its most concentrated and unrealistic target of achievement in the so-called 'free time spectrum'. Erotic love was, as it were, one of the treasures of the kingdom of leisure. It changed one in fundamental, unparalleled ways. According to Foucault (1981), it was believed to provide a route to the hidden inner world of authentic feeling and need. As Max Weber, no less, expressed it:

> the erotic relation seems to offer the unsurpassable peak of the request for love in the direct fusion of souls of one to another. The boundless giving of oneself is as radical as possible in opposition to all functionality, rationality and generality. It is displayed here as the unique meaning which one creature in his irrationality has for another, and only for this specific other. (Weber, quoted in Gane 1993: 171)

This is a taxing doctrine of erotic love. As Gane (1993: 156–72) demonstrates in detail, Weber signally failed to live up to it in his own erotic life, which was peppered with agonizing and disruptive acts of adultery. But more generally, cannot one see in the exclusivity of the doctrine the self-punishing, self-denying, unrealistic strand which runs through modernist thought? For those who fail to find this 'unsurpassable peak' in a 'specific other', or those who find 'unique meaning' in many others, experience feelings of unworthiness, guilt or self-reproach. Their lives are blighted by the sense of having failed themselves and others, the sense of being incomplete and abnormal. But then again, Weber is careful to mark this doctrine as 'irrational'. As Benjamin (1955) argued, the modern world perpetuates standardization, repetition and mechanically reproduced commodities which render 'the absolutely unique' object anomalous. Our quest for the unique is measured out in a series of encounters with the standardized object. The dissatisfaction that we accumulate from the quest is a result of the unrealistic targets set by modernism rather than the deficiencies of personality or circumstance. Modernity sets us idealized targets of self-disclosure, interpersonal feeling and erotic fulfilment which are achieved, at best perhaps, only intermittently.

This is perhaps what Bauman (1993: 32) means when he defines postmodernity as 'modernity without illusions'. For him, postmodernity carries with it the possibility of the general recognition of certain pretences as false and certain objectives not only as unattainable, but also as undesirable. The result is a more tolerant, richer civil society. Within the field of leisure studies what are the key modernist pretences and objectives which are undermined by postmodernism? Five points need to be made and it is perhaps most helpful to list them in a fairly formal way.

(1) Postmodernism goes some way towards correcting the modernist conviction that leisure is segmented from the rest of life as a charmed realm of self-fulfilment and life-satisfaction. With this the modernist convention of treating work as the central life interest of 'normal' people and the foundation of society is also challenged. Instead it maintains that the modernist practice of polarizing work and leisure is simply insupportable. Leisure experience is perfectly compatible with the office or the shop floor; and the experience of routine and confinement which is often associated with paid labour is quite consistent with many ordinary features of leisure experience. The symbolic role of 'work' and 'leisure' in structuring identity, association and practice is therefore directly confronted. Instead of treating the categories of work and leisure as centred on inflexible meanings, the flexibility and mobility of these categories are emphasized.

(2) Postmodernism reverses the tendency in modernist thought to oppose authentic experience with inauthentic experience and to privilege the former. By throwing the symbolic, processed character of social experience into sharp relief, postmodernism problematizes the realm of the authentic. In modernist leisure planning the commitment to active leisure management founded upon hard facts as opposed to the so-called empty signs of postmodernism is conventionally presented as evidence of the moral superiority of modernist practice over postmodern analysis. Postmodernist writers are conveniently branded as 'nihilists' and 'dreamers' who are totally out of touch with the real world. But this suggests a strategic distance of modernist leisure planning from the sign-world. Nothing could be more misleading. Signs and symbols are the common currency of modernist leisure planning.

If one were asked to cite an example of the generality of the empty sign in modernist leisure planning in the UK today, one could do no better than refer to the non-appearance of the disused Battersea power station. The scheme was announced in 1988. It was launched with the participation of the then Prime Minister, Margaret Thatcher, who even fired a laser gun from the top of the power station at the launch party to start work on the scheme. Planned by the same group that controls the UK's largest theme park, Alton Towers, the Battersea project was envisaged as 'an entertainment palace without parallel in the world'. Five floors, each fashioned to represent international landscapes, were planned, thus enabling customers to 'visit' China or take a voyage beneath the ocean without ever leaving South London. A high-speed transport link – the Battersea Bullet – was announced to transport 7,000 people per hour from Victoria station to a purpose built on-site terminal. The complex was due to be opened on 21 May 1990 at 2.30 p.m. precisely.[14] At the time of writing, Battersea power station stands virtually derelict. The London press regularly carries worried articles fretting that the listed building is in danger of permanent structural damage and even collapse. South London's 'entertainment palace without parallel in the world' is in reality a gloomy, rain-drenched façade, frequented only by pigeons and river-rats, with no firm prospect of being built.

For many critics the Battersea project exposes the feel-good, expansionist philosophy of the Thatcher–Reagan years. But of more importance for present purposes is the particularly clear illustration of the interweaving of signs with modernist leisure planning that it provides. For all practical purposes the Battersea leisure project only exists as an empty sign. Not that this interweaving between plan and sign is unique to the Battersea project. On the contrary, it is a general characteristic of Modernist leisure planning. At least since the cheerful hucksterism of the leisure entrepreneur P.T. Barnum in the nineteenth century,[15] the leisure industry has enticed customers with signs of amazing experiences and astonishing spectacles. The modernist leisure industry routinely manufactures signs of escape, pleasure and fulfilment as part of its marketing strategies. Far from being totally out of touch with the real world, postmodernist discussions of simulation and hyperreality are directly relevant to modernist planning strategies and the 'ordinary', 'normal' experiences of leisure in contemporary society.

(3) Postmodernism outflanks the notion of the integrated self which underpins modernist thought. It presents the self as a fissile entity which presents in different ways in different social settings. Modernism regarded the development of the self in strictly evolutionary terms. Childhood, adolescence, youth, middle age and old age are seen as stages on the road to maturity. Postmodernism presents the development of the self as a mix of continuous and discontinuous tendencies. Thus the preoccupations of adolescence are not seen as necessarily ending when one reaches middle age just as in old age the individual may cultivate many youthful characteristics. No correlation is recognized between age and maturity. Postmodernism therefore disrupts the modernist framework of the life-cycle which is one of the key grids for ordering modernist propositions about leisure conduct.

(4) Postmodernism treats the expansion of identity politics and the emergence of critical pluralism in civil society not as temporary aberrations but as the inevitable consequences of the circulation, production and consumption processes in advanced society. The tendency to accelerate the pace of life through an increase in the density and velocity of circulation of bodies, information, commodities and spectacles destabilizes the modernist order of homogenized categories of social life. The barriers between home and abroad, public and private life, work and leisure, childhood and old age, male roles and female roles, white and ethnic cultures cease to be treated as given 'facts' of life. Instead there is more emphasis on ambivalence, variability, flexibility and individualism. The fulcrum of politics shifts from modernist categories of class, race and gender to the more fragmented, diversified, contingent categories of gay and lesbian issues, eco-feminists, animal rights campaigners, ethnic subcultures, the unborn and the physically and mentally challenged.

(5) Postmodernism destabilizes the elitist authority structure of modernity. By emphasizing change, contingency, diversity and flexibility it disrupts the division between providers and users, experts and laypersons, legislators and

the public. Modernist criticism has focused on the *anomic* consequences of this tendency. It accuses postmodernism of seeking to subvert the authority of the established social leaders in society – politicians, professionals, civil servants, managers – and so to plunge society into an unmanageable state of chaos. But this ignores two things. First, the condition of *anomaly* which marginalized people recognize in the modernist order where their voices are systematically devalued or stifled. While this condition can produce protest among the marginalized it more typically ends in a demoralizing and demotivating sense of powerlessness and helplessness in the face of an apparently monotonous, impassive, unchangeable order of things. Second, the thrust of postmodernist criticism is directed not towards denying power but towards empowerment. Postmodernism aims to widen the circle of discussion, opinions and negotiation, to emancipate voices which have been suppressed or confined to the borderlines of society. Within the field of leisure this means abandoning the donatory culture of leisure policy which divides people into providers and users and transforming leisure-users into the key resource of management and strategy. Instead of fomenting nihilism, as modernist critics have argued, postmodernism operates to extend co-operation and participation. By emphasizing the fragmentary, the discontinuous, the contingent, the formless and the unfinished in human experience, postmodernism avoids the constraining absolutism of modernist politics.

If one should be wary of reaching conclusions about a social process which is still in mid-flight, one should be equally wary of reading the five points listed above as a categoric endorsement for every aspect of postmodernist thought. I have extracted here only what I take to be the most compelling positive features of postmodernism. I have done so because, not least in the fields of leisure studies and cultural studies, there is a tendency for modernist critics to caricature postmodernism as simply an adolescent adventure in social analysis. But I share the worries of modernist critics about the apocalyptic, unsupported and arrogant tone that one finds in much postmodernist writing. The trajectory of my discussion in this book has moved from considering capitalism, to modernity, to postmodernity. However, the reader should not assume that it follows from this that I am positing an evolutionary curve which climaxes in fully-fledged postmodernity. If the impetus of postmodernism is towards more co-operation and participation, there are many modernist obstacles in place to derail this movement, and many unanticipated consequences which might ambush its progress.

For all that, it is worth taking the postmodernist arguments of diversity, change, fragmentation, discontinuity, simulation and hyperreality seriously and not – in the manner of the most stuffy modernist critics – as a collection of irrelevant side-issues. Capitalism and modernity can be twinned together in their headlong dash for progressive order and stability and the orchestrated confinement, repression, anomaly and irrationality which this has brought in its wake. By exposing the partiality of capitalist and modernist notions of progressive order and stability, postmodernism creates the space to question social interaction at a truly elementary level – asking what being, identity, motive, collectivity, meaning, practice, pleasure, really mean – without kow-towing to the conventions of radical modernist thought. It places us beyond the epoch of the integrated, triumphant self and the utopia of the emancipated universal subject. This spot *may* be the road to nowhere; or it may afford new vantage to perceive society and leisure in more accurate ways. Either way it is rash of modernist critics to renounce postmodernism as a matter of no consequence.

9

CONCLUSION: *HOMO FABER/ HOMO LUDENS*

Is leisure an individual and societal need? It may seem strange to pose this question in the final chapter of the book. The preceding chapters have discussed leisure in capitalism, modernity and postmodernity. They show significant variations in leisure forms, but they also suggest that leisure is a consistent feature of life in these human gatherings. In other words they apparently indicate that leisure is something that human beings need just as they need food, shelter, warmth, security and production. At the same time our discussion of leisure under capitalism and modernity suggests that leisure is seen as quite low down on the scale of essential social values. Under these cultures a donatory view of leisure is maintained. That is, leisure is regarded as something to be given as a reward to the individual and society or withheld as a punishment or as a way of controlling social behaviour. Hence, public leisure provision has traditionally been seen as a soft target in public expenditure reviews (Henry 1993).

However, the subordination of leisure under capitalism and modernity exists in some tension with social theories of human needs. For example, Habermas (1971, 1973) argues that all human gatherings can be analysed in terms of two transcendent societal needs: work and communication. Work, or, in Habermas' term, 'purposive rational action', is oriented to the expansion of technical control over nature. It is the precondition for human emancipation from material wants. Communication refers to language systems and social rules. It includes the social institutions in which these systems and rules are formally embodied and practically reproduced: the family, mass media, leisure, sport, etc. Communication, maintains Habermas, is a need which is equal to work since it equips human beings with the personality structures and generalized norms to achieve mutual consensus.

An important part of Habermas' argument is the proposition that both work and communication needs are systematically distorted under late capitalism. Thus, the political and economic requirements of capitalism presuppose the dehumanization of workers by treating them as mere factors of production. Managerial coercion and deskilling cap the creative potential of workers and prevent them from experiencing labour as an emancipatory activity. At the same time, communication is distorted by the various commodification processes perpetuated by the culture industry. Non-work time is colonized by distraction activities, organized manipulation and the brutalization of human emotions. For Habermas, the basic human needs of work and communication are blocked by the mechanics of the capitalist power system. The solution, he argues, is to empower the workers through education and economic resources and to de-toxify the communication channels of society by the application of principles which guarantee maximum access and participation. His concept of the 'ideal speech situation' clarifies his view of what constitutes a society in which the needs of work and communication are truly emancipated. However, before coming to that, I want to probe more deeply into the place of leisure in the schema of human needs.

Basic Individual Needs and Basic Institutions

Following Habermas, Doyal and Gough (1984) have elaborated a theory of human needs. They propose that human beings have *basic individual needs* and that all societies face the question of supplying these needs. By the term *basic individual needs* the authors (1984: 10) understand 'those goals which must be achieved if any individual is to achieve any other goal – however idiosyncratic or culturally specific those other goals are'. Two general pairs of needs are identified: survival/health and autonomy/learning. The first pair is more or less self-explanatory. All individuals possess the need to survive and to maintain good health. The second pairing is slightly more complicated. According to Doyal and Gough, recognition of oneself as a distinct and separate person – an individuated being – is a basic personal need. Hand-in-hand with this is the recognition that the individual has the capacity to grow and develop through learning and education. Basic individual needs, continue the authors, are necessarily realized in a social context. For no individual is capable of growing up and existing alone. Since it is in the interest of society to produce the survival of its members and to ensure their good health, autonomy and growth through learning, society has evolved basic institutions for the achievement of individual needs. Doyal and Gough refer to these as *societal needs* and they distinguish four general categories:

(1) *Production*. This refers to the need of all societies to create the material prerequisites of survival, health and individuation. It encompasses technological and cultural institutions designed to extract use and value from nature as well as the total relations of exchange, distribution and consumption. Industrial, business, technical, administrative and scientific institutions are all examples.
(2) *Reproduction*. This refers to the need to ensure the biological reproduction, care and socialization of the members of society. The management of this need is associated with the development of specific family, kinship and formal care institutions.
(3) *Communication*. This refers to the need to equip members of society with an understanding of the techniques and rules which make orderly collective life possible. Although the authors do not mention it, play and leisure are two of a primary set of institutions through which individuals are

formally and informally socialized into the rules and mores of collective life. Examples include institutions of education (schools/universities), the mass media, sport and leisure.

(4) *Political authority*. This refers to the societal need to achieve a legislative and executive moral and physical force in collective life which will be universally recognized as ultimate, binding and legitimate. This force normally operates by persuasion and consent but it does have the right to formulate the law and other sanctions to regulate behaviour. Examples include the judiciary, the police and the armed forces.

Again, following Habermas, Doyal and Gough contend that there is a deep propensity in human beings to struggle for the optimization of basic individual needs. However, various social conditions are identified as hindering this propensity. Among the most important ones listed by the authors are class and gender inequality, poor communication networks, uneven provision of education and the absence of genuine participatory structures in the decision-making process. The authors call for a politics of liberation to reconcile basic individual needs with societal needs.[1] It is not necessary to go into the details of this politics here. What needs to be stressed at this stage of the discussion is that Doyal and Gough's theory of human needs suggests that leisure is an essential social institutional requirement for the fulfilment of basic individual needs. A society with no leisure provision – or one with very little leisure – is unlikely to achieve its production and reproduction requirements or to equip its members with the communicational competence and legitimate political structures necessary to accomplish the satisfaction of basic individual needs.

However, Doyal and Gough's theory stops well short of identifying leisure as a basic individual or social need. Rather, it is implicitly theorized as an institutional adjunct of the societal needs for production, reproduction and communication. That is, leisure is posited as one institutional means which enables individuals to satisfy their basic individual needs for survival, health, autonomy and learning. The point may appear to be somewhat pedantic. Actually it is a matter of real substance. For what follows from it is the proposition that leisure is a relatively elastic feature of human gatherings. That is, at the level of societal needs, the amount of resources devoted to leisure are flexible and variable. In contrast, the resources devoted to production, reproduction, communication and political authority are relatively inelastic.

This line of argument would appear to verify the subordinate position which has conventionally been assigned to leisure in social thought. However, there are problems with the way in which Habermas and Doyal and Gough define and use the concept of need. Four points must be made. In the first place, the taxonomies proposed by the authors identify need too closely with rational instrumentality. That is, existence is presented in Cartesian terms as the struggle of mind over the body and nature. What this marginalizes is the emotional, allegorical and irrational content of everyday life. For example, much ordinary leisure experience such as day-dreaming, fantasy-work, killing time, escape activity and *flânerie* cannot be satisfactorily explained by the Cartesian model. In this sense the theories of need proposed by Habermas and Doyal and Gough provide a distorted, partial view of human capacities and experience.

The second point is that Habermas and Doyal and Gough simply provide a description of human need. They fail to show how need is socially constructed and developed. As Turner (1984: 27) notes, a general problem shared by most theories of human need is that their propositions are, in the final analysis, banal. For example, to describe human beings *à la* Habermas as driven by the needs to work and communicate is merely a truism. What is missing is a convincing theory of power to explain how needs are socially mediated and reproduced. Habermas, Doyal and Gough do of course suggest that basic human needs are distorted by the capitalist power system. But there are problems with their arguments of how distortion operates and how it can be transcended. This brings me to my third point.

It is precisely in the area of emancipatory politics that the theories of need propounded by Habermas and Doyal and Gough break down. The authors describe human needs under capitalism as 'mutilated' and 'distorted'. Habermas (1979: 111–17) resorts to the notoriously problematic concept of the 'ideal speech situation' to illustrate how the real standards of work and communication under capitalism fall short of what is ideally possible. He argues that the prerequisites of 'ideal speech' are as follows:

(1) *Technical understanding.* That is, social actors should possess an accurate understanding of the technical issues involved in determining choices and managing actions.
(2) *Procedural understanding.* That is, social actors should possess the relevant methodological skills to pursue courses of action with the utmost efficiency.
(3) *Participatory competence.* That is, social actors should operate in a social context which guarantees full and open participation in decision-making processes.

In all three particulars Habermas judges capitalism to be deficient. The remedy, he suggests, is the extension of rights of education, the redistribution of economic wealth and the enforcement of genuine conditions of democracy. However, as Doyal and Gough (1984: 26) themselves acknowledge, these are old demands which, since the Enlightenment, have never been fully realized. By omitting to explain why present conditions provide a superior window of opportunity and failing to specify a compelling political strategy to achieve the aims of the ideal speech situation, Habermas is spurned for his alleged naïvety and utopianism. Yet in a peculiar act of auto-criticism Doyal and Gough (1984: 32–3) admit that their own efforts to translate their theory of needs into a convincing emancipatory politics scarcely get much further than Habermas. In chastising their own theoretical efforts, they draw attention to the 'highly abstract' and 'self-indulgent' character of their discussion of basic individual needs when set against the immediate 'tactical' and 'pragmatic' questions facing those who wish to operationalize basic individual needs; and they question if they really have understood the 'structural constraints' imposed by 'existing monopolies of power'. In short, Doyal and Gough raise the doubt that their project of the 'universal liberation' of human need is over-idealistic. Of course it does not follow from this that idealism and emancipatory politics have no place in studying leisure. Rather it emphasizes the necessity not to exaggerate what the state and education can accomplish in leisure provision and practice.

The fourth point refers back to the taxonomies of need proposed by Habermas and Doyal and Gough. The concept of 'basic human needs' is essentialist in character. It fails to encompass the capacity of humans to change needs through the ordinary processes of human action. In so far as a theory of basic human needs logically implies a basic political system to promote or protect human needs, there is obvious room for repression. This is certainly implicit in the authors' quite conventional treatment of leisure. Although couched in a language of emancipation their theories of need reinforce a *productivist* view of society which prioritizes the need to work over all other needs. At this juncture, it might be helpful to examine the productivist case in more detail. A good starting point is to examine two related questions. What do productivists mean by the need for work? And how do they see this need connecting up with leisure?

The Need to Work

In an interesting and important discussion Sayers (1987) identifies three basic human needs which work fulfils:

(1) *Activity*. Work satisfies the human need to be active. Individuals who are inactive are generally unhappy and frustrated.
(2) *Production*. Humans have an integral 'species need' to shape the external world. Work is the means through which we mould our environment and ourselves.
(3) *Sociality*. Work enables us to develop our social relations. Through it we develop a sense of identity and status and it increases our contacts with others.

To some extent Sayers' identification of work as a basic human need is polemical. He is concerned to rebut the argument made by 'leisure society' theorists that real freedom lies in leisure not work. He contends that radical politics which is founded in the objective of 'liberation from work' misunderstands human nature. It mistakenly presents work as a false and unnatural compulsion which will disappear when capitalism is dismantled. Against this Sayers maintains that work is an inalienable human need. Even in societies in which leisure is given a higher profile in the organization of everyday life there will be an acute need to work.

Interestingly Sayers (1987: 23) defines leisure as a basic human need. We need time off work for rest, relaxation and to pursue interests and capacities which are not fulfilled in work. However, he is careful to avoid holding that leisure needs are equal to work needs. Instead he regards leisure as the necessary, but lesser, 'complement' to work. The distinction is important because Sayers contends that the active, creative and disciplined traits of human behaviour spring from the realm of production or, to put it differently, from the experience of work. He uses two arguments to support the contention. In the first place he submits that the need for 'active' and 'positive' non-work activities is a consequence of the development of the forces of production. Pre-industrial society, he continues, possessed non-work time, but it tended to be filled with 'desultory', 'vacant' or 'limited' activity. 'The extensive, active, free and creative use of non-work time by working people', writes Sayers (1987: 23), 'is a development of modern industrial society.' This reading of pre-industrial leisure and the well-spring of creative and active conduct is controversial and I shall come to some of the criticisms that can be levelled against it in due course.

The second argument used by Sayers is that individuals who have a surplus of non-work time are typically unhappy and frustrated. He asserts that the experience of being jobless is 'profoundly demoralizing and unfulfilling' (1987: 21). Unemployment, Sayers argues, produces these psychological traits in an acute form. However, he maintains that they are also present in the case of retired people and women engaged solely in housework. Sayers approvingly quotes the findings of the social psychologist Marie Jahoda (1982) that people without work have difficulty in 'creating their own time structure', 'sharing goals and purposes with others' and maintaining active leisure pursuits.

Sayers' conclusion is that the socialist transformation of society requires the *extension* of work opportunities and the *enlargement* of work experience. Although no detailed policies are described, it is clear that he envisages putting the unemployed back to work and creating the conditions for the free, full and co-operative development of human capacities in the workplace. As with Marx, the elimination of the capitalist class is presented as placing the management of society in the hands of the 'associated producers'. In these conditions, Sayers contends, the alienation that derives from the coercive work routines of capitalism will disappear. At the same time the expansion of the leisure society is dismissed as the pursuit of folly. For Sayers, more leisure will actually lead to more unhappiness. The logical corollary of this position is that socialism requires a political apparatus to ensure that leisure is contained. However, Sayers does not explore this point in any theoretical or practical detail.

As Sayers (1987: 20) somewhat fastidiously points out, productivism is currently a rather unfashionable social philosophy. Essentially it identifies work as the seat of personal creativity, satisfaction and growth. Leisure is defined as a secondary sphere of life. One important implication of productivism is that full employment is seen as the essential moral precondition of 'the good society'. What makes this a particularly unfashionable position at the present time is that policies of full employment are now widely seen as unrealistic. Automation, computerization and other technological changes have led to an absolute fall in the work-time requirement. Moreover, socialist critics, like

André Gorz (1980), have developed powerful cases that true socialists should not lament this reduction in work time. Gorz emphasizes the dehumanizing effects of work under capitalism and points to leisure as the realm of real creativity and personal growth. In his view only a society which has abolished the need for work will succeed in creating the conditions for the free and full development of all individuals.

Sayers (1987: 24) dismisses Gorz's position as phoney libertarianism and he deplores the alleged cynicism of state policies which tolerate mass unemployment. He insists that socialism must be uncompromising in its insistence that work belongs to 'the realm of necessity' and devise realistic policies of work extension and job enlargement.

Is Sayers right? The productivist case stands or falls on the propositions regarding the character of pre-industrial leisure and the attributions of activity, productivity and sociality with work experience. In none of these particulars is the productivist case beyond criticism. To take the question of pre-industrial leisure first, there is a wealth of historical evidence to suggest that leisure activity was personally meaningful, enriching and socially disciplined. For example, carnival in the Middle Ages was a vital element in popular culture providing enjoyment and the release of tensions and harnessing and developing an extraordinary repertoire of symbols and rituals in the regeneration of sociality (Burke 1978; Bakhtin 1984; Stallybrass and White 1986). Similarly O'Loughlin (1978), writing on the Homeric, Roman and Christian traditions of leisure, supplies countless examples of the central institutionalized importance of leisure activity in moral remaking and civic integration. Furthermore, studies of aristocratic recreation in the sixteenth and seventeenth centuries and the 'grand tour' in the eighteenth century demonstrate that leisure activity was closely identified with personal growth, physical fitness and moral improvement (Veblen 1925; Vale 1977; Brailsford 1991; Black 1992). Industrialization certainly changed the form and content of many leisure activities. However, it is quite wrong to present it merely in discontinuous terms as a total break or rupture with the leisure of the pre-industrial past.

Turning now to the second productivist proposition. Unquestionably, there is a strong association in contemporary culture between work and creative, social and enriching experience. However, these characteristics are hardly exclusive to work experience. Indeed, as Sayers (1987: 18–21) notes, for many, perhaps the majority, work signally fails to deliver positive experience. For these individuals, as Gorz (1980) indicates, leisure is the creative and enriching area *nonpareil* in everyday life. Work is simply a means to securing the end of non-work time.

However, whereas Gorz (1980) calls for policies for abolishing work and the enriching of leisure through education and public provision, Sayers (1987: 18–21) continues to make the productivist demand for the 'right to work' and imaginative policies to eliminate alienation from the workplace. One might observe that productivism wants to have its cake and eat it. On the one hand, it claims that industrialization has increased the capacities of the workers for active, enriching pursuits. But against this it insists that the active, enriching pursuits which the workers have developed in their leisure time are necessarily subordinate to what occurs in the workplace. It is a strange argument to make, especially in the context of the deskilling of the work process identified by Braverman (1974) and others. To be sure, as we saw earlier (pp. 143–4), there are good grounds for arguing that industrial society in the postwar years has witnessed a trade-off between the deskilling of the worker through rationalization processes in the workplace and the reskilling of the worker through new communication activities in consumer culture.

As paid work becomes more routinized and mechanical, leisure becomes the axis for the development of creativity and personal enrichment. For example, Aronowitz (1985: 27–8) cites the experience of Brooklyn longshoremen who have suffered the relegation of paid work to the 'margins' of their existence. Productivist analysis would have us believe that the experience of long-term unemployment for these men is intensified social isolation, feelings of worthlessness and pointlessness and time-killing 'free time' activity such as watching TV or drinking in bars. Doubtless, all of these behavioural traits can be found in these communities if one looks for them. However, they are also balanced and to some extent surpassed by the enlargement of social activities and skills. Thus, workers have found more time to be involved with their wives in housework and child-rearing, voluntary sport and fitness activities and greater participation in the community. In this case, contrary to productivist assumptions, prolonged non-work experience did not in any automatic sense mean the end of self-esteem or the disintegration of the working-class community. Wheelock's (1990) study of house-husbands in the north of England produced similar findings.

Both Aronowitz and Wheelock note the importance of assured income plans in the form of unemployment pay, child support and national insurance entitlements in providing the unemployed with a basic level of subsistence. These studies suggest that the cultural values surrounding family life, the community and leisure are *more* important than the values derived from regular employment in sustaining the individual's sense of personal worth and growth.[2] And further, that a society which reduces the need for work guarantees subsistence levels and improves the opportunities for leisure, education and participatory experience enlarges social skills and contributes to the general enrichment of all. Of course, neither Aronowitz nor Wheelock is arguing for deliberate policies of mass unemployment. Rather their work questions the productivist emphasis on the necessary centrality of work in ensuring personal health and social order. By extension, it suggests that socialists need to rethink work and leisure in the context of the labour-saving possibilities associated with new technologies and administrative systems of production.

In general, the productivist case may be criticized for wrongly prioritizing production over culture. It has presented the experience of work as the seat of personal development. It has stubbornly dismissed as 'fashionable' the arguments of researchers like Gorz (1980) and Willis (1990: 15) that leisure is now the vital area of self-expression and real and symbolic personal growth in

society. Instead it has intensified calls for Keynesian policies to 'put the unemployed back to work'. By positing work not simply as one of a shifting and
malleable configuration of human needs, but as the true 'premise of human
existence', the productivist case produces a limited and dismissive view of the
potential for personal and social enrichment through leisure forms.

Homo Faber: The 'Labour Metaphysic'

Perhaps Wright Mills got it right when he complained that socialism is hood-
winked by the 'labour metaphysic' (quoted by Aronowitz 1985: 19). Certainly,
it is characterized by a horror of free time. As Aronowitz (1985: 39) observes,
the traditional response of organized labour to unemployment and the growth
of free time is not to plan for leisure but to defend and, wherever possible,
extend the right to work. Aronowitz writes of the 'introjection' of the work
ethic and the capacity of workers to extract more value from the workplace by
'stealing' time on the job for themselves and their compulsion to 'appear to be
busy' in the sight of the employer when they are actually 'doing nothing'.[3] For
Aronowitz this is socially divisive and personally demeaning. For in defending
one's own work one limits the work opportunities for the unemployed; and in
killing time at work one engages in wasteful 'performance' activity instead of
genuinely creative and productive work activity.

   All of this is a world away from the meaning of work in pre-industrial society. Applebaum's (1992) monumental study of ancient, medieval and modern
concepts of work shows that pre-industrial meanings of work were closely
interwoven with nature and culture. There was no clock-watching or separation of the working day from the rest of life. Rather work and leisure were
intertwined and operated as the general process of collective making and
remaking. Although frustration and dissatisfaction are an obvious and prominent feature of pre-industrial life, Applebaum's study suggests that the balance
between the needs for work and for leisure was in greater harmony than it is
today. This argument is generally reinforced in the historical literature (see, for
example, Pirenne 1936; Bloch 1962; Thompson 1967).

   However, Stedman-Jones (1977) and Sayers (1987: 23) complain that it is a
common fault in the literature to romanticize work experience in pre-industrial
society by painting it as a pastoral idyll. This is a legitimate criticism. But it
does not absolve productivist writers from the charge that they exaggerate
the effect of industrialization in enlarging the need for work and expanding
creativity and sociality. It was only with Locke that labour was recognized as
the source of all property. It was left to Smith and Marx respectively to claim
that it was the source of all 'wealth' and 'value'. Classical political economy
consistently overexaggerated the economic need for work and underestimated
other human needs. Industrialization may have vastly increased productivity
but it also atomized the worker, commodified work activity, alienated work
from leisure and fetishized 'labour' as the key to existence. It wrecked the traditional balance between personal development and the cohesion of the

community. It magnified the tendencies in society towards chronic *anomie*, fragmentation and restlessness.

Leisure was presented as an oasis of release and freedom. However, this condition always existed more as an ideal than a reality. Industrialization polluted leisure with a constant time-consciousness and guilt about activity which was not directly productive. It required that individuals did not merely enjoy free time but extracted value from it by adding to personal growth. Divorced from the deep values and mores of traditional communities, the atomized individual began to learn to look to leisure as the reward for work. In this sense leisure became enmeshed in general market activity.

Homo faber[4] began to pursue leisure activity as extending personal market capacity. The rational recreationists devised leisure offensives on idleness and wasteful leisure practice. Leisure became a form of rational purposive activity which complemented work. Because work was regarded as the fundamental human need and the centre of social existence, communication, play and sociality were marginalized, thus exacerbating the individual's sense of homelessness. Leisure became an artificial realm of freedom in which the pursuit of escape routinely ended in anti-climax and where fantasy and illusion flourished. It was therefore no accident that leisure practice under modernity became ever more dominated by the dreamworld of advertising. Escape and freedom became qualities of experience that could only be realized through images. The fantasy world of *homo faber* was necessarily over-heated and distorted because the rewards of satisfaction, fulfilment, excitement and release that leisure was meant to provide were never more than gestural. It was not that people failed to experience these qualities in leisure. Rather they experienced them in a momentary, fragmented form which only emphasized the illusory character of 'authentic' escape under modernity.

Homo Ludens

The discussions of the need to work in Habermas (1971, 1973) and Doyal and Gough (1984) bind it closely to the concepts of 'rationality' and 'culture'. Work and communication are identified as the primary channels through which cultural life is made and developed. They are regarded as the twin premises of human existence because no form of human existence is rationally conceivable without them. Yet there is one human need which is left out of these accounts and which cannot be subsumed under work and communication. It is also directly relevant to our understanding of leisure and the relation of leisure to the rest of society. This is the need of play. In his classic study of play the great Dutch historian Johan Huizinga (1947) argued that culture is *sub specie ludi*, that is, play precedes culture. For Huizinga it must therefore be recognized as the true first premise of human existence. In his view, ritual, poetry, music, dancing, battle knowledge, wisdom and philosophy all derive from play (1947: 173).

Furthermore, Huizinga (1947: 4) counters rational theories of human need by insisting that play is often irrational. This stress on the irrational element in human need opens up a different line of thinking about need and society. It is certainly a line which is neglected by Habermas and his followers. Huizinga's argument is richly illustrated with evidence from biology, history, psychology and sociology. However, in essence he identifies four characteristics of play and relates them to the development of culture and civilization:

(1) *Freedom*. Whereas much leisure performs a cultural function by fulfilling ritual obligations or duties, play follows the dictate of voluntary enjoyment. While many play-elements have been co-opted by leisure to contribute to social integration – one thinks above all of sport – the essence of play is enjoyable activity conducted for its own sake.

(2) *Imagination*. Play mobilizes the imagination. It thrives on projection, irony, allusion and fantasy. It is distinguished by an 'only pretending' quality, as when we imagine ourselves to be different people or in swapping places and times. Through imagination we develop our sense of difference, otherness and identity.

(3) *Disinterestedness*. *Homo ludens* pursues the pleasures of motor activity and the poetry and comedy of existence as ends in themselves. The enjoyment comes from the practice, not necessarily the calculations or effects which surround the practice.

(4) *Tension*. Play forms typically involve testing, chance and contest. Through play *homo ludens* lives out emotions which are either repressed or diverted by the rest of life.

How did these characteristics influence the development of culture and civilization? Huizinga supplies a host of examples. Here, we must confine ourselves to a brief consideration of three of the most striking ones: law, philosophy and war.

At first sight, nothing can be further removed from play than the law. The law is usually regarded soberly as the cement of civilization. It reconciles conflict and is the foundation of order. In Durkheim's sociology the law properly belongs to the realm of 'the sacred' – a realm which seems far removed from the comedy and disinterestedness of the play form. However, as Huizinga (1947: 76–88) points out, the essence of the law is contest. The conventions of prosecution and defence revolve around imagination, testing, chance and irony. Moreover the costumes of the wig and gown relay an 'only pretending' quality. Play tactics and styles are integral to the dynamics of legal argument and counter-argument.

The second example is play and philosophy. A general part of Huizinga's arguments is that play is integral to language. Puns, witticisms, *double entendres,* frivolous connections and word-play abound. But philosophy has traditionally prided itself on its clarity and precision. For Huizinga this pride is a delusion. Philosophy began, he argues, as a sacred riddle-game which was simultaneously ritual and festival entertainment. In Ancient Greek society the sophist practised flights of imaginative fancy and dexterity, astounding his audience with the mobility and richness of his reason. But he was also engaged in a contest to defeat his rival in a public arena. Disputations and declamations were the prime themes in public competition. Huizinga traces the play spirit embodying competition and tension through the lubrications and 'pengames' of Roman, Scholastic, Renaissance and Enlightenment philosophy.

The last example that I want to briefly refer to here is Huizinga's (1947: 89–104) discussion of play and war. In traditional society combat and tournament figured as methods for training warriors. Even today 'mock combat' drills, games of chance and fictional battles are crucial elements in military training and practice. The game of chess evolved as a method of imparting and refining the principles of military strategy. Military tactics are replete with 'let's pretend' strategies, mock battles, calculated tension games and dressing up. Play forms also developed ideas of chivalry, honour, nobility, courage and self-control – all of which have been adapted by warrior groups. Huizinga (1947: 104) refers to the 'immemorial conception' of war as a noble game. For him play is both the origin of modern warfare and the principal means through which modern battle skills and tactics are extended.

Huizinga's discussion of *homo ludens* is diametrically opposed to the model of *homo faber* that emerges in the work of Habermas (1971, 1973) and Doyal and Gough (1984). Drawing on the ideas of Weber (1976) these latter writers present play as a human capacity which has been subordinated by the needs for survival, work and order. Reason is portrayed as subduing the irrational content of life; and play is presented as confined to the margins of society. Here leisure appears to be nothing but the cultural codification of play needs and play forms. Culture has, as it were, triumphed over nature. Against this, Huizinga asserts the developmental and structural priority of play. In his view, play is the origin of culture and the foundation of human association and practice. To restrict it to 'the leisure sphere' is to misread its inalienable presence in human life.

Support for Huizinga's view comes from Bauman (1993: 169–74). He argues that the *flâneur* was the quintessential representative of *homo ludens* under modernity. The arcades and shop window displays were the new aesthetic playgrounds of industrial culture. Browsing, meeting, watching and being watched were the typical experiences of *flânerie*. In traditional society leisure was enmeshed in the dense fabric of community life. In modernity *homo ludens* survives as an atomized being who thrives on the fantasy content of city life and who experiences nothing but disjointed, episodic contact with others. Bauman's discussion of *homo ludens* is of particular interest because it includes a summary of the conditions of play needs and play forms under postmodernity. According to Bauman (1993: 177–9), the defining feature of these needs and forms is the interiorization of aesthetic space. The *flâneur* treated the street map of the metropolis as a labyrinth of pleasure and seduction; the postmodern *homo ludens* still wants to play with pleasure and seduction but only in a voyeuristic way which guarantees his or her absolute personal security. Play under postmodernity is mediated through *telecity*. The exterior with all of its uncertainties and threats is 'telemediated'. For *homo ludens* the window on the world is supplied by television, video, computer games and security cameras. External life is reduced to a series of surface appearances and disappearances. In the aesthetic space of telecity others exist solely as objects of amusement. Togetherness for the postmodern *homo ludens* is 'fortuitous', 'incidental' and 'casual'. Multiple TV households, equipped with personal stereos, portable disc-players and game consoles for each member of the household are warrens of solitary pleasure. Indeed Bauman (1993: 178) proposes that 'life in [this] aesthetic space is, essentially, a *solitaire*.'

Bauman therefore presents life under postmodernity as a game. For many critics this is a prodigal and implausible vision implying, as it does, that the poor, the homeless and the unemployed have a lot to laugh about. However, this criticism perhaps says more about the ideological dominance of *homo faber* as a model of being than it does about the actual condition of these groups. Anyone with a moment's acquaintance of the people who make up these groups knows that the need to play is not extinguished. Rather in each group play forms remain a vital channel for expressing sociality and identity. Irony, exercise, competition, parody, allusion and projection are all evident in the behaviour of their members. Of course play needs are expressed and developed in conditions of material deprivation. Yet they remain a palpable feature of ordinary life. This might be taken to say something about the powers of human adaptability; but surely it says more about the indomitable character of play needs, thus lending support to Huizinga's and Bauman's contention that play is central in understanding social life. Moreover, can one not argue that the opportunities for expressing play needs have vastly increased in the ad-drenched, TV-saturated world of today? In the moral universe prescribed by the *homo faber* model of existence, *homo ludens* appears either as an object of pity (the 'workless') or as an object of allure (the 'leisure class'). Play, for *homo faber,* is the reward for discipline and effort. It is, as it were, a surplus pleasure, to be enjoyed only after the pleasures of wealth creation and the duties of social responsibility have been fulfilled. Play outside of leisure was seen as something that had to be curtailed. The rational recreation campaigns at the end of the nineteenth century and during the interwar years were programmes of moral regulation dedicated to confining leisure to its proper place at the margins of society.

As I stated at the beginning of the chapter, in general, capitalism and modernity advanced a donatory view of leisure. That is, leisure was regarded as the reward for work which could be extended or contracted at the will of the donator. The donator reflects the authority structure of society and can be variously conceived of as husbands, parents, employers, the able-bodied, the colonial force or the state. As Bauman (1993) suggests, it is only with postmodernity that one can speak of the mass democratization of leisure. For it is only in this condition that accessibility to leisure data and relations becomes an ordinary part of mass culture. Through advertising, television, popular music and the other branches of the mass media everyone gains entry to the main symbolic leisure capital of the culture at little or no cost. The society of *telecity* is a society in which leisure codes have been inextricably linked with work codes. 'Leisureliness' is not necessarily confined to leisure institutions. *Homo ludens* is released from the rule of *homo faber*.

Conclusion

The renewal of interest in the *homo ludens* model of human relations sharply emphasizes the one-sided view of the significance of play and leisure in most nineteenth- and twentieth-century traditions of social thought. The centring of creativity and self-development on the *homo faber* model was basically a product of the nineteenth century. To be sure, Puritans had stressed the importance of a calling for work in the sixteenth and seventeenth centuries. But it was only in the nineteenth century that work was universally and deliberately constructed as the fundamental human need and the central life interest in society.

The *homo faber* model was essentially atomistic. That is, it envisaged society as a collection of private individuals intent on maximizing personal profit as the ultimate end of existence. In this scheme of things leisure is narrowly conceived as relating primarily to those interests and activities pertaining to recharging the energies of the individual for renewed effort in the workplace. True, leisure is also associated with escape and personal enrichment. But Modernity 1 tended to assess lives built around leisure as morally inferior or at least morally suspect. Thus the cosmology of Modernity 1 situated leisure on the periphery of life. It regarded it as a crucial part of a well-ordered existence but it also cast it in a supporting role to workplace experience. For it was taken for granted that in the workplace individuals create the objects and effects which transform their living conditions and produce genuine growth. From Bentham to Mill in the nineteenth century, and later in the writings of F.W. Taylor and the school of scientific management, the view is expressed that work is the core of personal health and the survival of society,

As early as the Romantic movement in the late eighteenth century one can detect a strong reaction to the narrow identification of the need to work with the workplace. Writers like Goethe, Coleridge, Wordsworth and Blake demand a more rounded model of *homo faber*. In particular, they associate creativity with the actions of the imagination, the spirit and the emotions. They criticize industrial culture for making a fetish of economic value and restricting the expression of human capacities. Their thought is further distinguished by a respect for nature and the desire for humanity to form a common bond with the natural world. Free time is regarded as the true axis of self-expression and personal development because it is only then that the individual is unencumbered by the cares of meeting the requirements of existence. Implicit in this tradition of thought is the proposition that leisure is a basic human need and that work in industrial society is disfiguring and damaging.

These ideas influenced the utopian socialists who were prominent in the early decades of the nineteenth century. Leading figures here included Charles Fourier, Saint-Simon and Robert Owen. They followed mainstream social thought in arguing that work is a creative and liberating force that would positively transform both the worker and his or her world. At the same time they insisted that the existing institutions in society deformed work experience for the mass of workers. They demanded the transformation of these institutions in order to make work more meaningful. The need for leisure was acknowledged. However, these writers tended to hold a productivist view of society in which the need for work is recognized as the paramount human need. These ideas were an important influence on Marx, who critically developed them in his discussion of alienation and the necessity for the 'associated producers' to dismantle capitalism and build communism.

The social reaction to the limited, dominant nineteenth-century perspective on *homo faber* drew extensively on Enlightenment ideas on the meaning of labour. Critics argued that industrial capitalism had betrayed the Enlightenment legacy by restricting the concept of labour to productivity, narrowly conceived of as the creation of economic value. What, then, was the Enlightenment view of labour? This is obviously a many-sided question. Rather than speak of *the* Enlightenment view it is perhaps more accurate to speak of Enlightenment *views*. Certainly the differences between Hobbes, Locke, Rousseau, Voltaire, Diderot, Adam Smith, Ferguson, Comte, Condorcet and Benjamin Franklin on this matter were more than a question of nuance. As Applebaum (1992: 369–407) demonstrates, these writers are divided by important differences on the question of the significance of labour and play in the organization of society. However, to do credit to those differences here would be to embark upon a lengthy and separate task. Instead I want to turn to the work of Kant and Hegel to provide a flavour of Enlightenment thought on labour. My object is to show how the Enlightenment concept of labour, which recognized play and leisure as fundamental human needs, was truncated by the *homo faber* model which rose to ascendancy in the nineteenth century. For reasons of space, the following discussion will focus only on the Kantian and Hegelian traditions.

Kant (1970: 43) identified labour with the realization of reason. He argued that the development of reason was the spur to human progress. At the same time he insisted that it was, so to speak, 'pre-given' by nature. We do not choose it, we are, so to speak, 'innately' predisposed to exercise and advance it. However, by our standards Kant's concept of labour is very generous. Our view is shaped by the *homo faber* model which dominated industrial capitalism. This associated labour with the production of necessities or, to quote Habermas again, the practice of 'purposive rational action'. In contrast, Kant used the concept to refer to *any* activity which contributes to the realization of reason. On this account play and leisure are subsumed under the general concept of labour. Writing, drawing, observing, debating and playing all deploy and develop reason. There is nothing pre-eminent about the workplace or the creation of economic value. The labour involved in playing a game with one's neighbours is just as decisive in developing reason as the labour involved in constructing a table or a chair. Leisure is not situated at the periphery of life.

At the same time, Kant's thought may be criticized for overexaggerating the centrality of reason in human relations. He also recognized a tension between the personal pursuit of reason and the generalized use of reason to effect social improvement. As he put it:

> Man has an inclination to live in society, since he feels in this state more like a man, that is, he feels able to develop his natural capacities. But he also has a great tendency to live as an individual, to isolate himself, since he also encounters in himself the unsocial characteristic of wanting to direct everything in accordance with his own ideas. He therefore expects resistance all around, just as he knows of himself that he is in turn inclined to offer resistance to others. It is this very resistance which awakens all man's powers and induces him to overcome his tendency to laziness. (Kant 1970: 44)

Kant here posits an inviolable antagonism between the egoistic needs of the individual and social needs of labour. In following one's personal inclinations one achieves self-expression; but at the same time one's personal inclinations may be contrary to the inclinations of society. In Kant's view reason, and therefore progress, is stimulated by this conflict. His idea of 'resistance all around' provides an important parallel with Hegel's discussion of labour.

Hegel, like Kant, regards labour as the main pathway to self-creation. However, his discussion of the antagonism between personal needs and the social context in which these needs are realized is more developed. For Hegel, labour is the articulation of the individual's confrontation with the natural, external world. Through labour *homo faber* objectifies his immanent powers by expressing them in an external product or effect. Hegel regards this process of self-objectification as necessarily social in character. For it is only through our relations with others that the creation and exchange of products and effects occurs. However, self-objectification requires labour to be unfettered. According to Hegel, the organization of industrial society produces precisely the opposite consequence. The division of labour has been the vehicle of immense wealth creation but it also forces the worker to engage in work practice which is highly specialized and fragmented. The worker lacks control of the work process. The experience of labour therefore becomes ever more abstract and alienating. Leisure here operates as nothing more than the means to replenish the stultified energies of the worker. Because it is also fragmented and divided from the rest of life it cannot provide the basis for true self-expression. The human need for fulfilling leisure cannot be satisfied because work fragments and divides the needs of the worker. Hegel's analysis applies to industrial culture. He contrasts the labour experience of the industrial worker with that of the farmer. He argues that the worker is a slave to a world of abstract needs and inner strife. For his part, the farmer is represented as experiencing the labour process as concrete and, because it is in tune with nature, personally rewarding. Marx, of course, drew extensively on Hegel in developing his theory of alienation and his critique of capitalism.

However, the point that needs to be stressed here is that Hegel's philosophy rejected the notion of divisions in social life in favour of an integrated model of society. This is crucial because, from a Hegelian standpoint, the division of leisure from the rest of life is a symptom of the alienation which tarnishes industrial society. The segregation of leisure from the rest of life is paralleled by the artificial divisions within the human psyche. These divisions are akin to a permanent rent in the constitution of the human psyche which retards human capacities and potentials. Marx, of course, seized upon this point to develop a political analysis to remedy this condition.

Many aspects of Enlightenment thought are of more than passing interest to current debates on leisure. In particular the refusal to subsume leisure under work in favour of a more general concept of labour and creativity; the rejection of leisure as a separate part of life with its own rhythms and laws; and the commitment to achieving managed social harmony retain relevance and fascination. At the same time, the Enlightenment faith in the power of reason to create an orderly society is now widely criticized. We now have a better understanding of the negative and harmful unintended consequences that spring from the attempt to create the planned society. In addition we are more critical of the practice of treating reason as the sovereign element of humanity.

The growing interest in the sociology of the body and the emotions undoubtedly counter-balances the Enlightenment and post-Enlightenment focus on reason as the centre of things. At the same time it is dangerous to believe – as some postmodernist accounts maintain – that reason has run its course and that we can surrender ourselves to the 'ecstasy' of the emotions (Tucker 1993). The *homo faber* model of human relations that emerged in its fully developed form under Modernity 1 constructed leisure as the realm of freedom. The limitations on self-making which the world of work necessarily imposed upon the individual were rewarded with the gift of 'free time'. The struggle to negotiate 'free time' activity in the context of limited escape opportunities allied with the gradual commercialization of free time experience greatly enhanced fantasy content in leisure activity. Personal and collective reveries of absolute excitement, choice and self-determination crystallized in the symbol of the leisure society. Aristocratic ideals of a labour-free existence fused with modernist ideals of self-expression to divert super-charged hopes and expectations into leisure. Play and spectacle may have had their origins in communal life, but they were gradually reabsorbed as privatized, commodified experiences. Maffesoli's (1990, 1991) neo-tribes – those flexible, elastic, semi-detached collectivities which cluster in intense bursts to consume a sports fixture, the latest movie or some other organized play form but then disperse to their automobiles and homes – are today the primary nexus of public leisure.

Finally, what emerges most forcefully from the discussion is the sheer paradox of leisure. Leisure is a luminous goal in culture. It is associated with freedom, choice, escape and life-satisfaction. Yet it is prosaically constructed through social means and its meaning varies historically so that commonsense, essentialist definitions and treatments are unsustainable. As I said in my introductory remarks to the book, leisure is one place on the map of the human world where we are constantly trying to land, but which perpetually evades our reach. I do not mean by this that we are incapable of experiencing freedom, choice, escape and life-satisfaction. Rather, this experience is often revealed in memory and even during the moments of direct experience as illusory or artificially induced. We are driven by the desire to own our leisure; yet at the same time we sense that our leisure never really belongs to us. To be sure, it often seems to be an insubstantial, virtual thing, a thing which is constantly beyond our grasp even when we feel that we attain the necessary external conditions required to support it. This sense of insubstantiality is exacerbated by the media, which paint leisure with images of colour and excitement which are rarely sustained in ordinary life.

Western culture presents leisure as a realizable utopia. Perhaps this is why we often feel that our leisure does not belong to us and that it eludes our grasp. For it is in the nature of utopia to be perpetually out of reach and on the edge of our existence (Bauman 1976). In struggling to achieve that longed-for state of freedom, choice and life-satisfaction, we find ourselves trapped in new, unanticipated obligations and chains. We discover that our images of freedom, choice and life-satisfaction are barred by undreamt-of contingencies and hazards. Leisure becomes one more problem in an existence already surrounded with problems. We feel deceived and short-changed. The standards of freedom, choice, life-satisfaction and escape that we hoped for seem like mere plaster-board constructions. Our leisure expectations which are born in hope and expectation seem to survive only by being wrapped in veils of dissatisfaction and poignancy. Things always seem less than they could be.

It is the fate of modernism to regard these responses as subjects to be remedied; and it is the condition of postmodernism to perceive the remedy as the problem. By committing ourselves to decentring leisure we emancipate leisure from the modernist burden of *necessarily* connoting freedom, choice, life-satisfaction and escape with leisure. We recover what the illusions of modernism have concealed.

NOTES

Introduction

1. See, in particular, the work of functionalist writers such as Dumazedier (1967, 1974) and Parker (1981).

2. Bauman (1976: 9–11) makes a similar point with regard to utopia. The links between Western conceptions of leisure and utopia have been under-explored. However, there is an obvious sense in which leisure is associated with 'the good life', richness and a more desirable, fulfilling existence.

3. However, it will be apparent to the reader that I am not a proponent of the 'cultural studies' approach to the study of leisure. Culture, as Williams (1981: 10) remarked, is an 'exceptionally complex term'. He distinguishes a variety of meanings of the term. For our purposes the two most important distinctions are the *idealist* and the *materialist*. Williams defined the idealist distinction as 'the informing spirit' and 'signifying system' which invests human practices and communication. He regarded the materialist meaning of culture as referring to 'a whole social order', a complete set of institutions and processes. To some extent the dichotomy between idealism and materialism is false. However, in my view the primary weakness of the cultural studies approach is the conflation of class and culture in pursuit of a *basically* materialist explanation of society. It follows that the approach that I take here assigns more autonomy to the place of ideas, reverie and imagination in the organization of everyday life.

4. The term 'universal market' comes from the work of Braverman (1974). It refers to the global commodification of natural resources and human sentiments. As Braverman (1974: 279) puts it, 'corporate institutions . . . have transformed every means of entertainment and "sport" into a production process for the enlargement of capital.'

5. See Lisa Buckingham, Andrew Gilf and Suzanne Goldberg, 'The Battle for Global Vision', *Guardian*, 23 October 1993.

6. Drawing on Durkheimian sociology, Burns and Stalker (1961) make an early and useful distinction between 'mechanical' and 'organic' forms of organization. Mechanical forms are hierarchical, rule-bound, inflexible and perpetuate deferential authority systems. They tend to predominate in markets where the conditions of trading are relatively fixed and predictable. Organic forms are less hierarchical, more flexible and tie authority to knowledge. They tend to predominate in markets where conditions are unpredictable and subject to change. The postmodernist case is, of course, that mechanical forms are dinosaurs which are incapable of functioning in the postmodern market.

7. In Schivelbusch's case the qualities that he singles out are velocity (1980), light (1988) and ambience (1992); for Sennett it is the disappearance of public space and for Lasch it is the continuous and intense examination of the self.

8. For examples, see Rojek (1993a: 146–60).

9. Commodity fetishism is the general worship of commodities above human relationships. The concept is closely associated with *reification*, that is, the transformation of human relations into objects so that they have an unchangeable 'thing-like' quality.

Chapter 1   Capitalism: Production

1. In classical Marxist terms, of course, profit is the surplus value extracted from the worker as a condition of the capitalist labour process.

2. This is an example of a Fordist analysis of society. Fordism treats the labour process and the consumption process as an integrated whole. Thus the needs and conditions of workers must be managed in the home with the same rigour as in the workplace. The ideal is to subject the worker to a universal system of control and to engineer compliance through a commitment to 'steadily improving lifestyle'.

3. For discussions of the rational recreation movements in Britain and the USA, see Yeo (1976), Cunningham (1980), Bailey (1987), Ewen (1976), Ewen and Ewen (1982).

4. The same image is realized cinematically in Fritz Lang's classic film *Metropolis* (1926). Here the city of the twenty-first century is envisaged as a robotic order in which a master race and slave class participate in a mutually annihilating order of domination with mathematical precision.

5. The Frankfurt School is the name attributed to the privately funded Institute for Social Research founded in Frankfurt in the mid-1920s. The School assembled a dazzling array of sociologists, philosophers, literary critics, psychologists, economists and political scientists including Theodor Adorno, Max Horkheimer, Walter Benjamin, Erich Fromm, Otto Kirchheimer, Leo Lowenthal, Herbert Marcuse, Franz Neumann and Friedrich Pollock. Following the minatory ascent to power of the Nazis in Germany, Adorno and Horkheimer relocated the School in the USA in the late 1930s. They returned to Germany after the war, but Fromm, Lowenthal and Marcuse remained in America to continue the tradition of Frankfurt research.

6. Marcuse's position changed rather significantly. His *One-Dimensional Man* (1964) was, as it were, the apogee of pessimism. It identified no prospect of breaking the strangle-hold of commodity fetishism and cultural manipulation organized by capitalism. However, in *The Aesthetic Dimension* (1978) he softens his position by allowing room for resistance and opposition.

7. The now widely discredited work of Althusser and Poulantzas emerged to fill the gap.

8. Althusser (1971) distinguished between the *repressive state apparatus* and *ideological state apparatus*. The *repressive state apparatus* referred to the coercive mechanisms of the state, such as the police, the army, the judiciary and the prisons; while the *ideological state apparatus* referred to the state-funded and -controlled machinery to organize consent and conformity by the manipulation of consciousness. Examples include the education system, the media and the Church.

9. Their work is also clearly influenced by Durkheim and Foucault.

10. Although, of course, many functionalist writers continue to support them with ardour undimmed.

11. That these 'contextualizations' are never elucidated by Clarke and Critcher is a major weakness of their analysis. It invites the criticism that they see racial conflict as subsumed under class domination.

12. Hughes thus suggests that racism pre-dated capitalism and therefore provides an historical basis for challenging the class analysis of Clarke and Critcher.

13. This is not quite the same as saying that capitalism is irrelevant. Rather, capitalism is the necessary but not the sufficient context for studying racism.

Chapter 2 Capitalism: Reproduction

1. It is worth noting that patriarchy and the feminist reaction against it is a dichotomy constructed under modernity. It is therefore no surprise that the dichotomy should come under fire at a moment when postmodernism is become more fashionable. Postmodernism challenges the dichotomies installed under modernity.

2. *Post-feminisms* is probably a more accurate term to use in this context than post-feminism.

Chapter 3 Modernity 1: The Roots of Order

1. Examples of this type of functionalist analysis in the literature are Parker (1983), Roberts (1978, 1981), Olszweska and Roberts (1989).

2. For a general account of survey material in the study of leisure, see Veal (1987).

3. Pluralism is therefore closely related to conservatism. It tends to celebrate difference and diversity without explaining the roots of social divisions. Interestingly postmodernism is associated with a version of *critical pluralism* in the form of *identity politics*. The latter stresses the variety of attitudes and divisions between groups. However, it combines this with a radical approach to the organization of power in society.

4. Rybczynski's (1991) slack book on leisure time is a leading example of this position. I use the word 'slack' because Rybczynski makes no attempt to situate his position in the available literature. There is therefore an anecdotal, unprepared quality to his discussion of leisure which diminishes its interest for students in the field.

5. There are, of course, strong connections between the regulation school and Fordism.

6. The 'there is no alternative' attitude associated with the Thatcher–Reagan years is a good example of this attitude.

7. The back to basics campaign foundered in the first months of 1994 as the press revealed a series of moral scandals involving senior members of the Conservative Party. The campaign's failure illustrates the problems that moral regulation campaigners face in conditions of critical pluralism.

8. These projects are now, of course, widely scorned as objects of shame and regret in white culture.

9. One of the principal arguments in the book is that leisure should be understood as the dream-world of modernity. That is, the qualities of escape, relaxation and rest associated with the concept of leisure are *idealist* constructs which reflect the materialist limitations of life under modernity.

10. Indeed, from the standpoint of figurational sociology the notion of autonomous action is rather eccentric. Elias and his followers emphasize the chained, interdependent qualities of human action. One interesting implication of this – which has not been explored in the literature – is that it suggests that uniqueness in human affairs is a delusion. One might speculate that interesting parallels might be drawn between Elias and Benjamin on the questions of interdependence and reproduction.

11. The history of the book is quite well known by now. However, for the benefit of readers who do not know, Elias' *Über den Prozeß der Zivilisation* was published in two volumes in 1939 in Basel by Verlag Haus zum Falken. The war put paid to much serious academic activity, not least reviews and discussions of challenging new books in sociology. Elias fled Nazi Germany and spent many difficult years re-establishing an academic career in England. He was appointed to a post in the Department of Sociology at Leicester University in 1954. Under the direction of the colourful, and much misunderstood, Ilya Neustadt, Leicester was arguably the most important provincial centre of sociological activity in the 1950s and 1960s. Chris Bryant, John Eldridge, Paul Hirst, Graeme Salaman and Bryan Wilson number among its most illustrious graduates; and Neustadt employed some of the leading figures in postwar British sociology, including Martin Albrow, Sheila Allen, Joe and Olive Banks, Richard Brown, Percy Cohen, Eric Dunning, Anthony Giddens, John H. Goldthorpe, Mary McIntosh, Nicos Mouzelis and Sami Zubaida. All of these figures came into contact with Elias. But with the notable exception of Eric Dunning, none of them made a strong allegiance to figurational sociology and few refer to his work in their own publications. Yet in personal conversations with most of these people it is clear that Elias made a strong impression on them.

I was an undergraduate and postgraduate student in Leicester between 1973 and 1979. Elias was still on campus at that time as an Emeritus Professor and his paper 'Problems of Involvement and Detachment', published by the *British Journal of Sociology* in 1956, was widely referenced by members of the department. I came across *The Civilizing Process* via my third-year Sociology tutor, Eric Dunning, who allowed me to read his handwritten translation in 1976. However, it was not until 1978 that the first volume was published by Blackwell. Perhaps typically, given the history of Elias's bad luck in making the book available to readers, there was a four-year delay before the crucial second volume was published in English. The result is that the first volume was initially generally misunderstood as a mere 'history of manners'. The second volume, which provided a sociological framework for explaining the historical changes in personality structure described in Chapter 1, was widely misperceived as a separate book.

12. In fairness to figurational sociologists, the notion of 'full testing' is something of a *non sequitur*. Hypotheses and testing methods are themselves *in process*. All thought is therefore conditional.

13. Perhaps the notion that we do not torture or butcher our enemies is too complacent. Peters (1985) quotes Victor Hugo's claim made in 1874 that 'torture has ceased to exist'. According to Peters, torture is used routinely in one of every three countries.

14. To some extent this disapproval is more symbolic than real. Throughout the writing of the book, the tragedy in former Yugoslavia unfolded and the response of the United Nations was widely criticized for being muddled and tokenistic.

15. Interestingly, Elias never wrote much about the institution of psychiatry. The sole exception is his paper on sociology and psychiatry (1969).

16. It is worth making this point given the view in the secondary literature that the approach is associated with intellectual arrogance.

Chapter 4 Mechanisms of Regulation

1. Marxist sociology posits that 'a realm of freedom' can be reached through the transformation of society by working-class revolution. Marx (1977, III: 820) writes: 'The realm of freedom actually begins only where labour which is determined by necessity and mundane considerations ceases. . . . Freedom in this field can only consist in socialized man, the associated producers, rationally regulating their interchange with Nature, bringing it under common control, instead of being ruled by it as by the blind forces of Nature; and achieving this with the least expenditure of energy and under conditions most favourable to, and worthy of, their human nature.' Marx's commitment to key elements in the Enlightenment project is evident in this passage.

2. Exceptions include the feminist sociology of sport associated with Hargreaves (1994) and the sociology of culture associated with Craik (1993).

3. They acquire a 'sacred' quality. Just as Durkheim (1915: 475) intimated in his remarks on the role of 'collective remaking' available for leisure in organic society.

4. This expansionist, feel-good philosophy has suffered in the economic retrenchment in California that occurred in the 1980s and 1990s.

5. Smiles was of course a Victorian paterfamilias who took it for granted that the economy of the home is based in a rigid division of labour between males and females.

6. There are parallels between Bourdieu's use of the term 'habitus' and Veblen's use of the terms 'emulation' and 'conspicuous consumption'. Both authors operate with the notion that leisure behaviour is shaped by distinct social strata.

7. It might be argued, of course, that continued participation in fox-hunting is a mark of distinction – a way of defying the 'political correctness' of critics.

8. Bourdieu here invites comparison with Elias' sociology.

9. 'Fictive' in the sense that most of the crucial elements of 'nation' and 'nationalism' subsist at the level of the symbolic and hence are capable of 'adaptations', 'extensions' and 'interpretations'.

10. Most of the jobs were concentrated in ironworks, chemical and rubber plants and fertilizer units.

11. Opponents are also incensed over plans to acquire hundreds of acres of land around the monument for a huge national park; and also to raise the entrance fee from 2 to 100 rupees. The latter is seen as a move to appease foreign tourists by limiting the access of locals who 'spoil' the sight.

12. It is good that this sense of wonderment is being retrieved by these and other writers. Too many neo-Marxist critiques of consumer society have presented consumption experience in terms of coercion, manipulation and brutalization (see Marcuse 1964; Clarke and Critcher 1985).

13. These examples, of course, support feminist accounts of the rigid stereotypes of leisure behaviour constructed under patriarchy.

14. A common fault in social science is to over-simplify complex processes of transformation by providing a 'one-sided' account of the origin and trends of development. It is worth making the

point in this context as it can be argued with equal force that regulatory mechanisms expanded the human life-world by bringing new standards of security and restraint into daily life.

Chapter 5 Modernity 2: The Disorder of Things

1. In the funeral oration delivered at Highgate Cemetery, London, on 17 March 1883, Engels (1968: 429–30) credits Marx with discovering 'the law of development of human history', 'the special law of motion governing the present day capitalist mode of production and the bourgeois society that this mode of production has created'.

2. 'Abstract, indeterminate beauty' was the motor behind modernist utopias such as the unpolluted fatherland of the Nazis and the society of equality and freedom dreamt of by the revolutionary Bolsheviks.

3. Maffesoli (1993) has perhaps done most in recent years to adapt Nietzsche's Dionysian philosophy to consumer culture and present-day leisure practice.

4. This is indeed strange because one can speculate with some confidence that 'a dark area' of deviant leisure activity is an ordinary part of contemporary experience. For example, one is struck by the popularity of drug-taking and trespassing in the 'free time spectrum'.

Chapter 6 The Phenomenology of Leisure

1. 'What is really going on' was Goffman's obsession.

2. Typifications are, of course, open to processes of negotiation and bargaining. While Schutz's (1982) sociology recognizes that the typification operates as a basis for 'maintaining' social interaction, he also insists that human actors are knowledgeable and capable agents who routinely challenge notions of 'order' and 'normality'.

Chapter 7 Postmodernity and Postmodernism

1. Tester (1993) uses the term 'without bounds' to identify the primary characteristic of postmodernity. Modernity 1 attempted to lay down clear boundaries to govern human relations. Modernity 2 was associated with revealing the contradictions of these boundaries and constructing alternative boundaries which were believed to enrich human relations. Postmodernity plays with the boundaries of Modernity 1 and Modernity 2 and politically aims to expose their limitations.

2. Bauman (1992, 1993) argues that postmodernity widens tolerance and enhances morality. 'In so far as the modern obsession with purposefulness and utility,' writes Bauman (1993: 36), 'and the equally obsessive suspicion of all things autotelic (that is, claiming to be their own ends, and not means to something else than themselves) fade away, morality stands the chance of being finally coming into its own. It may stop being cajoled or bullied to present its credentials; to justify its right to exist by pointing to the benefit it brings to personal survival, standing or happiness, or the service it renders to collective security, law and order. This is a seminal chance.'

Chapter 8 Postmodern Leisure

1. The symbolic and material differences between whites and non-whites is a symptom of modernist consciousness. It attempted to set clear, unambiguous standards between 'advanced' and 'backward' conduct; but these standards were themselves untenable and only sustainable by the use of physical force.

2. The position of Bauman (1992, 1993) and Tester (1993) contrasts radically with this interpretation of postmodernity. Bauman and Tester emphasize the potential for richness in postmodern experience.

3. Simmel (1978) produced the seminal understanding of restlessness through his sociology of modern consciousness.

4. This is of course radically different from the position in functionalist, Marxist and feminist traditions of leisure, which tend to emphasize the evolutionary universals in leisure practice.

5. Postmodernism suggests that the 'steering capacity' of states to regulate morality and govern social conduct is seriously weakened by postmodern conditions.

6. These secular events might be said to be an important channel of 'collective remaking'. One is again struck by the prescience of Durkheim's (1915: 475) speculation that leisure and recreation have the capacity to replace the religious function in industrial, secular societies.

7. This also reflects the omnipotence that is attributed to celebrities by the star system organized by the cultural industry. Death is simply treated as another thing that the industry can fix.

8. The crime shelves of bookshops are full of accounts of real murders which invite readers to 'discover' for themselves what really happened. The Murder Club, based in North Audley Street, London, invites members to become armchair detectives and points out that criminology is no longer the exclusive domain of scientists, lawyers and writers. The Club produces a bi-monthly bulletin devoted to every aspect of real-life murder cases – 'new cases, old cases to marvel at, cases to solve'. Members receive their own unique badge, membership card and personal certificate of membership. Research programmes and 'notorious locations' tours and presentations are offered. In 1989 Harrap in association with the Murder Club published a series of guides to 'true tales of dark deeds and arch fiends' in all of the main regions of the UK.

9. According to the story, a glass canopy collapsed on the passenger and *despatched* him.

10. She is known locally as 'Kate' and is thought to be the ghost of Catherine of Aragon.

11. All of the references to Shropshire's 'ghostly tours' and 'ghostly breaks' come from the *Breakaway* programme broadcast on BBC Radio 4 on 23 October 1993.

12. Ironically, Adorno's forays into 'real art' in the form of his own musical composition are widely regarded to be minor pastiches and 'repro versions' of Schoenberg's music.

13. Although, of course, the roots of dissatisfaction with modernist theory reach back to the 1960s.

14. All quotations and details regarding the Battersea project come from 'Leisure Leader Guns for Disney', *Guardian*, 9 June 1988.

15. Phineas Taylor Barnum has some claim to being regarded as the first great leisure entrepreneur in American culture. He began in 1835 by exhibiting a slave who he alleged had been George Washington's nurse and whom he announced as being 161 years old. He faked freaks such as the Fejee Mermaid, who he claimed was half-human (actually it was the top part of a mummified monkey attached to the bottom part of a dried fish); he managed genuine freak attractions such as the midget Tom Thumb, the giantess Anna Swan and the Siamese twins Eng/Chang; and he created the American Museum in 1841 on Broadway where he exhibited 'educated dogs, industrious fleas, automatons, jugglers, ventriloquists, living statuary'. Barnum's (1869) autobiography is a rich and important document in the history of the leisure entrepreneur.

Chapter 9 Conclusion: *Homo Faber/Homo Ludens*

1. However, they are notably less forthcoming about what this liberation politics would look like. The position is therefore subject to the charge of being too utopian.

2. Of course, this is not a satisfactory apology for the condition of unemployment. Rather it simply suggests that this condition cannot be accurately understood in stereotypical terms.

3. For Aronowitz (1985: 39–40) this introjection signifies the compliance of the workforce to capitalist domination. As he writes: 'The political climate is unfavourable even for a substantial reduction of working hours, a measure which would certainly share the available work among a larger group of people and would not threaten the underlying moral structure that income should

be a consequence of hard work. . . . The sad fact is that workers and their unions . . . have sur-
rendered the shorter working week demand not only because in most cases the labour movement
has been so severely weakened that it could not win; but also because it has lost the will to oppose
the institutions of surplus repression.'

4. The *homo faber* model was the corollary of this grid-like structure. It emphasized purposive-
rational action in the organization of life. The need for work is conceived as generating
self-discipline and extending the creativity and knowledge of the individual. The *homo faber*
model connects up with the agency–structure dichotomy that has traditionally dominated mainstream leisure theory. This dichotomy presents personal and social development in terms of a
dialectic between agency and structure. Agency is generally conceived of as actions and practices
which bring about change. Agency approaches to leisure relations are usually reinforced with vol-
untaristic paradigms which emphasize the choice, will, freedom and self-determination of the
social actor. In contrast, structure is generally conceived as either the social contexts which nur-
ture change or the barriers which condition action in leisure behaviour. Structure approaches tend
to endorse deterministic paradigms of life, i.e. paradigms which highlight the importance of structural influences such as class, race, gender, nationalism and so forth in shaping personal conduct.

The agency–structure dichotomy has recently been the subject of intense debate within sociology. The chief catalyst behind this has been Giddens' (1979, 1984) claims to have transcended the
dichotomy with his custom-built 'structuration theory'. While paying due respect to the importance and ambition of Giddens' work, several influential critics have rounded on these claims,
attacking some of the basic premises of structuration theory (see, in particular, Craib 1991; Turner
1992). This is not the place to consider this matter in detail. Rather it will be enough to comment
on the influence of the agency–structure dichotomy in the study of leisure and to draw attention
to some of its primary defects.

As I have noted elsewhere (Rojek 1989, 1992), the agency–structure dichotomy has dominated
social thought on leisure. The work of Parker (1983), Roberts (1978) and Young and Wilmott
(1973) can be numbered among leading representatives of agency theory; while the work of Clarke
and Critcher (1985), Bialeschki and Henderson (1986), Green et al. (1987) and Scraton and
Talbot (1989) may be referred to as examples of structure approaches. Because I have given a fairly
full account of the relative strengths and weaknesses of these two approaches elsewhere (Rojek
1989, 1992) I will confine myself here to a critical consideration of the strengths and weaknesses
of the dichotomy as a whole.

On the strengths side, the dichotomy clearly identifies a motivating force to explain change – the
conflict between personal actions and contextual limits, agency and structure – in leisure and
social conduct. With this comes theoretical clarity and boldness in the formulation of propositions. Of course it is possible to complain that this clarity is an illusion and that this boldness is
misplaced. However, at this point it should be recognized that there is considerable momentum in
formulating questions of change in terms of the dichotomy between agency and structure. It
allows for an exhaustive explanation of social life. Besides exhaustiveness, a second benefit is the
containment of difficult and perhaps insoluble epistemological issues. By treating the individual
and society, the agent and the structure, as integral, solid, separate entities, one avoids the entire
subject of the discursive level of agency and structure. By concentrating on the discursive level, it
is arguable that strategies of change are paralysed because discussion focuses not on action and its
objects but on the ambiguities of action and the unintended consequences of intended actions.

However, critics dismiss these strengths as mirages. Three basic weaknesses are generally identified with the agency–structure paradigm. First of all it is regarded as overestimating either the
freedom of social actors or the mechanical reproductive effects of structures. For example, in
leisure studies, agency theories have presented the social actor as possessing either freedom,
choice or self-determination, while structure models have often depicted personal conduct as the
determined consequence of structural forces.

The second basic weakness that critics draw attention to is the tendency in the paradigm to present the two sides as alternatives. The possibility of a fluid, diverse, interactive, developing
relationship between social actors and social structures is somewhat understated. Instead fairly
crude functionalist assumptions are made. For example, the feminist sociology of leisure tends to
present the structure of patriarchy as operating in a homogeneous way to oppress women. The

class, race and lifestyle differences between women are thus marginalized, just as the criticism of patriarchy from within the orders of masculinity is neglected. Similarly, pluralist writers like Veal (1987) tend to assign freedom, choice and flexibility to the actor without revealing the historical and contextual dimensions of these characteristics. The result is an unsatisfactory ahistorical view of the social actor which is incapable of accounting for changes in the organization of leisure in society.

The third major defect of the agency–structure paradigm is its neglect of the subject of embodiment. In agency theory the premise of all meaningful social life is the knowledgeable actor operating creatively upon nature and culture to produce change. For its part, structure theory commences with the premise that all social action is generated and shaped by layered social structures. However, from the standpoint of the emerging sociology of leisure, each premise is misplaced (Gehlen 1988; Turner 1984, 1992; Synott 1993; Classen 1993). From this standpoint the body is the first fact of social existence. Before we are in a position to act or to be shaped by social structures we experience bodily sensations and an acute sense of our own body as separate from other things in the world.

REFERENCES

Abercrombie, N., Hill, S. and Turner, B.S. (1980) *The Dominant Class Thesis*, London, Allen & Unwin

Abercrombie, N., Hill, S. and Turner, B.S. (1986) *Sovereign Individuals of Capitalism*, London, Allen & Unwin

Addison, W. (1953) *English Fairs and Markets*, London, Batsford

Adorno, T.W. (1991) 'Resignation', pp. 171–5 in *The Culture Industry* (ed. with an Introduction by J.M. Bernstein), London, Routledge

Adorno, T.W. and Horkheimer, M. (1944) *Dialectic of Enlightenment*, London, Verso

Aglietta, M. (1979) *A Theory of Capitalist Regulation*, London, New Left Books

Allison, L. (1994) 'Home as Away', *Times Higher Education Supplement*, 23 July

Althusser, L. (1971) *Lenin and Philosophy and Other Essays*, London, New Left Books

Altman, D. (1986) *AIDS and the New Puritanism*, London, Pluto

Alvarez, A. (1971) *The Savage God*, Harmondsworth, Penguin

Anderson, P. (1983) *In the Tracks of Historical Materialism*, London, New Left Books

Andrew, E. (1981) *Closing the Iron Cage*, Montreal, Black Rose Books

Ang, I. (1985) *Watching Dallas*, London, Methuen

Anger, K. (1975) *Hollywood Babylon*, New York, Dell

Anger, K. (1984) *Hollywood Babylon 2*, London, Arrow

Applebaum, H. (1992) *The Concept of Work*, Albany, State University of New York Press

Aronowitz, S. (1981) 'A Metatheoretical Critique of Immanuel Wallerstein's *The Modern World System*,' *Theory and Society*, 10: 503–20

Aronowitz, S. (1985) 'Why Work?', *Social Text*, 12: 19–42

Bachelard, G. (1968) *The Psychoanalysis of Fire*, Boston, Beacon Press

Bachelard, G. (1969) *The Poetics of Reveries*, Boston, Beacon Press

Bachelard, G. (1971) *The Poetics of Space*, Boston, Beacon Press

Bailey, P. (1987) *Leisure and Class in Victorian England*, London, Methuen

Bakhtin, M. (1984) *Rabelais and his World*, Cambridge, MA, MIT Press

Banton, M. (1967) *Race Relations*, London, Routledge & Kegan Paul

Barrett, M. (1980) *Women's Oppression Today*, London, Verso

Barrett, M. and McIntosh, M. (1982) *The Anti-Social Family*, London, Verso

Barthes, R. (1973) *Mythologies*, St Albans, Paladin

Baudelaire, C. (1964) *The Painter of Modern Life and Other Essays*, New York, Da Capo

Baudelaire, C. (1970) *Paris Spleen*, New York, New Directions

Baudelaire, C. (1983) *Intimate Journals*, San Francisco, City Lights

Baudrillard, J. (1975) *The Mirror of Production*, New York, Telos Press

Baudrillard, J. (1983a) *Simulations*, New York, Semiotext(e)

Baudrillard, J. (1983b) *In the Shadow of the Silent Majorities*, New York, Semiotext(e)

Baudrillard, J. (1986) *Forget Foucault*, New York, Semiotext(e)

Baudrillard, J. (1987) *The Ecstasy of Communication*, New York, Semiotext(e)

Baudrillard, J. (1990) *Fatal Strategies*, New York, Semiotext(e)

Baudrillard, J. (1993) *Symbolic Exchange and Death*, London, Sage

Bauman, Z. (1976) *Socialism: The Active Utopia*, London, Allen & Unwin

Bauman, Z. (1979) 'The Phenomenon of Norbert Elias', *Sociology*, 13(1): 117–25

Bauman, Z. (1987) *Legislators and Interpreters*, Oxford, Blackwell

Bauamn, Z. (1989) *Modernity and the Holocaust*, Cambridge, Polity

Bauman, Z. (1992) *Intimations of Postmodernity*, London, Routledge

Bauman, Z. (1993) *Postmodern Ethics*, Oxford, Blackwell

Bayley, S. (1986) *Sex, Drink and Fast Cars*, London, Faber & Faber

Beck, U. (1991) 'Die blaue Blum der Moderne', *Der Spiegel*, 33: 50–1

Beck, U. (1992a) 'From Industrial Society to Risk Society: Questions of Survival, Structure and Ecological Enlightenment', *Theory, Culture and Society*, 9: 97–123

Beck, U. (1992b) *Risk Society*, London, Sage

Becker, H. (1963) *Outsiders*, New York, Free Press

Beckford, J. (1989) *Religion in Industrial Society*, London, Unwin Hyman

Bell, D. (1960) *The End of Ideology*, New York, Free Press

Bell, D. (1974) *The Coming of Post-Industrial Society*, London, Heinemann

Bell, D. (1976) *The Cultural Contradictions of Capitalism*, London, Heinemann

Bella, L. (1989) 'Women and Leisure: Beyond Androcentrism' pp. 151–81 in E. Jackson and T.L. Burton (eds), *Understanding Leisure and Recreation: Mapping the Past, Charting the Future*, State College, Venture Publishing

Benjamin, W. (1955) *Illuminations*, London, Jonathan Cape

Benjamin, W. (1970) *Charles Baudelaire*, London, Verso

Benjamin, W. (1979) *One Way Street*, London, New Left Books

Bennett, T. and Mercer, C. (1986) *Popular Culture and Social Relations*, Milton Keynes, Open University Press

Berger, P., Berger, B. and Kellner, H. (1973) *The Homeless Mind*, Harmondsworth, Penguin

Berman, M. (1982) *All that is Solid Melts into Air*, London, Verso

Bernstein, J. (1991) 'Introduction', pp. 1–25 in Adorno (1991)

Berridge, V. and Edwards, G. (1987) *Opium and the People*, New York, Yale University Press

Bessel, R. (ed.) (1987) *Life in the Third Reich*, Oxford, Oxford University Press

Bialeschki, D. and Henderson, K. (1986) 'Leisure in the Common World of Women', *Leisure Studies*, 5(3): 299–308

Black, J. (1992) *The British Abroad: The Grand Tour in the Nineteenth Century*, Stroud, Alan Sutton

Bloch, E. (1962) *Feudal Society* (2 vols), London, Routledge

Bogdan, R. (1988) *Freakshow: Presenting Human Oddities for Amusement*, Chicago, Chicago University Press

Bolla, P., Dawson, D. and Harrington, M. (1991) *Women and Leisure in Ontario*, Toronto, Ministry of Tourism and Recreation

Borzello, F. (1987) *Civilizing Caliban: The Misuse of Art 1875–1980*, London, Routledge

Boskind-Lodhal, M. (1976) 'Cinderella's Stepsisters: A Feminist Perspective on Anorexia Nervosa', *Signs*, 2(2): 342–56

Bourdieu, P. (1984) *Distinction*, London, Routledge & Kegan Paul

Bourdieu, P. (1990) *Photography*, Stanford, Stanford University Press

Brailsford, D. (1991) *Sport, Time and Society*, London, Routledge

Braverman, H. (1974) *Labour and Monopoly Capital*, New York, Monthly Review Press

Bromley, R. (1988) *Lost Narratives*, London, Routledge

Bruch, H. (1977) *The Golden Cage: The Enigma of Anorexia Nervosa*, Cambridge, MA, Harvard University Press

Burke, P. (1978) *Popular Culture in Early Modern Europe*, London, Temple Smith

Burns, T. (1973) 'Leisure in Industrial Society', pp. 40–55 in M. Smith, S. Parker and C. Smith (eds), *Leisure and Society in Britain*, London, Allen & Unwin

Burns, T. and Stalker, G.M. (1961) *The Management of Innovation*, London, Tavistock

Callinicos, A. (1989) *Against Postmodernism: A Marxist Critique*, Cambridge, Polity

Campbell, C. (1987) *The Romantic Ethic and the Spirit of Modern Consumerism*, Oxford, Blackwell

Cannadine, D. (1983) 'The Context, Performance and Meaning of Ritual: The British Monarchy and the "Invention of Tradition" 1820–1977', pp. 101–64 in E. Hobsbawm and T. Ranger (eds), *The Invention of Tradition*, Cambridge, Cambridge University Press

Carnegie, A. (1903) *The Empire of Business*, London, Harper

Castells, M. (1989) *The Informational City*, Oxford, Blackwell

Chaney, D. (1983) 'The Department Store as a Cultural Form', *Theory, Culture and Society*, 1(3): 22–31

Chaney, D. (1990) 'Subtopia in Gateshead: The Metrocentre as a Cultural Form', *Theory, Culture and Society*, 7(4): 49–62

Chaney, D. (1992) 'The Representation of Holidays and Holidays as Representation for the Ageing', mimeo, University of Durham

Chaney, D. (1993) *Fictions of Collective Life*, London, Routledge

Chaney, D. (1994) *The Cultural Turn*, London, Routledge

Christiansen, R. (1988) *Romantic Affinities: Portraits from the Age*, London, Sphere

Clark, D. (ed.) (1991) *Marriage, Domestic Life and Social Change*, London, Routledge

Clarke, J. (1992) *New Times and Old Enemies*, London, HarperCollins

Clarke, J. and Critcher, C. (1985) *The Devil Makes Work*, London, Macmillan

Classen, C. (1993) *Worlds of Sense*, London, Routledge

Cloward, R.A. and Ohlin, L. (1960) *Delinquency and Opportunity*, Glencoe, IL, Free Press

Cody, D. (1991) 'All Hail, the Renaissance!', *Delta Airlines Sky Magazine*: 10–18

Cohen, A. (1955) *Delinquent Boys*, Glencoe, IL, Free Press

Cohen, S. and Taylor, L. (1992) *Escape Attempts*, London, Routledge

Collins, J. (1989) *Uncommon Cultures*, London, Routledge

Collins, M. and Strelitz, Z. (1982) 'Families and Leisure', in M. Rapaport, M. Fogarty and R. Rapaport (eds), *Families in Britain*, London, Routledge

Corrigan, P. and Sayer, D. (1985) *The Great Arch*, Oxford, Blackwell

Craib, I. (1991) *Anthony Giddens*, London, Routledge

Craik, J. (1993) *The Face of Fashion*, London, Routledge

Cross, M. and Keith, M. (eds) (1993) *Racism, the City and the State*, London, Routledge

Cunningham, H. (1980) *Leisure in the Industrial Revolution*, London, Croom Helm

Curtis, J. (1986) 'Isn't it Difficult to Support Some Notions of "The Civilizing Process"? A Response to Dunning', pp. 57–66 in C.R. Rees and A.W. Miracle (eds), *Sport and Social Theory*, Champaign, IL, Human Kinetics

Debord, G. (1967) *Society of the Spectacle*, London, Rebel Press

De Certeau, M. (1984) *The Practice of Everyday Life*, Berkeley, University of California Press

Deem, R. (1986) *All Work and No Play?*, Milton Keynes, Open University Press

Dingle, A.E. (1980) *The Campaign for Prohibition in Victorian England*, New Brunswick, NJ, Rutgers University Press

Dixey, R. and Talbot, M. (1982) 'Women, Leisure and Bingo', mimeo, Leeds, Trinity and All Saints College

Donnelly, P. (1986) 'The Paradox of the Parks: Politics of Recreational Land Use Before and After the Mass Trespasses', *Leisure Studies*, 5(2): 211–32

Dorn, N. and South, N. (1989) 'Drugs and Leisure Prohibition and Pleasure', pp. 171–90 in C. Rojek (ed.), *Leisure for Leisure: Critical Essays*, London, Macmillan

Douglas, M. (1966) *Purity and Danger*, London, Routledge & Kegan Paul

Dower, M., Rapaport, R., Strelitz, Z. and Kew, S. (1981) *Leisure Provision and People's Needs*, London, HMSO

Doyal, L. and Gough, I. (1984) 'A Theory of Human Needs', *Critical Social Policy*, 10: 6–38

Dumazedier, J. (1967) *Towards a Sociology of Leisure*, London, Collier-Macmillan

Dumazedier, J. (1974) *The Sociology of Leisure*, Amsterdam, Elsevier

Dunning, E. (1992) 'Figurational Sociology and the Sociology of Sport', pp. 221–84 in E. Dunning and C. Rojek (eds), *Sport and Leisure in the Civilizing Process*, London, Macmillan

Dunning, E., Murphy, P. and Williams, J. (1988) *The Roots of Football Hooliganism*, London, Routledge

Durkheim, É. (1902) *The Division of Labour in Society*, New York, Free Press

Durkheim, É. (1915) *The Elementary Forms of Religious Life*, New York, Free Press

Durkheim, É. (1958) *Professional Ethics and Civic Morals*, London, Routledge

Eco, U. (1986) *Faith in Fakes*, London, Secker & Warburg

Elias, N. (1969) 'Sociology and Psychiatry', pp. 117–44 in S.H. Foulkes and G. Steward Prince (eds), *Psychiatry in a Changing Society*, London, Tavistock

Elias, N. (1978) *The Civilizing Process.* Vol. 1: *The History of Manners*, Oxford, Blackwell

Elias, N. (1982) *The Civilizing Process.* Vol. 2: *State Formation and Civilization*, Oxford, Blackwell

Elias, N. and Dunning, E. (1986) *Quest for Excitement: Sport and Leisure in the Civilizing Process*, Oxford, Blackwell

Engels, F. (1968) 'Speech at the Graveside of Karl Marx', pp. 429–30 in Marx and Engels (1968)

Ewen, S. (1976) *The Captains of Consciousness*, New York, McGraw-Hill

Ewen, S. (1988) *All Consuming Images*, New York, Basic Books

Ewen, S. and Ewen, E. (1982) *Channels of Desire*, New York, McGraw-Hill

Fazio, J.R. (1979) 'Parks and Other Recreational Resources', pp. 197–232 in H. Ibrahim and J. Shivers (eds), *Leisure: Emergence and Expansion*, Los Angeles, Hwong

Featherstone, M. (1982) 'The Body in Consumer Culture', *Theory, Culture and Society*, 1(2): 18–33

Featherstone, M. (1991) *Consumer Culture and Postmodernism*, London, Sage

Ferguson, H. (1992) 'Watching the World Go Round: Atrium Culture and the Psychology of Shopping', pp. 21–39 in Shields (1992)

Findlay, J.M. (1992) *Magic Lands: Western Cityscapes and American Culture after 1940*, Berkeley, University Press of California

Finlay, K. (1991) 'Karen Finlay', pp. 41–9 in A. Juno and V. Vale (eds), *Angry Women*, San Francisco, Re/Search Publications

Fiske, J. (1987) *Television Culture*, London, Methuen

Fiske, J. (1989a) *Reading the Popular*, London, Unwin Hyman

Fiske, J. (1989b) *Understanding Popular Culture*, London, Unwin Hyman

Flink, J. (1975) *The Car Culture*, Cambridge, MA, MIT Press

Ford, J. (1977) *This Sporting Land*, London, New English Library

Foster, H. (ed.) (1985) *Postmodern Culture*, London, Pluto

Foucault, M. (1973) *The Order of Things*, London, Routledge & Kegan Paul

Foucault, M. (1974) *The Archaeology of Knowledge*, London, Routledge & Kegan Paul

Foucault, M. (1975) *Discipline and Punish*, Harmondsworth, Penguin

Foucault, M. (1981) *History of Sexuality*, Harmondsworth, Penguin

Foucault, M. (1982) 'The Subject and Power', in H.L. Dreyfus and P. Rabinow (eds), *Michel Foucault*, Brighton, Harvester

Foucault, M. (1988) '[Auto]biography, Michel Foucault 1926–84', *History of the Present*, Spring, 4: 13–15 [adopting the pseudonym of Maurice Florence]

Freud, S. (1939) *Civilization and its Discontents*, Harmondsworth, Penguin

Friedmann, G. (1950) *Anatomy of Work*, Glencoe, IL, Free Press

Frisby, D. (1985) *Fragments of Modernity*, Cambridge, Polity

Frisby, D. (1989) 'Simmel and Leisure', pp. 75–91 in C. Rojek (ed.), *Leisure for Leisure: Critical Essays*, London, Macmillan

Game, A. (1991) *Undoing the Social*, Milton Keynes, Open University Press

Gane, M. (1993) *Harmless Lovers*, London, Routledge

Garber, M. (1992) *Vested Interests*, London, Routledge

Gehlen, A. (1988) *Man, his Nature and Place in the World*, New York, Columbia University Press

Gellner, E. (1992) *Postmodernism, Reason and Religion*, London, Routledge

Gelsthorpe, L. (1992) 'Response to Martyn Hammersley's Paper "On Feminist Methodology"', *Sociology*, 26(2): 213–18

Gibbon, F. (1934) *William A. Smith of the Boys' Brigade*, Glasgow, Collins

Giddens, A. (1979) *Central Problems in Social Theory*, London Macmillan

Giddens, A. (1984) *The Constitution of Society*, Cambridge, Polity

Giddens, A. (1990) *The Consequences of Modernity*, Cambridge, Polity

Gilroy, P. (1987) *Ain't No Black in the Union Jack*, London, Routledge

Glyptis, S. (1989) *Leisure and Unemployment*, Milton Keynes, Open University Press

Glyptis, S., McInnes, H. and Patmore, A. (1987) *Leisure and the Home*, London, Sports Council/ESRC

Godbey, G. (1989) 'Anti-Leisure and Public Recreation Policy', pp. 74–86 in F. Coalter (ed.), *Freedom and Constraint*, London, Routledge

Goffman, E. (1959) *Asylums*, Harmondsworth, Penguin

Goffman, E. (1963) *Stigma*, Harmondsworth, Penguin

Goffman, E. (1967) *Interaction Ritual*, New York, Pantheon

Goffman, E. (1971) *Relations in Public*, Harmondsworth, Penguin

Goffman, E. (1974) *Frame Analysis*, New York, Harper & Row

Golby, J.M. and Purdue, A.W. (1984) *The Crowd in Civilization*, London, Batsford

Gold, S.M. (1980) 'Future Leisure Environments in Cities', pp. 125–40 in T.L. Goodale and P.A. Witt (eds), *Recreation and Leisure*, State College, Venture Publishing

Goldman, A. (1981) *Elvis Presley*, Harmondsworth, Penguin

Goldman, A. (1989) *The Lives of John Lennon*, New York, Bantam

Goldmann, L. (1981) *Towards a Sociology of the Novel*, London, Tavistock

Gorz, A. (1980) *Farewell to the Working Class*, London, Pluto

Gramsci, A. (1971) *Selections from Prison Notebooks*, London, Lawrence & Wishart

Gray, R. (1981) *The Aristocracy of Labour in Nineteenth-Century Britain*, London, Macmillan

Green, E., Hebron, S. and Woodward, D. (1987) 'Women's Leisure in Sheffield', mimeo, Dept of Applied Social Studies, Sheffield University

Griffin, C. (1985) *Typical Girls?*, London, Routledge

Habermas, J. (1971) *Knowledge and Human Interests*, London, Heinemann Educational Books

Habermas, J. (1973) *Legitimation Crisis*, London, Heinemann Educational Books

Habermas, J. (1979) *Communication and the Evolution of Society*, London, Heinemann Educational Books

Habermas, J. (1984) *The Theory of Communicative Action*. Vol. 1: *Reason and the Rationalization of Society*, Boston, Beacon Press

Habermas, J. (1985) 'Modernity – an Incomplete Project', pp. 3–15 in Foster (1985)

Habermas, J. (1987) *The Theory of Communicative Action*. Vol. 2: *Lifeworld and System*, Boston, Beacon Press

Hall, S. and Jacques, M. (1989) *New Times*, London, Lawrence & Wishart

Hall, S. and Jefferson, T. (eds) (1975) *Resistance through Rituals*, London, Hutchinson

Hall, S., Critcher, C., Jefferson, T. and Roberts, B. (eds) (1978) *Policing the Crisis*, London, Macmillan

Hall, S., Hobson, D., Lowe, A. and Willis, P. (eds) (1980) *Culture, Media and Language*, London, Heinemann Educational Books

Hammersley, M. (1992) 'On Feminist Methodology', *Sociology*, 26(2): 187–206

Hargreaves, J. (1986) *Sport, Power and Culture*, Cambridge, Polity

Hargreaves, J. (1989) 'The Promise and Problems of Women's Leisure and Sport', pp. 130–49 in C. Rojek (ed.), *Leisure for Leisure: Critical Essays*, London, Macmillan

Hargreaves, J. (1992) 'Sex, Gender and the Body in Sport and Leisure: Has There Been a Civilizing Process?', pp. 161–82 in E. Dunning and C. Rojek (eds), *Sport and Leisure in the Civilizing Process*, London, Macmillan

Hargreaves, J. (1994) *Sporting Women*, London, Routledge

Harriman, A. (1982) *The Work/Leisure Trade Off*, New York, Praeger

Harrington, M., Dawson, D. and Bolla, P. (1992) 'Objective and Subjective Constraints on Women's Enjoyment of Leisure', *Society and Leisure*, 15(1): 203–21

Harvey, D. (1985) *Consciousness and the Urban Experience*, Oxford, Blackwell

Harvey, D. (1989) *The Condition of Postmodernity*, Oxford, Blackwell

Haug, W.F. (1983) *Critique of Commodity Aesthetics*, Cambridge, Polity

Haworth, L. (1977) *Decadence and Objectivity*, Toronto, University of Toronto Press

Hayden, D. (1981) *The Grand Domestic Revolution*, Cambridge, MA, MIT Press

Hebdige, D. (1979) *Subculture*, London, Methuen

Hebdige, D. (1987) *Cut 'n' Mix*, London, Comedia

Hebdige, D. (1988) *Hiding in the Light*, London, Comedia

Hebdige, D. (1993) 'Redeeming Whiteness: In the Tracks of the Homeless Vehicle Project', *Cultural Studies*, 7(2): 173–223

Heidegger, M. (1949) *Essential Writings*, London, Routledge

Heller, A. (1978) *Renaissance Man*, London, Routledge & Kegan Paul

Henderson, K.A. and Bialeschki, D. (1992) 'Leisure Research and the Social Structure of Feminism', *Leisure Studies*, 15(1): 63–75

Henry, I. (1993) *The Politics of Leisure Policy*, London, Macmillan

Hewison, R. (1987) *The Heritage Industry*, London, Methuen

Hobsbawm, E. (1969) *Industry and Empire*, Harmondsworth, Penguin

Hobsbawm, E. (1975) *The Age of Capital*, London, Cardinal

Hobsbawm, E. (1987) *The Age of Empire*, London, Cardinal

Horkheimer, M. (1974) *Critique of Instrumental Reason*, New York, Continuum

Hughes, R. (1993) *The Culture of Complaint*, Oxford, Oxford University Press

Huizinga, J. (1947) *Homo Ludens*, London, Routledge & Kegan Paul

Humphries, S. (1981) *Hooligans or Rebels?*, Oxford, Blackwell

Huyssen, A. (1986) *After the Great Divide*, Bloomington, Indiana University Press

Isaacs, R. (1991) *Gropius*, Boston, Bulfinch

Jahoda, M. (1982) *Employment and Unemployment*, Cambridge, Cambridge University Press

Jameson, F. (1984) 'The Politics of Theory: Ideological Positions in the Postmodernism Debate', *New German Critique*, 33: 53–65

Jameson, F. (1991) *Postmodernism, or The Cultural Logic of Late Capitalism*, London, Verso

Jarman, D. (1987) *The Last of England*, London, Constable

Jarman, D. (1991) *Modern Nature*, London, Constable

Jary, D. and Horne, J. (1987) 'The Figurational Sociology of Sport and Leisure of Elias and Dunning and its Alternatives', *Society and Leisure*, 10(2): 177–94

Jencks, C. (1984) *The Language of Postmodern Architecture*, London, Academy Press

Jenkins, R. (1992) *Pierre Bourdieu*, London, Routledge

Jhally, S. (1990) *The Codes of Advertising*, London, Routledge

Jusserand, J.J. (1888) *English Wayfaring Life in the Middle Ages*, London, Fisher-Unwin

Kant, I. (1970) 'Idea for a Universal History with a Cosmopolitan Purpose', pp. 41–53 in *Kant's Political Writings* (ed. K. Reiss), Cambridge, Cambridge University Press

Kaplan, M. (1975) *Leisure: Theory and Practice*, New York, Wiley

Kaplan, M. (1984) 'Leisure: Toward a Theory and Policy in Israel', pp. 42–61 in H. Ruskin (ed.), *Leisure*, New Jersey, Associated University Press

Kasson, J.E. (1978) *Amusing the Millions: Coney Island at the Turn of the Century*, New York, Hill and Wang

Kelly, J. (1987) *Freedom to Be: A New Sociology of Leisure*, New York, Macmillan

Kerr, C., Dunlop, J.T., Harbison, F.H. and Meyers, C. (1973) *Industrialism and Industrial Man*, (2nd edition), Harmondsworth, Penguin

Kidson, P., Murray, P. and Thompson, P. (1962) *A History of English Architecture*, Harmondsworth, Penguin

King, A. (1980) 'A Time for Space and a Space for Time: The Production of the Vacation House', pp. 193–227 in A. King (ed.), *Buildings and Society*, London, Routledge & Kegan Paul

Kolakowski, L. (1972) *Positivist Philosophy*, Harmondsworth, Penguin

Kracauer, S. (1975) 'The Mass Ornament', *New German Critique*, 2: 67–76

Kraus, R. (1987) *Recreation and Leisure in Modern Society*, Glenview, IL, Scott Foresman

Kroker, A. and Cook, D. (1986) *The Postmodern Scene*, New York, St Martin's Press

Kuhn, T.S. (1970) *The Structure of Scientific Revolutions* (2nd edition), Chicago, University of Chicago Press

Lasch, C. (1979) *The Culture of Narcissism*, London, Abacus

Lasch, C. (1984) *The Minimal Self*, London, Picador

Lash, S. (1990) *Sociology of Postmodernism*, London, Routledge

Lash, S. and Urry, J. (1987) *The End of Organized Capitalism*, Cambridge, Polity

Lash, S. and Urry, J. (1994) *Economies of Signs and Space*, London, Sage

Laslett, P. (1965) *The World We Have Lost*, London, Methuen

Le Corbusier (1929) *The City of Tomorrow*, London, Architectural Press

Lefebvre, H. (1991a) *Critique of Everyday Life*, London, Verso

Lefebvre, H. (1991b) *The Production of Space*, Oxford, Blackwell

Levy-Bruhl, L. (1966) *Primitive Mentality*, London, Allen and Unwin
Lewis, I. (1988) *Ecstatic Religion*, London, Routledge
Lipietz, A. (1987) *Mirages and Miracles*, London, Verso
Lowenthal, D. (1985) *The Past is a Foreign Country*, Cambridge, Cambridge University Press
Lyotard, J.-F. (1984) *The Postmodern Condition*, Manchester, Manchester University Press
Lyotard, J.-F. (1988) *The Inhuman*, Stanford, Stanford University Press
Lyotard, J.-F. (1992) *The Postmodern Explained*, Minneapolis, Minnesota University Press
Maas, J. (1984) *Holman Hunt and the Light of the World*, London, Scolar Press
McCann, G. (1988) *Marilyn Monroe*, Cambridge, Polity
MacCannell, D. (1976) *The Tourist*, New York, Schocken
MacCannell, D. (1992) *Empty Meeting Grounds*, London, Routledge
McCracken, G. and Pollay, R. (1981) 'Anthropology and the Study of Advertising', mimeo, University of British Columbia
McGuigan, J. (1992) *Cultural Populism*, London, Routledge
McHugh, P. (1980) *Prostitution and Victorian Social Reform*, London, Croom Helm
MacIntyre, A. (1981) *After Virtue*, London, Duckworth
Mackenzie, J. (ed.) (1986) *Imperialism and Popular Culture*, Manchester, Manchester University Press
MacLeod, S. (1981) *The Art of Starvation*, London, Verso
McLuhan, M. (1967) *The Gutenberg Galaxy*, London, Routledge & Kegan Paul
McLuhan, M. (1973) *Understanding Media*, London, Routledge & Kegan Paul
McRobbie, A. (1978) 'Working-Class Girls and the Culture of Femininity', in CCCS Women's Studies Group, *Women Take Issue*, London, Hutchinson
McRone, K. (1988) *Sport and the Physical Emancipation of English Women 1870–1914*, London, Routledge
Maffesoli, M. (1988) 'Jeux de Masques: Postmodern Tribalism', *Design Issues*, 4: 141–51
Maffesoli, M. (1990) 'Post-modern Sociality', *Telos*, 85: 89–92
Maffesoli, M. (1991) *Les Temps des Tribus*, Paris, Livre de Poche
Maffesoli, M. (1993) *The Shadow of Dionysus: A Contribution to the Sociology of the Orgy*, New York, State University of New York Press
Malcolmson, R. (1973) *Popular Recreations in English Society 1700–1850*, Cambridge, Cambridge University Press
Manchester City Art Galleries (1987) *Parks for the People*, Manchester, Manchester City Art Galleries
Mangan, J. (1985) *The Games Ethic and Imperialism*, New York, Viking
Marcus, G. (1989) *Lipstick Traces*, London, Secker & Warburg
Marcuse, H. (1964) *One-Dimensional Man*, London, Abacus
Marcuse, H. (1978) *The Aesthetic Dimension*, London, Macmillan
Marcuse, H. (1988) 'On Hedonism', pp. 159–200 in *Negations*, London, Free Association Books
Marshall, G. (1982) *In Search of the Spirit of Capitalism*, London, Hutchinson
Marshall, T. (1977) *Class, Citizenship and Social Development*, Chicago, Chicago University Press
Marx, K. (1964) *Economic and Philosophic Manuscripts*, New York, International Press
Marx, K. (1977) *Capital* (3 vols), London, Lawrence & Wishart
Marx, K. and Engels, F. (1954) *The German Ideology*, London, Lawrence & Wishart
Marx, K. and Engels, F. (1968) *Selected Works*, London, Lawrence & Wishart
Massey, D. (1984) *Spatial Divisions of Labour*, London, Macmillan
Mennell, S. (1985) *All Manners of Food*, Oxford, Blackwell
Mennell, S. (1989) *Norbert Elias: An Introduction*, Oxford, Blackwell
Merton, R.K. (1940) 'Bureaucratic Structure and Personality', *Social Forces*, 17: 560–8
Mestrovic, S. (1993) *The Barbarian Temperament*, London, Routledge
Miles, R. (1993) *Racism, After Race Relations*, London, Routledge
Moorhouse, H. (1989) 'Models of Work, Models of Leisure', pp. 15–35 in C. Rojek (ed.), *Leisure for Leisure*, London, Macmillan
Mort, F. (1987) *Dangerous Sexualities: Medico-Moral Politics in England since 1830*, London, Routledge & Kegan Paul

Mumford, L. (1967) *The Myth of the Machine: Technics and Human Development*, London, Secker & Warburg

Nairn, T. (1988) *The Enchanted Glass*, London, Radius

Newburn, T. (1992) *Permission and Regulation*, London, Routledge

Nietzsche, F. (1968) *Twilight of the Gods*, Harmondsworth, Penguin

Nietzsche, F. (1973) *Thus Spake Zarathustra*, Harmondsworth, Penguin

Nietzsche, F. (1979) *Ecce Homo*, Harmondsworth, Penguin

Nietzsche, F. (1980) *Samtliche Werke: Kritische Studienausgabe* (15 vols), (ed. by G. Colli and M. Montinari), vol. 6, Munich/Berlin/New York, DTV, de Gruyter

Nietzsche, F. (1983) *Untimely Meditations*, Cambridge, Cambridge University Press

Nietzsche, F. (1994) 'The Anti-Christ', in *The Portable Nietzsche* (ed. R.J. Hollingdale) Harmondsworth, Penguin

Norris, C. (1990) 'Lost in the Funhouse: Baudrillard and the Politics of Postmodernism', pp. 114–53 in R. Boyne and A. Rattansi (eds), *Postmodernism and Society*, London, Macmillan

Oakley, A. (1974) *The Sociology of Housework*, Oxford, Martin Robertson

Olmsted, F. (1979) 'Public Parks and the Enlargement of Towns', in S.B. Sutton (ed.), *Civilizing American Cities: A Selection of Frederick Law Olmsted's Writings on City Landscape*, Cambridge, MA, MIT Press

O'Loughlin, M. (1978) *The Garlands of Repose*, Chicago, University of Chicago Press

Olszweska, A. and Roberts, K. (eds) (1989) *Leisure and Life-style*, London, Sage

Parker, S. (1981) 'Choice, Flexibility, Spontaneity and Self-Determination', *Social Forces*, 60(2): 323–31

Parker, S. (1983) *Leisure and Work*, London, Unwin Hyman

Pearson, G. (1987) *The New Heroin Users*, Oxford, Blackwell

Pemble, J. (1987) *The Mediterranean Passion*, Oxford, Oxford University Press

Perry, R. (1992) 'Colonizing the Breast: Sexuality and Maternity in Eighteenth Century England', pp. 107–38 in J.C. Fort (ed.) *Forbidden History*, Chicago, Chicago University Press

Peters, E. (1985) *Torture*, Oxford, Blackwell

Pirenne, H. (1936) *Economic and Social History of Medieval England*, London, Methuen

Plant, S. (1992) *Most Radical Gesture*, London, Routledge

Plumb, J.H. (1983) 'Commercialization and Society: The Commercialization of Leisure', pp. 265–85 in N. McKendrick, J. Brewer and J.H. Plumb, *The Birth of Consumer Society*, London, Hutchinson

Plummer, K. (ed.) (1992) *Modern Homosexualities*, London, Routledge

Poggi, G. (1983) *Capitalism and the Calvinist Spirit*, London, Macmillan

Poole, R. (1983) 'Oldham Wakes', pp. 71–98 in J. K. Walton and J. Walvin (eds), *Leisure in Britain 1780–1939*, Manchester, Manchester University Press

Popper, K. (1962) *The Open Society and its Enemies*, Vol. 2, London, Routledge & Kegan Paul

Porter, R. (1993) 'Baudrillard: History, Hysteria and Consumption', pp. 1–21 in C. Rojek and B.S. Turner (eds), *Forget Baudrillard?*, London, Routledge

Ramazanoglu, C. (1989) *Feminism and the Contradictions of Oppression*, London, Routledge

Ramazanoglu, C. (ed.) (1992) 'On Feminist Methodology: Male Reason versus Female Empowerment', *Sociology*, 26(2): 207–12

Rearick, C. (1985) *Pleasures of the Belle Époque: Entertainment and Festivity in Turn-of-the-Century France*, New Haven, CT, Yale University Press

Richards, J. (1984) *The Age of the Dream Palace*, London, Routledge

Riese, R. and Hitchens, N. (eds) (1988) *The Unabridged Marilyn*, London, Corgi

Riesman, D. (1960) *Thorstein Veblen: A Critical Introduction*, New York, Scribners

Riesman, D. (1964) *Abundance for What and Other Essays*, London, Chatto & Windus

Rigauer, B. (1981) *Sport and Work*, New York, Columbia University Press

Ritvo, H. (1987) *The Animal Estate: The English and Other Creatures in the Victorian Age*, Cambridge, MA, Harvard Education Press

Roberts, K. (1978) *Contemporary Society and the Growth of Leisure*, London, Longman

Roberts, K. (1981) *Leisure* (2nd edition), London, Longman

Robertson, R. (1992) *Globalization: Social Theory and Global Culture*, London, Sage

Rojek, C. (1985) *Capitalism and Leisure Theory*, London, Tavistock

Rojek, C. (1986) 'Problems of Involvement and Detachment in the Writings of Norbert Elias', *British Journal of Sociology*, 37(4): 584–96

Rojek, C. (1988) 'The Convoy of Pollution', *Leisure Studies* 7(1): 21–31

Rojek, C. (1989) 'Leisure and Recreation Theory', pp. 69–88 in E. Jackson and T.L. Burton (eds), *Understanding Leisure and Recreation: Mapping the Past, Charting the Future*, State College, Venture Publishing

Rojek, C. (1992) 'The Eye of Power: Moral Regulation and the Professionalization of Leisure Management from the 1830s to the 1950s', *Society and Leisure*, 15(1): 355–75

Rojek, C. (1993a) *Ways of Escape: Modern Transformations in Leisure and Travel*, London, Macmillan

Rojek, C. (1993b) 'Disney Culture', *Leisure Studies*, 12(1): 121–35

Rojek, C. (1993c) 'Restlessness', *Vrijetijd en Samenleving*, 10(4): 5–17

Rojek, C. (1994) 'Leisure and the Dreamworld of Modernity', mimeo

Rorty, R. (1989) *Contingency, Irony and Solidarity*, Cambridge, Cambridge University Press

Rutherford, J. (1992) *Men's Silences*, London, Routledge

Rybczynski, W. (1991) *Waiting for the Weekend*, New York, Viking

Said, E.W. (1978) *Orientalism*, London, Routledge

Saisselin, R.G. (1985) *Bricabracomania: The Bourgeois and the Bibelot*, London, Thames & Hudson

Savage, M., Barlow, J., Dickens, P. and Fielding, T. (1992) *Property, Bureaucracy and Culture*, London, Routledge

Sayer, D. (1991) *Capitalism and Modernity*, London, Routledge

Sayers, S. (1987) 'The Need to Work', *Radical Philosophy*, 46: 17–26

Schivelbusch, W. (1980) *The Railway Journey: Trains and Travel in the Nineteenth Century*, Oxford, Berg

Schivelbusch, W. (1988) *Disenchanted Light: The Industrialization of Light in the Nineteenth Century*, Oxford, Berg

Schivelbusch, W. (1992) *Tastes of Paradise: A Social History of Spices, Stimulants and Intoxicants*, New York, Vintage

Schneemann, C. (1979) *More than Meat Joy: Complete Performance Works and Selected Writings*, New York, McPherson/Documentext

Schneemann, C. (1991) 'Carole Schneemann', in A. Juno and V. Vale (eds), *Angry Women*, San Francisco, Re/Search Publication

Schutz, A. (1982) *Life-forms and Meaning Structure*, London, Routledge & Kegan Paul

Scraton, S. (1993) 'Feminism, "Post-feminism" and Leisure', mimeo, International Leisure Studies Association

Scraton, S. and Talbot, M. (1989) 'A Response to 'Leisure, Life-style and Status: A Pluralist Framework for Analysis', *Leisure Studies*, 8(2): 155–8

Seidler, V. (1989) *Rediscovering Masculinity*, London, Routledge

Seidler, V. (ed.) (1992) *Men, Sex and Relationships*, London, Routledge

Sennett, R. (1977) *The Fall of Public Man*, Cambridge, Cambridge University Press

Sennett, R. (1980) *Authority*, London, Faber

Sennett, R. (1992) *The Conscience of the Eye*, London, Faber

Shields, R. (1990) 'The System of Pleasure', *Theory, Culture and Society*, 7(10): 39–72

Shields, R. (1991) *Places on the Margin*, London, Routledge

Shields, R. (ed.) (1992) *Lifestyle Shopping*, London, Routledge

Simmel, G. (1971) *On Individuality and Social Forms*, Chicago, University Press of Chicago

Simmel, G. (1978) *The Philosophy of Money*, London, Routledge & Kegan Paul

Simmel, G. (1991) 'The Berlin Trade Exhibition', *Theory, Culture and Society*, 8(3): 119–24

Skopcol, T. (1979) *States and Social Revolution*, Cambridge, Cambridge University Press

Smart, B. (1992) *Modern Conditions, Postmodern Controversies*, London, Routledge

Smiles, S. (1859) *Self-Help*, London, Murray

Smiles, S. (1894) *Character*, London, Murray

Smith, D. (1984) 'Norbert Elias: Established or Outsider?', *Sociological Review*, 32: 367–89

Smith, N. (1992) 'Contours of a Spatialized Politics: Homeless Vehicles and the Production of Geographical Scale', *Social Text*, 33: 54–81

Smoodin, E. (1993) *Animating Culture*, New Brunswick, NJ, Rutgers University Press

Springhall, J. (1977) *Youth, Empire and Society*, London, Croom Helm

Stallybrass, P. and White, A. (1986) *The Politics and Poetics of Transgression*, London, Methuen

Stanley, L. and Wise, S. (1992) *Breaking Out*, London, Routledge

Stedman-Jones, G. (1977) 'Class Expression versus Social Control? A Critique of Recent Trends in the Social History of Leisure', *History Workshop Journal*, 4: 162–70

Summerfield, P. (1986) 'Patriotism and Empire: Music-Hall Entertainment', pp. 17–48 in Mackenzie (1986)

Suttles, G. (1968) *The Social Order of the Slum*, Chicago, University of Chicago Press

Synott, A. (1993) *The Body Social*, London, Routledge

Talbot, M. (1988) '"Their Own Worst Enemy?" Women and Leisure Provision', pp. 161–76 in Wimbush and Talbot (1988)

Taylor, F.W. (1964) *Principles of Scientific Management*, New York, Harper

Tester, K. (1993) *The Life and Times of Postmodernity*, London, Routledge

Tester, K. (ed.) (1994) *The Flâneur*, London, Routledge

Theweleit, K. (1987) *Male Fantasies*. Vol. 1, Cambridge, Polity

Theweleit, K. (1988) *Male Fantasies*. Vol. 2, Cambridge, Polity

Thompson, E.P. (1963) *The Making of the English Working Class*, Harmondsworth, Penguin

Thompson, E.P. (1967) 'Time, Work-Discipline and Industrial Capitalism', *Past and Present*, 38: 56–97

Thompson, E.P. (1975) *Whigs and Hunters: The Origins of the Black Act*, Harmondsworth, Penguin

Toffler, A. (1981) *The Third Wave*, London, Pan

Tomlinson, A. (1989) 'Whose Side are They On? Leisure Studies and Cultural Studies in Britain', *Leisure Studies*, 8(2): 97–106

Tomlinson, A. (ed.) (1990) *Consumption, Identity and Style*, London, Routledge

Touraine, A. (1974) *The Post-Industrial Society*, London, Wildwood House

Touraine, A. (1992) 'Beyond Social Movements', *Theory, Culture and Society*, 9(1): 125–46

Tucker, K. H. (1993) 'Aesthetics, Play, and Cultural Memory: Giddens and Habermas on the Postmodernist Challenge', *Sociological Theory*, 11(2): 194–211

Tunstall, J. (1962) *The Fishermen*, London, McGibbon & Kee

Turner, B.S. (1984) *The Body and Society*, Oxford, Blackwell

Turner, B.S. (1992) *Regulating Bodies*, London, Routledge

Urry, J. (1988) 'Cultural Change and Holiday Making', *Theory, Culture and Society*, 5: 35–55

Urry, J. (1990a) *The Tourist Gaze*, London, Sage

Urry, J. (1990b) 'Time and Space in Giddens' Social Theory', pp. 160–75 in C. Bryant and D. Jary (eds), *Giddens' Theory of Structuration*, London, Routledge

Urry, J. (1993) 'Time, Leisure and Social Identity', mimeo, ASSET conference, Dartington

Vale, M. (1977) *The Gentleman's Recreations: Accomplishments and Pastimes of the English Gentleman 1580–1630*, Ipswich, Brewer

Vattimo, G. (1992) *The Transparent Society*, Cambridge, Polity

Veal, A.J. (1987) *Leisure and the Future*, London, Allen & Unwin

Veblen, T. (1925) *The Theory of the Leisure Class*, London, Allen & Unwin

Venturi, R., Scott-Brown, D. and Izenour, S. (1972) *Learning from Las Vegas*, Cambridge, MA, MIT Press

Virilio, P. (1986) *Speed and Politics*, New York, Semiotext(e)

Virilio, P. (1991) *The Aesthetics of Disappearance*, New York, Semiotext(e)

Wallerstein, I. (1979) *The Capitalist World Economy*, Cambridge, Cambridge University Press

Wallerstein, I. (1980) *The Modern World System II: Mercantilism and the Consolidation of the European World Economy*, New York, Academic Press

Wallerstein, I. (1984) *The Politics of the World Economy*, Cambridge, Cambridge University Press

Walton, J. (1983) *The English Seaside Resort: A Social History 1750–1914*, Leicester, Leicester University Press

Walvin, J. (1992) *A Child's World: A Social History of English Childhood 1800–1914*, Harmondsworth, Penguin

Watney, S. (1987) *Policing Desire: Pornography, Aids and the Media*, London, Comedia

Wearing, B. (1992) 'Leisure and Women's Identity in Late Adolescence: Constraints and Opportunities', *Society and Leisure*, 15(1): 323–43

Wearing, B. and Wearing, S.L. (1988) 'All in a Day's Leisure: Gender and the Concept of Leisure', *Leisure Studies*, 7: 111–23

Weber, M. (1961) *General Economic History*, New York, Collier

Weber, M. (1968) *Economy and Society* (3 vols), New York, Bedminster Press

Weber, M. (1970) *From Max Weber* (ed. by H. Gerth and C. Wright Mills), London, Routledge & Kegan Paul

Weber, M. (1976) *The Protestant Ethic and the Spirit of Capitalism*, London, Routledge & Kegan Paul

Weeks, J. (1991) *Against Nature: Essays on History, Sexuality and Identity*, London, Rivers Oram Press

Wheelock, J. (1990) *Husbands at Home*, London, Routledge

Wigley, J. (1980) *The Rise and Fall of the Victorian Sunday*, Manchester, Manchester University Press

Williams, R. (1973) *The Country and the City*, London, Hogarth Press

Williams, R. (1981) *Culture*, Glasgow, Fontana

Williams, R.H. (1982) *Dream Worlds: Mass Consumption in Late Nineteenth-Century France*, Berkeley, University of California Press

Willis, P. (1990) *Common Culture*, Milton Keynes, Open University Press

Wilson, B. (1976) *Contemporary Transformation of Religion*, Oxford, Oxford University Press

Wilson, E. (1985) *Adorned in Dreams: Fashion and Modernity*, London, Virago

Wilson, J. (1988) *Politics and Leisure*, London, Unwin Hyman

Wimbush, E. (1986) *Women, Leisure and Well-Being*, Edinburgh, Centre for Leisure Research, Dunfermline College of Physical Education

Wimbush, E. and Talbot, M. (eds) (1988) *Relative Freedoms: Women and Leisure*, Milton Keynes, Open University Press

Wolff, J. (1990) *Feminine Sentences*, Berkeley, University of California Press

Wood, M. (1974) 'Nostalgia or Never: You Can't Go Home Again', *New Society*, 7 November: 343–6

Woodward, D., Green, E. and Hebron, S. (1989) 'The Sociology of Women's Leisure and Physical Recreation: Constraints and Opportunities', *International Review for the Sociology of Sport*, 24(2): 121–34

Wright, P. (1992) 'Home is Where the Cart is', *Independent on Sunday*, 12 January

Yeo, S. (1976) *Religion and the Voluntary Sector*, Beckenham, Croom Helm

Young, M. and Wilmott, P. (1973) *The Symmetrical Family*, London, Routledge & Kegan Paul

Young Woman's Guide to Domestic Happiness (1834) London, Thomas Kelly

Zukin, S. (1988) *Loft Living: Culture and Capital in Urban Change*, London, Radius

Zukin, S. (1991) *Landscapes of Power: From Detroit to Disney World*, Berkeley, University of California Press

AUTHOR INDEX

Abercrombie, N. 19
Adorno, T. 7, 16–18, 20
Althusser, L. 18
Andrew, E. 14
Ang, I. 95
Anger, K. 164
Applebaum, H. 183, 189
Aronowitz, S. 182

Bachelard, G. 123
Bailey, P. 12
Bakhtin, M. 85
Barrett, M. 29
Barthes, R. 122
Baudelaire, C. 5, 80, 91, 122
Baudrillard, J. 7, 9, 10, 139–40, 150, 168
Bauman, Z. 6, 8, 53, 135–6, 138, 156–7, 168, 170, 186–7, 192
Beck, U. 113, 152–5
Bell, D. 115–16
Benjamin, W. 11, 84, 91, 96, 100, 170
Berger, P. 6, 110
Berman, M. 4, 37, 80, 101
Bernstein, J. 18
Bialeschki, D. 28, 30, 32
Bogdan, R. 86
Borzello, F. 14, 66
Bourdieu, P. 67–9
Braverman, H. 18, 182
Burns, T. 67

Campbell, C. 56, 114, 116
Cannadine, D. 86
Castells, M. 143
Chaney, D. 14, 24, 57, 63, 125, 148
Clarke, J. 20–5, 53
Cohen, S. 4, 88, 89, 107–8
Cook, D. 8, 9, 110
Corrigan, P. 18, 19, 43, 44, 72
Craik, J. 94
Critcher, C. 20–5
Cunningham, H. 44

Debord, G. 14, 89
De Certeau, M. 106, 132
Deem, R. 28, 30, 31, 34

Donnelly, P. 101
Doyle, L. 176–9
Dumazedier, J. 38
Dunning, E. 50–6
Durkheim, E. 19, 66, 135, 152

Eco, U. 149, 164
Elias, N. 50–6
Engels, F. 4, 5, 10
Ewen, S. 14, 75

Fazio, J. 14
Featherstone, M. 64, 113, 121
Ferguson, H. 117
Findlay, J. 61, 62
Finlay, K. 115
Fiske, J. 106
Foucault, M. 59, 60, 147
Freud, S. 54
Frisby, D. 11, 27, 80, 109

Game, A. 31, 34, 61
Gane, M. 170
Gelsthorpe, L. 31
Giddens, A. 113
Gilroy, P. 27
Glendenning, R. 97
Godbey, G. 41
Goffman, E. 48–9, 105, 124
Goldman, A. 163
Gorz, A. 181
Gough, I. 176–91
Gramsci, A. 21, 42
Gray, R. 14, 44
Griffin, C. 29

Habermas, J. 69, 111, 176, 178, 184
Hall, S. 19, 20
Hammersley, M. 30
Hargreaves, J. 28
Harriman, A. 76
Harvey, D. 7, 8, 13, 19, 43, 142, 143
Haworth, L. 133
Hayden, D. 32, 91
Hebdige, D. 17, 26, 93–4, 166
Hegel, G. 190

Heidegger, M. 105
Heller, A. 118, 126
Henderson, K. 28, 30, 32
Henry, I. 131, 142, 176
Hughes, R. 25
Huizinga, J. 184–6

Jacques, M. 19, 20
Jahoda, M. 180
Jameson, F. 8, 10, 119, 137, 165
Jarman, D. 99

Kant, I. 187–90
Kaplan, M. 39, 40
Kasson, J. 57, 83, 86–7, 123
Kelly, J. 9, 62
Kolakowski, L. 37
Kracauer, S. 17
Kraus, R. 40–1
Kroker, A. 8, 9, 10

Lasch, C. 9, 112–14, 116, 154–5
Lash, S. 136, 143
Laslett, P. 65
Lefebvre, H. 97–8, 102
Lowenthal, D. 119
Lyotard, J.-F. 6, 8, 132–4

MacCannell, D. 48, 67, 124, 125, 149
MacIntyre, A. 37, 54
Maffesoli, M. 151–2, 156, 191
Marcuse, H. 16, 17, 77, 92–3
Marshall, T. 72
Marx, K. 3–5, 10, 14–16, 83
Massey, D. 94
McCann, G. 16
McGuigan, J. 106
McLuhan, M. 92
McRobbie, A. 29
Mennell, S. 53
Merton, R. 70
Mestrovic, S. 54
Miles, R. 26
Moorhouse, H. 38
Mumford, L. 2

Nairn, T. 71
Nietzsche, F. 80–3

Olszweska, A. 39

Ramazanoglu, C. 31, 32
Riesman, D. 48, 76, 102
Roberts, K. 39
Robertson, R. 93

Rojek, C. 2, 4, 24, 32, 52, 73, 96, 136, 157
Rorty, R. 169

Said, E. 25
Sayer, D. 4, 18, 19, 44, 72
Sayers, S. 179–81
Schivelbusch, W. 9
Schneemann, C. 114
Seidler, V. 33
Sennett, R 9, 109–11, 135
Shields, R. 24, 87–8, 102, 125, 148
Simmel, G. 6, 11, 109, 110, 128
Smart, B. 158
Smiles, S. 64, 90
Smith, N. 166
Smoodin, E. 44
Springhall, J. 14
Stallybrass, P. 87

Talbot, M. 28, 32–3
Taylor, F.W. 13
Taylor, L. 4, 88, 89, 107–8
Tester, K. 6, 24, 156
Theweleit, K. 71, 87
Thompson, E.P. 12, 45
Tomlinson, A. 24
Turner, B.S. 33, 61, 178

Urry, J. 4, 61, 120, 136, 143, 144

Vale, M. 71
Vattimo, G. 138, 140, 150
Veblen, T. 47–50, 71, 113
Venturi, R. 147–8
Virilio, P. 7, 158–9

Wallerstein, I. 95
Walton, J. 97
Walvin, J. 57
Wearing, B. 29, 31, 34
Weber, M. 3, 43, 45–7, 69–70, 127, 170
Weeks, J. 59, 65
Wheelock, J. 182
White, A. 87
Williams, R. 21
Willis, P. 74, 145, 182
Wilson, J. 64, 91
Wimbush, E. 28
Wood, M. 120
Woodward, D. 34
Wolff, J. 91

Yeo, S. 14

Zukin, S. 121–2, 146–7

SUBJECT INDEX

Aesthetics 165–9
AIDS 98–9
Alienation 14–16
Amusement parks 86–7, 97
Anorexia nervosa 63
Anti-leisure 42
Apollonian culture 80–3

Body 61–4
Bureaucracy 69–70

Capitalism 2–4, 12
Carnivalesque 85–8
Circulation 83–5
Citizenship 72–4
Civilizing process 50–6
Conservative theory 40–2
Conspicuous consumption 47–50
Contingency 156–7
Core 95–6
Cultural studies 20–5
Culture industry 16–18
Cyberspace 147–8

Decentring 131–2
Denial 161
Desacralization 163
Deviance 99–101
Dionysian culture 80–3
Disembedding 147
Distraction factories 11
Dreamworlds 88–92

Elvis wars 118
Emotional disengagement 154
Escape 74–6
Ethics 165–9

Family 64–6
Fantasy voyaging 154
Fatalism 154–5
Feminism 28–33
Flânerie 90–2, 123, 186
Flexible accumulation 142
Fordism 12–14, 141–2
Freakshows 86–7
Functionalism 36–8

Gaze 61
Globalization 92–6

Habitus 67–9
Hedonism 114
Hegemony 21–3
Heterotopic space 147
Homelessness 110–12
Hyperreality 149–51

Intertextuality 10

Labour metaphysic 183–4
Life chances 127
Liminal zones 87–8

Magic lands 62
Modernity 4–6
Moral regulation 19, 42–5
Myth 126

Narcissism 112–24
Nationalism 71–2
Necro-fever 160–4
Neo-tribalism 151–2, 191
Nostalgia 118–22

Order 38–40

Patriarchy 33
Patrism 33
Periphery 95–6
Pluralism 37
Positivism 37
Post-feminism 33–5
Postmodernism 6–8
Power 60
Productivism 179–83
Protestant ethic 45–7

Racism 25–7
Rational recreation 14
Reflexive accumulation 143
Religion 66–9
Repetition 83–5
Risk 152–5

Scandalization 161–2
Sign-economy 10–11
Simulation 9–10
Society for Creative Anachronism 125
Spectacular society 14, 89–90
Speed 157–60
Staged authenticity 124–5
State 18–20
Stonehenge 73
Strength through Joy 42, 71

Taj Mahal 73, 74
Taxation 43
Telecity 186

Universal market 13–16
Urban planning 75

Work 14–24